RE-VIEWING JAMES BALDWIN

things not seen

RE-VIEWING JAMES BALDWIN

things not seen

Edited by

D. Quentin Miller

Foreword by **David Adams Leeming**

TEMPLE UNIVERSITY PRESS
Philadelphia

Temple University Press, Philadelphia 19122
Copyright © 2000 by Temple University
All rights reserved
Published 2000
Printed in the United States of America

⊗ The paper used in this publication meets the requirements of the American
National Standard for Information Sciences—Permanence of Paper for Printed
Library Materials, ANSI Z39.48-1984

Library of Congress Cataloging-in-Publication Data

Re-viewing James Baldwin: things not seen / edited by D. Quentin Miller:
foreword by David Adams Leeming.
    p.   cm.
    Includes bibliographical references.
    ISBN 1-56639-736-7 (alk. paper). — ISBN 1-56639-737-5 (pbk. : alk. paper)
    1. Baldwin, James, 1924–1987—Criticism and interpretation.   2. Afro-Americans
in literature.   3. Gay men in literature.   4. Race in literature.   I. Miller,
D. Quentin (Daniel Quentin), 1967– .
818'. 5409—dc21   99-33993
                                                                          CIP

I would like to acknowledge generous support from Dr. Elizabeth Baer, Dean of
the Faculty at Gustavus Adolphus College, for funding the costs of reproducing
the photographs in Chapter 7 of this volume.

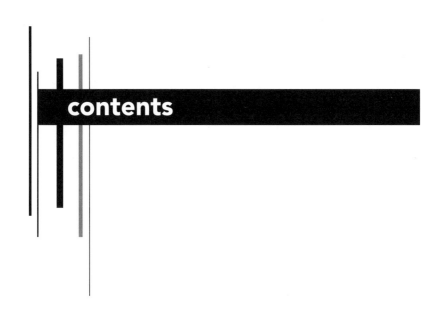

contents

foreword

DAVID ADAMS LEEMING

In *Re-Viewing James Baldwin,* Quentin Miller and his contributors provide us with a much needed assessment of the late works of James Baldwin. For too many readers of Baldwin, the interest in his work stops with *The Fire Next Time.* To a great extent, the unawareness of the late work and the gradual obscurity of some of the early work can be attributed to the critical establishment's resentment of Baldwin's apparent change of attitude in the mid-sixties.

The author of the autobiographical first novel, *Go Tell It on the Mountain,* met the liberal need to sympathize with the plight of a sensitive youth and his tortured family hidden away in that foreign country called Harlem. The first two books of essays, *Notes of a Native Son* and *Nobody Knows My Name,* although strong in their protest against racial injustice in America, were not antagonistic toward whites. The reader of "Equal in Paris" or "Stranger in the Village" or even the essay "Notes of a Native Son" itself, were exposed in no uncertain terms to the horrors of racism from the point of view of an African American man. But this black man's style was reminiscent of Henry James rather than of Bigger Thomas. And the author seemed to be holding our hands, promising that nothing bad would happen to us if we went with him to the Paris jail, the streets of Harlem, or the restaurant in New Jersey where he threw a glass at the waitress who refused to serve him. We were enlightened by the early James Baldwin, but we were safe with him. The same could be said of the great "homosexual novel," *Giovanni's Room* or the bisexual epic, *Another Country*. These novels were upsetting, but we were liberal enough in the late fifties and early sixties to accept with minimal discomfort the message that sexual honesty was important and that sexual honesty was inevitably related to honesty about other issues—art, race, politics. As to *The Fire Next Time*, it was, after all, first published in *The New Yorker*, and although Baldwin was fascinated by Elijah Muhammad, he did not come down on the side of the Muslims. Instead, speaking right out of the tradition of Martin Luther King, Jr., perhaps flavored by a bit of Malcolm X, he warned us that those of us—black and white—who were liberal enough could prevent the fire by working together for justice.

But then came the terrifying short story, "Going to Meet the Man," in which a lynching is somehow associated with the sexual problems of a white sheriff, and the even more bothersome play, *Blues for Mr. Charlie*, in which there seems to be an almost insurmountable barrier between Black Town and White Town and the black preacher at the end of the play, Malcolm X style, has a gun in his Bible. People—especially white people—were made uncomfortable by those works and they found it convenient to blame the discomfort on the author's failing powers rather than on the real problem that faced us in the mid-sixties. People with Baldwin's prophetic understanding already were beginning to see by that time that those whites who had linked arms to overcome racism in the "movement" were not willing or able to open the collective pocketbook or the collective neighborhood of white America in any significant way to alleviate inequality. They were willing to march in the nonviolent safety of Martin's shadow but were not in the sunlight of Malcolm's or Stokely Carmichael's early calls to battle.

So Baldwin became disillusioned, and he expressed that disillusionment in the words of characters that included Tish in *If Beale Street Could Talk*, Black Christopher in the autobiographical *Tell Me How Long the Train's Been Gone*, in the tragic lives of Arthur, Jimmy, and Julia in the much underrated—in fact, ignored—family blues epic, *Just Above My Head*, and in the moving and sometimes powerful poetry of *Jimmy's Blues*. And he expresses it in the late prose works, in which critics almost uniformly have been bothered by his "unreasonable bitterness." In fact, Baldwin was never bitter; he was, as Maya Angelou has reminded us, just angry—angry about the plight of the inner-city black, angry about the sacrifice of so many modern "buffalo soldiers" in the Vietnam War and black children in the drug war, and angry about a "new South" that masked old injustices with architectural and economic glitz. He expressed his anger in several late works of nonfiction—*The Devil Finds Work, No Name in the Street,* and *The Evidence of Things Not Seen,* all segments of an autobiography that began with the first two books of essays and *The Fire Next Time.*

In this much-needed collection we finally find a serious consideration of this late, angry, and still articulate James Baldwin, who understands that the fire is smoldering under the brush of complacency, who knows that "he who collaborates is doomed, bound forever in the unimaginable and yet very common condition which we weakly suggest as *Hell.*"[1]

NOTE

1. James Baldwin, *The Evidence of Things Not Seen* (New York: Holt, Rinehart and Winston, 1985), 125.

RE-VIEWING JAMES BALDWIN

things not seen

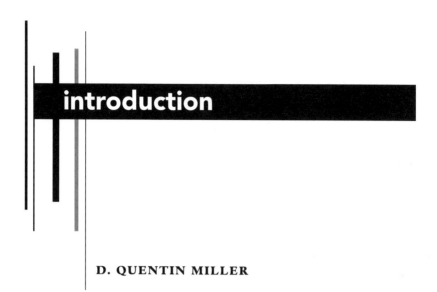

introduction

D. QUENTIN MILLER

In her posthumous tribute to James Baldwin, Toni Morrison writes, "You are an artist after all and an artist is forbidden a career in this place; an artist is permitted only a commercial hit" (Troupe 76). In the same volume of essays, another artist, Mary McCarthy, reluctantly admits, "After [reading *Go Tell It on the Mountain*], I read *The Fire Next Time* and was moved, maybe shaken a little by it. And, after that, I'm sorry to say, I read no more of Jimmy. The reason was simple: I was afraid to. From what I heard, I did not think I would like *Giovanni's Room* or the books that followed and I preferred to keep my sense of Jimmy's gift pure and intact in my mind. (When we stop reading an author we like, that is usually why, I imagine: we do not want to change the idea we have of him)" (Troupe 48). From different viewpoints, these two novelists approach the same question: What is behind the tendency to limit our reading of an author's works? Morrison, who claims to have "pored again through the 6,895 pages of [Baldwin's] published work" (Troupe 76) before writing her tribute, clearly believes that true artists like Baldwin are underappreciated, and that their careers are often reduced to the legacy of their one commercial success, if they even have one. McCarthy expresses a different anxiety: She can't imagine an author has transcended the perfection of that one commercial success, and she doesn't want that perfection compromised by other works that might not measure up. For better or worse, more of Baldwin's readers are like

McCarthy than Morrison, largely because he was an artist who refused to stand for any one single thing or to write in any one single voice.

An author's reputation rarely should, but too often does, rest on the reputation of one or two books. It is impossible, of course, to have read all the works by every author we have ever dipped into; time constraints and an appetite for variety prevent us from fully absorbing one author before moving on to another. We are often introduced to an author by forces beyond our control—forces dictated by the sometimes-whimsical taste of anonymous critics or by the marketing strategists of publishers. The recent list of the one hundred "best" novels of the past century—a shameless marketing ploy of the Modern Library—caused as much flak as Harold Bloom's top one hundred list in *The Western Canon* did five years ago; yet sales of the books that appeared on these lists jumped instantly. If the judges of the National Book Award select an unknown author, sales of that author's book also will increase; and if Oprah Winfrey selects that author for her televised book club, sales will go through the roof (for example, Wally Lamb hit the jackpot with his first novel *She's Come Undone,* which Oprah promoted). An individual publisher might decide to market one of its authors aggressively—as Cormac McCarthy happily discovered—and readers reach for their wallets.

Lists, prizes, and publishers aside, the reading public is frequently introduced to an author in a college literature course, and the "representative" work by that author may be selected for any number of reasons: it is that author's best work, the work that best represents a certain category, or the one that coincides best with the other works in the course. Rarely is it the author's *only* work. Yet when professors consistently teach the same work by an author, the association becomes so strong that the writer's other works are obscured, and eventually obscure. Anyone familiar with, say, all of the works by James Joyce from *Dubliners* through *Finnegans Wake,* no doubt has felt the frustration of speaking with someone who has read only *A Portrait of the Artist as a Young Man* and has claimed to have "gotten" Joyce. Similarly, the devotee of Jane Austen's novels has no doubt said something like, "But she was so much *more* than *Pride and Prejudice.*" Something has been lost when a writer's reputation has been so reduced.

In the case of James Baldwin, what has been lost is a complete portrait of his tremendously rich intellectual journey that illustrates the direction of African American thought and culture in the late twentieth century. Also lost has been a widely varied oeuvre of an experimental writer who never was content with retelling the same story, using the same voice, or speaking to the same audience. Lost, too, is the legacy of Baldwin's considerable influence: as one strong yet invisible presence informing the majestic novels of Toni Morrison, the screenplay for Spike Lee's influential film *Malcolm X* (based upon a screenplay that Baldwin had published in 1973 as *One Day When I Was Lost*), or the recent debates over the curricular uses of black English.

Baldwin himself seems to have gotten lost, or, at least, misplaced. To some degree, he has realized the anxious prophecy evident in his book titles *No Name in the Street* or *Nobody Knows My Name*. Ironically, his own tireless refusal to allow himself to be labeled probably has led to his uncertain place in the annals of literary history. Throughout his career he took pains to remind friends and interviewers that he was Jimmy Baldwin rather than the representative of some group. He repeatedly echoes Emersonian ideals of individualism even as he attempts to define for his readers what it means to be an American. In a 1960 address at San Francisco State College, he proclaimed, "A country is only as strong as the people who make it up and the country turns into what the people want it to become. Now, this country is going to be transformed. It will not be transformed by an act of God, but by all of us, by you and me" (*Nobody* 126). This rhetorical move from an external authority (God) to a group consensus (all of us) to the individual (you and me) underscores the supreme importance of the individual, especially in terms of the individual's need to escape the labels that imprison him or her. In his final interview he tells Quincy Troupe, "I was not born to be defined by someone else, but by myself, and myself only" (Troupe 193). But writers rarely are remembered as individuals. If they are to be remembered, they are subject to classification, and it remains unclear a decade after his death what Baldwin's legacy will be. On one level—the level of popularity or fame—he seems to have "arrived": the austere Library of America recently issued a two-volume set of his works, edited by Toni Morrison, and Quincy Troupe's collection of essays by famous people and literary luminaries, though anecdotal, attests to Baldwin's fame as a public figure as well as author. Karen Thorsen's acclaimed documentary of Baldwin's life, *The Price of the Ticket* (1989), is a magnificent portrait of his life and contributions, while the positive reception of David Leeming's biography *James Baldwin* (1994) is testimony to Baldwin's enduring legacy as an author of merit.

Yet when it comes to literary history, Baldwin seems to have been overlooked, or unjustly reduced. Despite the fact that his influence is so wide and varied, and that there is so much to say about the impact of his art and his vision, critics, scholars, and teachers tend to skip over his works quickly. Although Hilton Als recently proclaimed him "the greatest Negro writer of his generation" (72), Baldwin's novels are certainly less likely to be included in American literature courses than novels by the three most prominent African American novelists of the past half-century: Richard Wright, Ralph Ellison, and Toni Morrison. The argument may go that—as Thomas Cooley has summarized the critical response to Mark Twain—Baldwin "is a great writer who never wrote a great book" (ix). But I believe that Baldwin's fate in literary history is more complex, and that it rests upon his refusal to attach himself to any single ideology, literary form, or vision. Because he never let himself be labeled as a gay writer, a black writer, a protest writer, a modern writer, a fiction writer, an essay writer, or a prophetic writer, his legacy is not entirely stable. Perhaps he achieved his succinct goal as stated at the beginning of his career: "I want to be an honest man and a good writer" (*Notes* 9). Honesty and goodness may describe Baldwin, but they are not useful categories for the literary historian.

Critics and anthology compilers generally have focused on three of Baldwin's works to represent his achievement: his first collection of essays, *Notes of a Native Son* (1955), his first novel, *Go Tell It on the Mountain* (1953), and a short story from his first collection, "Sonny's Blues" (1957).[1] Without calling into question the merit of these works—all of which regularly appear on my own syllabi—I took it upon myself to discover what (if anything) was being done with Baldwin's other works, the less visible ones: books that I loved, yet which I did not hear as much about. Through contact at conferences and a few informal solicitations, I discovered that there is an active subculture in literary studies currently unearthing and examining evidence of things not seen, to borrow Baldwin's final book title. His three "representative" works actually have served as starting points for these scholars and readers rather than end points. Baldwin's reputation is not fixed; it is in flux now, as it always has been, and future generations of Baldwin readers may be exposed to *Jimmy's Blues* or *Tell Me How Long the Train's Been Gone* before they read his earliest books. I hope that this collection will contribute to the process of revision that might (or might not) result in such a change. First, however, I would like to consider why Baldwin's reputation currently rests as it does largely on the three aforementioned works by tracing some significant patterns in Baldwin scholarship.

The most recent volume of scholarship devoted to Baldwin is Trudier Harris's edited collection *New Essays on Go Tell It On the Mountain* (1996). In her introduction, Harris points out that "*Go Tell It on the Mountain* has remained the primary novel through which readers come to Baldwin's works" (22). She attributes the novel's relative endurance to the power of its language—"its repetitious constructions, its realism, its evocative force, its almost hypnotic effect" (22)—as well as to its inventive use of church traditions, its autobiographical value, its place in the tradition of the *bildungsroman,* its portrayal of female characters, and its subtle (nearly invisible) treatment of race relations and homosexuality, which become overt topics in later works. These qualities do summarize the novel's appeal for critics, but they don't necessarily explain why it enjoys a greater reputation than subsequent works. Considering his novels alone for now, there are six to choose from; each is daring, inventive, and experimental, and each engages with the power of language in a fresh way.

Since it is rare that writers completely lose their talents over the course of a career, other forces must be at work in the selection of *Go Tell It* as Baldwin's finest novel. Writer and editor Mel Watkins claims,

> Among his fictional works—although he never wrote the great book that critics predicted he would—Baldwin's first novel, *Go Tell It on the Mountain* (1953), remains his highest achievement. . . . Baldwin's next novel, *Giovanni's Room* (1955), was a sketchy, tentatively drawn tale of a triangular love affair set in Paris. . . . Baldwin's next novel, *Another Country* (1962)—perhaps his most ambitious and controversial—and his last two, *If Beale Street Could Talk* (1974) and *Just Above My Head* (1979), like *Giovanni's Room,* were greeted with either mixed or less than enthusiastic critical response. Although these books seemed to strive for the large-scale social statement that his critics had demanded of him, they were not able to overcome blatant structural flaws and the Achilles' heel that plagued his fiction from the outset—a penchant for excessive rhetoric. (Troupe 113–14)

It will come as no surprise to the Baldwin scholar that Watkins neglects to mention *Tell Me How Long the Train's Been Gone* (1968) since it has been completely overlooked (and, alas, continues to be overlooked in this collection despite my efforts to find someone to write about it). More important is Watkins's accurate summary of the reception of Baldwin's novels: critics wanted a "large-scale social statement," yet they were put off by "excessive rhetoric." Driven by their expectations of a black writer, in other words, Baldwin's readers wanted him to be something he was not, some perfect hybrid of Ralph Ellison and Richard Wright. What these readers would term as Baldwin's failure to write "the great book that critics predicted he would," Baldwin would view as his own triumph as an individual, to have defined himself rather than allowed others to define him. These critics need only return to the conclusion of "Everybody's Protest Novel," the second essay in *Notes of a Native Son,* which speaks directly to their criticism: "The failure of the protest novel lies in its rejection of life, the human being, the denial of his beauty, dread, power, in its insistence that it is his categorization alone which is real and which cannot be transcended" (23).

But the fact remains that *Go Tell It* is widely seen as the closest Baldwin came to a great novel. Hilton Als confidently proclaims *Go Tell It* Baldwin's "first and best novel" (76), preferable to the "melodramatic plot" of *Giovanni's Room* that sets up "the sentimental, histrionic tone of Baldwin's later, unwieldy novels, notably *Another Country,*" which he deems "an artistic disaster" (77).[2] Certain questions should plague us: Are we still judging novels on the same scales of "greatness" that Baldwin's contemporary critics and reviewers used? Are we still reading or studying novels only because of their intrinsic greatness? And are we still trying to make Baldwin conform to our expectations, whether they are based on assumptions about aesthetics, race, or homosexuality?

Only half of Baldwin's critics regard him primarily as a novelist, though; the other half regard him as an essayist. Reflecting upon his first meeting with Baldwin, Henry Louis Gates, Jr. writes, "James Baldwin *was* literature for me, especially the essay" (Troupe 163), and in co-editing *The Norton Anthology of African American Literature* with Nellie McKay, Gates selected four of Baldwin's essays to represent him (all from *Notes of a Native Son*) along with one story ("Sonny's Blues"). Editors of essay collections have tried to claim Baldwin for their own; Gilbert H. Muller, for instance, describes Baldwin as a "novelist, short story writer, dramatist and, above all essayist" (166) whose job was to probe the American consciousness of race. (I take on the absence of "poet" from Mueller's list in my essay at the end of this volume.) After dismissing all of Baldwin's novels after *Go Tell It* and before calling his plays "ill-conceived and poorly written" (79), Hilton Als asserts, "It was in Baldwin's essays, unencumbered by the requirements of narrative form, character, and incident, that his voice was most fully realized" (77). Baldwin himself declared in the 1984 preface to *Notes of a Native Son,* "I had never thought of myself as an essayist: the idea had never entered my mind" (xi). When David Estes followed up on that statement in a 1986 interview, asking Baldwin if he considered either his fiction or his essays more important, Baldwin responded, "No, as a matter of fact I didn't. I thought of myself as a writer. I didn't want to get trapped in any particular form. I wanted to try them all" (Standley and

Pratt 276). Yet there is no question that he became famous in his ᴏ.. lifetime as a result of his powerful essays in addition to his fiction.

After *Notes of a Native Son* (and, to a lesser degree, *Nobody Knows My Name*) Baldwin's nonfiction, like his fiction, became more experimental. Essays from these first two collections are brilliant for their rhetoric, their topicality, and their undeniable beauty: in short, they are perfect examples of the genre. Critics have had a much harder time characterizing a book like *The Devil Finds Work* (1976), an extended meditation on American film, or *Nobody Knows My Name,* something between a memoir and an essay. In the final years of an extraordinary career Baldwin had to take his manuscript for *The Evidence of Things Not Seen* (1985) to a publisher he had not worked with before, a fact that reflects not only the book's controversial subject matter but also how far he had departed from his early successes. Baldwin's extended essay on race relations, *The Fire Next Time* (1963), was the piece that truly made him a superstar; but it also sealed off the early part of his career. It can only get worse now that it's gotten so good, to paraphrase Mary McCarthy's apology for not having read more of Baldwin's writings. Horace Porter, in the introduction to his acclaimed study of Baldwin's oeuvre, *Stealing the Fire* (1989), writes without apology or explanation, "My perceptions and insights are drawn from the body of Baldwin's work, ranging from his earliest essays and reviews published during the late 1940s to an address delivered to the National Press Club in December 1986, but, except by implication and in brief allusions, I do not go beyond *The Fire Next Time* published in 1963" (xii). By 1963, it seems, readers felt that the news was all in on Baldwin. We can stop reading him now; he's just going to try our patience, like Joyce did with *Finnegans Wake,* or like the Beatles did with *The White Album.* Apparently, artists risk the favor of critics and readers when they deviate too far from their early successes. But the fact that they take such risks may make them "true artists," to recall Morrison's assessment of Baldwin.

The time has come to reconsider some of Baldwin's lesser-known and later writings. This collection is not the first book to suggest that some of his work has been overlooked or undervalued critically. Louis H. Pratt in his 1978 study *James Baldwin* attempts to address "the compelling need for a more thorough assessment of Baldwin's writings," including "several of the virtually unexamined aspects of Baldwin's art" (9). Yet written as it was before the publication of *Just Above My Head, The Evidence of Things Not Seen,* and *Jimmy's Blues,* Pratt's effort cannot be comprehensive, and it also predates two decades of development in literary theory and the methods of interpretation that have shaped the way we think about literature. A more recent study like Trudier Harris's *Black Women in the Fiction of James Baldwin* (1985) is admirable both for its feminist approach and for its engagement with all of Baldwin's fiction; still, it is of necessity limited to a single approach to his work, and it examines only his fiction.

The chapters in this volume examine works by Baldwin that have not received much critical attention in the past, approach some of his more canonical works from fresh critical perspectives, or both. Although many of the chapters refer to the three widely read works, none focuses on these early works. David Leeming asserts that "*The Amen Corner* stands with *Notes of a Native Son* as a continuation of the story of the Baldwin hero begun in *Go Tell It on the Mountain*" (107), yet the play—originally produced in 1955 and published in 1968—has received little critical attention, either as a companion piece to Baldwin's famous works or on its own. Saadi Simawe's chapter "What Is in a Sound? The Metaphysics and Politics of Music in *The Amen Corner*" casts the play in terms of a broad discussion of music and its relationship to philosophy and ideology. Music, particularly the blues, is a touchstone of Baldwin criticism, and it clearly is essential to even a surface understanding of all of Baldwin's fiction from *Go Tell It* through *Just Above My Head*. Simawe's chapter fills in this context considerably with an expansive consideration of music in terms of Baldwin as well as the philosophical underpinnings of music. In "Staying Out of the Temple: Baldwin, the African American Church, and *The Amen Corner*," Michael Lynch considers the impact of Baldwin's relationship with the church as it develops out of *Go Tell It* and into *The Amen Corner*, and he also addresses why the play is overlooked in favor of the novel.

Baldwin's second novel, *Giovanni's Room*, is an excellent example of how the widespread desire to label his works has affected their reputation. As one of the first American novels to discuss homosexuality overtly, and as one of the most honest and enduring engagements with the topic, *Giovanni's Room* has the dubious distinction of being Baldwin's "gay novel" even though Baldwin claimed that "*Giovanni's Room* is not really about homosexuality. It's the vehicle through which the book moves" (Troupe 176). Kathleen Drowne's chapter "'An Irrevocable Condition': Constructions of Home and the Writing of Place in *Giovanni's Room*" departs from the critical trend of considering this novel strictly in terms of its treatment of homosexuality and explores the moral significance Baldwin attaches to landscape, both in terms of actual space and psychological placement. Taking a psychological approach to Baldwin's novel, Susan Feldman addresses normative readings of *Another Country* and offers a fresh counterreading that considers how Baldwin's representation of love and sexuality in that novel seeks to overcome false oppositions between private and social realms in America more generally. In her chapter "Another Look at *Another Country:* Reconciling Baldwin's Racial and Sexual Politics," Feldman explores bisexuality as a quintessential Baldwinian motif, analyzing it through both psychological and historical lenses. Charles Toombs's chapter "Black-Gay-Man Chaos in *Another Country*" focuses on the three intertwined facets of Rufus Scott's identity in the novel—race, repressed homosexuality, and masculinity—to discuss Baldwin's chaotic and complex aesthetic. No single facet of Rufus's personality explains the novel's themes adequately; the key, according to Toombs, is to examine their interaction.

Masculinity, homosexuality, and race are three of the aspects of identity construction that Baldwin bifurcates and then deconstructs throughout his career, according to Yasmin DeGout. In "Masculinity and (Im)maturity: 'The Man Child' and Other Stories in Baldwin's Gender Studies Enterprise," DeGout argues that Baldwin's theories prefigured current trends in gender studies theory, and she illustrates her argument through some of the critically overlooked stories in *Going to Meet the Man.* Joshua Miller, in his chapter "'A Striking Addiction to Irreality': *Nothing Personal* and the Legacy of the Photo-Text Genre," examines a book that has become his most obscure: his 1964 collaboration with photographer Richard Avedon, *Nothing Personal.* Miller contextualizes this book within the genre's development, then considers African American variations on the genre, and departs from there to arrive at an understanding of the ultimate impact and purpose of Baldwin and Avedon's book. Cassandra Ellis also engages with one of Baldwin's undervalued works, *The Devil Finds Work,* in "The Black Boy Looks at the Silver Screen: Baldwin as Moviegoer." Analyzing this book and many of Baldwin's others with an approach that borrows from film studies, literary theory, and history, Ellis casts Baldwin in the familiar role of witness, but a witness of American cinema in particular rather than of America more generally.

In the final years of his career Baldwin continued to experiment and attempted a number of ambitious works, refusing to repeat the styles and modes of inquiry that garnered critical acclaim for his early successes. Warren Carson's chapter on Baldwin's final novel, "Manhood, Musicality, and Male Bonding in *Just Above My Head*" studies the importance of music to the novel, but moves into a consideration of male relationships as they are expressed in the book. The final chapter is my own contribution, "James Baldwin, Poet," in which I analyze the critical abandonment of Baldwin's only commercially published book of poetry, *Jimmy's Blues,* and discuss how his spare, lucid presentation of his lifelong themes earn Baldwin the title of poet, even though he never has been regarded as one. I realize that the title labels Baldwin, even though my intention is to correct for other generic labels that have been applied to him. By calling Baldwin a poet, I hope to encourage readers to rethink him, to see the aspects of his career which have gone unseen.

As all of the chapters show, there is ample evidence to make the case for Baldwin as a true artist with far more breadth and scope than his few early commercial successes would indicate. Just three years before his death, in an interview in *The Paris Review,* Baldwin stated, "I hope, certainly, that my best work is before me.... I certainly have not told my story yet" (Standley and Pratt 242). Literary critics are still telling Baldwin's story, too; and it turns out that it has more than one version.

NOTES

1. "Sonny's Blues" has long been the story included in both the *Heath Anthology of American Literature,* McGraw Hill's *The American Tradition in Literature,* and the *Prentice-Hall Anthology of American Literature* as well as the recently published *Norton Anthology of African American Literature.* In its new fifth edition, the *Norton Anthology of American Literature* substituted "Going to Meet the Man" for "The Fire Next Time."

2. Reflecting the common trend in appraisals of Baldwin's work, Hilton Als fails to even mention *Tell Me How Long the Train's Been Gone, If Beale Street Could Talk,* and *Just Above My Head* in his article.

WORKS CITED

Als, Hilton. "The Enemy Within." *The New Yorker,* 16 February 1988, 72–80.

Baldwin, James. *Notes of a Native Son.* Boston: Beacon, 1955.

———. *Nobody Knows My Name.* New York: Dell, 1961.

Baym, Nina et al., eds. *The Norton Anthology of American Literature,* 5th ed. New York: Norton, 1999.

Cooley, Thomas et al., eds. *Adventures of Huckleberry Finn.* 2d. ed. New York: Norton, 1977.

Gates, Henry Louis Jr. and Nellie Y. McKay, eds. *The Norton Anthology of African American Literature.* New York: Norton, 1997.

Harris, Trudier. *Black Women in the Fiction of James Baldwin.* Knoxville: University of Tennessee Press, 1985.

———, ed. *New Essays on Go Tell It on the Mountain.* Cambridge: Cambridge University Press, 1996.

Lauter, Paul, ed. *The Heath Anthology of American Literature,* 3rd ed. Boston: Houghton Mifflin, 1998.

Leeming, David A. *James Baldwin: A Biography.* New York: Knopf, 1994.

McMichael, George, ed. *Concise Anthology of American Literature,* 4th ed. Upper Saddle River, N.J.: Prentice Hall, 1998.

Perkins, George and Barbara Perkins, eds. *The American Tradition in Literature,* 9th ed. Boston: McGraw Hill, 1999.

Porter, Horace. *Stealing the Fire: The Art and Protest of James Baldwin.* Middletown, Conn.: Wesleyan University Press, 1989.

Pratt, Louis. *James Baldwin.* Boston: Twayne, 1978.

Standley, Fred L. and Louis H. Pratt, eds. *Conversations With James Baldwin.* Jackson: University Press of Mississippi, 1989.

Troupe, Quincy. *James Baldwin: The Legacy.* New York: Simon & Schuster, 1989.

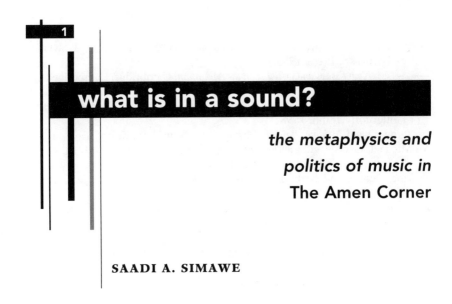

what is in a sound?

the metaphysics and
politics of music in
The Amen Corner

SAADI A. SIMAWE

This ferment, this disturbance, is the responsibility and the neces-
sity, of writers. It is, alas, the truth that to be an American writer
today means mounting an unending attack on all that Americans
believe themselves to hold sacred. It means fighting an astute and
agile guerrilla warfare with that American complacency which so
inadequately masks the American panic.   —James Baldwin

My models—my private models—are not
Hemingway, not Faulkner, not Dos Passos, or indeed
any American writer. I model myself on jazz
musicians, dancers, a couple of whores and a few junkies.
                                                  —James Baldwin

"THE BLUES IS MAN"

In almost all his work, James Baldwin aspires to become what
he views as the supreme artist, namely, the musician—in particular the
blues singer.[1] Further, Baldwin seems to have felt a link between his
vision of himself as "the incorrigible disturber of the peace" ("The Creative Process," 316) and music, the medium traditionally perceived as
the ideal subversive art, the one that eludes the control of mind and

rationality to appeal directly to passions and emotions, even instincts, in order to liberate them. Baldwin's crusade against the established moral order and the ideological apparatuses that support it, with music as his primary weapon, does not seem a lonely crusade or an isolated incident if examined in the broader context of the traditional hostility between the philosopher, the statesman, the ideologue, or the doctrinaire on the one hand, and the musician, the singer, the dancer, or the artist on the other. This hostility is articulated in Plato's *Republic,* where the philosopher declares his distrust of music, primarily due to its uncontrollable effect on human passions and emotions.

In this chapter, I will examine Baldwin's concept of music and its power, as depicted in his 1955 play *The Amen Corner,* in the broader context of the philosophical debate over the uneasy relationship between music and ideology or religion.[2] Before discussing the role that African American music plays in *The Amen Corner* in subverting repressive realities and ultimately liberating the major characters, I will situate Baldwin's concept of music in the traditional philosophical battle between music and ideology. Two confluent themes in *The Amen Corner,* white oppression and repressive religious puritanism, seem to make music the only medium that constantly eludes the reach of repression for Baldwin. In this context, it is illuminating to read Baldwin's characterization of music as subversion in the clash between music and proscriptive systems of morality and ideology. At the same time, this broader context will help highlight the universality and existentiality of Baldwin's vision of music as the archetypal medium of boundless humanity.

In his seminal work *The Philosopher and Music: An Historical Outline,* Julius Portnoy concludes his systematic study of traditional philosophical views of music and the musician by emphasizing the moral philosopher's perennial fear of the effect of music:

> The philosopher has persistently believed throughout history, with few exceptions, that music without words is inferior to music with words. It is the embodiment of emotion in tone and rhythm that awakens in us feelings that the composer felt to some degree when producing the music. But the philosopher is never sure that feelings can be trusted. He insists that words added to music conceptualize feeling, make the indefinite definite, and move the art of music from the lower level of emotion to the exalted plane of reason. (5)

Moral philosophers, ideologues, religious leaders, and doctrinaires—including Plato, Aristotle, Saint Augustine, Luther, Kant,

Descartes, Hegel, Schopenhauer, Kierkegaard, Cotton Mather, William James, and Allan Bloom—all rationalize, in distinct ways, their fear and distrust of music and the musician.[3] Aware of music's power over humans, Plato in the *Republic* distrusts pure melody, which he sees as lacking specific meaning. According to Plato, the danger of music lies in its very nature. Rhythm and harmony "most of all insinuate themselves into the innermost part of the soul and most vigorously lay hold of it in bringing grace with them; and they make a man graceful if he is correctly reared [in music], if not, the opposite" (80). Significantly, Plato warns the overseers of the Republic of music's decisive political power: "For never are the ways of music moved without the greatest political laws being removed." In order to contain music's unwanted effect, Plato insists on imposing words on music to make it make sense (90; 101–2; 77–78). Naturally, the act of making sense, the choice of words, the very nature of meaning, and the established concept of reason are all symptoms of the dominant ideology that ultimately determine the acceptable discourse. Likewise, Aristotle is keenly aware of the unlimited power of music in his *Politics* and he raises doubts and fears concerning music and its spiritual and educational value. "Music," he says, "has a power of forming the character, and should therefore, be introduced into the education of the young." But because music can affect all human passions, whether noble or ignoble, he distrusts its unrestricted effect in education (1306–12). More significantly, the father of Western theology, Saint Augustine, in his *Confessions* (c. 400), warns the faithful against the inherent sexual and erotic appeal of even religious music and songs (261–62).

In *The Amen Corner,* more than in any other of his works, Baldwin captures this rivalry and hostility between religious leaders and church musicians, let alone secular musicians in the street. As far as I know, no evidence exists that Baldwin was aware of the debate between the moral philosopher and the musician that permeates Western philosophy and culture. But that is not relevant, as many thinkers and critics have shown convincingly that writers are naturally influenced by cultural, historical, and even archetypal forces that they may be unaware of. In this context, Roland Barthes's concept of intertextuality in his *Image, Music, Text* (1977) proves illuminating: "We know now that a text is not a line of words releasing theological meaning (the 'message' of the 'author-God') but a multi-dimensional space in which a variety of writings, none of them original, blend and clash. The text is a tissue of quotations drawn from the innumerable centers of culture" (146). Accordingly, Baldwin's quarrel—and that of his musician- or his music-loving characters—with the established ideology is in fact one battle in the ongoing war between the musician and the ideologue. The clash with the church, reason, mind, conventions, morality, and rationality can be seen as one front in the struggle of the spirit, or the soul, as it is fully reflected in music, against the tyranny of rationality and ideology. Baldwin's well-known experimentation with bluesification or jazz-ification of fiction and style thus may be understood as genuine and ingenious attempts at liberating the soul from what he views as one of the ideological grids, the prison-house of language.

Baldwin's titles indicate how much his vision is informed by his interest in music, especially African American music. Titles such as *Go Tell It on the Mountain* (1953), *The Amen Corner* (1955), "Sonny's Blues" (1957), *The Fire Next Time* (1963), *Blues for Mister Charlie* (1964), *Tell Me How Long the Train's Been Gone* (1968), *If Beale Street Could Talk* (1974), and *Just Above My Head* (1979) all, with their evident allusions to traditional African American songs, inform the faith and trust Baldwin has put in the subversive, liberatory, and counter-spiritual power of African American music. In many of his essays and interviews, Baldwin underscores the spiritual role that music plays in sustaining and empowering African Americans in their struggle. In the 1951 essay "Many Thousands Gone," Baldwin points to the multifaceted power of music as a mask, as a subversive weapon, as a narrative for a story that language cannot grasp, and as a system of symbols and signs:

> It is only in his music, which Americans are able to admire because a protective sentimentality limits their understanding of it, that the Negro in America has been able to tell his story. It is a story which otherwise has yet to be told and which no American is prepared to hear. As is the inevitable result of things unsaid, we find ourselves until today oppressed with a dangerous and reverberating silence; and the story is told, compulsively, in symbols and signs, in hieroglyphics. (*Price of the Ticket* 65)

This masking that music provides—simultaneously a subversive technique and a liberating force for the silenced—later is accentuated by Baldwin in a 1972 interview with Nikki Giovanni:

> What we call black literature is really summed up for me by the whole career, let's say, of Bessie Smith, Ray Charles, Aretha Franklin, because that's the way it's been handed down. . . . We had to smuggle information, and we did it through our music and we did it in the church. (Giovanni and Baldwin 75)

Another essential component of the ideal condition of the blues, as Baldwin defines it, is its ability to make people learn, mature, and ultimately gain wisdom from suffering, which may be seen as the blues connection to the Biblical concept of suffering as a way to wisdom. The problem with religion, according to Baldwin, is that it frightens people and forces them to hide in a self-deluding myth of eternal safety. "There is something monstrous about never having been hurt, never having been made to bleed, never having lost anything, never having gained anything because life is beautiful and in order to keep it beautiful you're going to stay just the way you are and you're not going to test your theory against all the possibilities outside" ("The Uses of the Blues" 131–32). By contrast, the blues experience, as Baldwin sees it, is clear-eyed and sardonic in the face of harsh realities. Baldwin's blues artist, in many ways reminiscent of Nietzsche's subversive Dionysian musician,[4] is not afraid that he has no hopes. "Ray Charles, who is a great tragic artist, makes of a genuinely religious confession something triumphant and liberating. He tells us that he cried so loud he gave the blues to his neighbor next door" ("The Uses of the Blues" 241).

Even before he lost faith in formal religion and left the church in 1942, Baldwin discovered that he was a natural verbal improviser when he gave sermons:

> I would improvise from the texts, like a jazz musician improvises from a theme. I never wrote a sermon—I studied the texts. I've never written a speech. I can't read a speech. It's kind of give and take. You have to sense the people you're talking to. You have to respond to what they hear. (Sandley and Pratt 234–35)

Moreover, it was music—not religion or literature or the consolation of philosophy—that helped Baldwin reconcile himself to his African American heritage and eventually inspired him to write his first novel, *Go Tell It on the Mountain:*

> There [in Switzerland], in that absolutely alabaster landscape, armed with two Bessie Smith records and a typewriter, I began to try to recreate the life that I had first known as a child and from which I had spent so many years in flight.
>
> It was Bessie Smith, through her tone and her cadence, who helped me to dig back to the way I myself must have spoken when I was a pickaninny, and to remember the things I had heard and seen and felt. I had buried them very deep. I have never listened to Bessie Smith in Amer-

ica (in the same way that, for years I would not touch watermelon), but in Europe she helped to reconcile me to being a "nigger." (*The Price of the Ticket* 172)

On many other occasions, Baldwin describes his performance as a writer of fiction in terms of music, especially African American music. Without claiming any knowledge of music as an art, Baldwin nevertheless continues describing himself as a "blues singer" or "jazz musician" and hopes that readers receive his fiction as they would hear black music. "I would like to think that some of the people who liked it [*Another Country* (1962)] responded to it in the way they respond when Miles [Davis] and Ray [Charles] are blowing" (Campbell 181). With the typical hostility of the musician toward ideology and intellectuality, Baldwin often protests "I am not an intellectual . . . and do not want to be" (Campbell 181). Literary critics, Baldwin once declared, can make sense only "[w]hen I understand that they understand Ray Charles" (Giovanni and Baldwin 84). In an interview with Quincy Troupe a few months before Baldwin died in 1987, he states that in his last novel, *Just Above My Head* (1978), he attempts to face his "own legends," that is, the deep down spaces he has been scared to venture into. And in this Orphic descent into hell, music acts as both his guide and guardian: "The key to one's life is always in a lot of unexpected places. I tried to deal with what I was most afraid of. That's why the vehicle of the book is music. Because music was and is my salvation" (Troupe 26).

In Baldwin's mind, as his statements suggest, music is associated with liberation, security, mystical power, self-reconciliation, a more democratic divine power, unrestricted humanism, and sexuality that is inseparable from spirituality. Early in his life when Baldwin was under his religious father's control, secular African American music seems to have heightened his awareness of his individuality, of the world outside the church and Harlem, and thus legitimized his rebellion against father and church and any stifling ideologies, whether religious or nationalistic (Leeming 18). His new love was art, not religion:

> Beauford Delaney's small studio with a black stove and paintings everywhere and music always playing—the kind of music Baldwin's stepfather would never have in the house was part of the Harlem culture—Ma Rainey, Louis Armstrong, Bessie Smith, all the greats of the twenties and thirties—became a second home for Jimmy Baldwin. (Weatherby 30)

Baldwin embraced the world of art with the same religious passion with which he had earlier embraced the church: as a haven of security and safety. As his biographer James Campbell has noted in *Talking at the Gates: A Life of James Baldwin,* Baldwin rejected the concept of a God that cannot "make us larger, freer, and more loving." Yet to the very end of his career, Baldwin's life

> was based on a faith that can only be called religious, just as his thought was infused with religious belief. His scripture was the old black gospel music:
>
> > *Just above my head*
> > *I hear music in the air*
> > *And I really do believe*
> > *There's a God somewhere. (281)*

It is very significant that Baldwin, who once found in formal religion a safe haven from both the white world and his tyrannical father, decided later in his uncompromising search for self to replace religion with music. The essential similarity between religion and music, in terms of the appeal each holds, may indicate that Baldwin had not in fact strayed far from religion when he replaced it with music. Both have the power to create a temporary sense of immortality. In music, as Hegel has illustrated, the subjective and the objective momentarily collapse, and a sense of absoluteness takes over the listener (907–8).[5] In *The Raw and the Cooked: Introduction to a Science of Mythology,* a study of the nature and power of myth, Claude Lévi-Strauss sees surprising similarity in the ways myth (or, by extension, religion,) and music affect humans through a common fundamental characteristic. That is, myth and music

> share of both being languages which, in their different ways, transcend articulate expression, while at the same time—like articulate speech, but unlike painting—requiring a temporal dimension in which to unfold. But this relation to time is of a rather special nature: it is as if music and mythology needed time only in order to deny it. Both, indeed, are instruments for the obliteration of time. Below the level of sounds and rhythms, music acts upon a primitive terrain, which is the physiological time of the listener; this time is irreversible and therefore irredeemably diachronic, yet music transmutes the segment devoted to listening to it into a synchronic totality, enclosed within itself. Because of

the internal organization of the musical work, the act of listening to it immobilizes passing time; it catches and enfolds it as one catches and enfolds a cloth flapping in the wind. It follows that by listening to music, and while we are listening to it, we enter into a kind of immortality. (Lévi-Strauss 15–16)

Despite this essential similarity in their functions, music and myth (or religion) differ in their connections to language: while music can achieve its maximum power without language, as Kierkegaard has remarked,[6] myth is restricted by language and ideology. This purportedly absolute freedom that music promises seems to have fascinated Baldwin, and with almost the same religious passion, he embraced the music of his ancestors. Ralph Ellison, a musician and a writer, articulates what Baldwin and many African American writers seem to perceive as a natural nexus between music and freedom:

As a slave was, to the extent that he was a musician, one who expressed himself in music, a man who realized himself in the world of sound. Thus, while he might stand in awe before the superior technical ability of a white musician, and while he was forced to recognize a superior social status, he would never feel awed before the music which the technique of white musician made available. His attitude as a "musician" would lead him to seek to possess the music expressed through the technique, but until he could do so he would hum, whistle, sing or play the tunes to the best of his ability on any available instrument. And it was indeed out of the tension between desire and ability that the technique of jazz emerged. This was likewise true of American Negro choral singing. *For this, no literary explanation, no cultural analyses, no political slogans—indeed, not even a high degree of social or political freedom—was required. For the art—the blues, the spirituals, the dance—was what we had in place of freedom.* (Ellison 254–55, italics added)

MUSIC AS RELIGION, MUSIC VERSUS ESTABLISHED RELIGION IN *THE AMEN CORNER*

In *The Amen Corner,* Baldwin treats the same haunting themes as he does in his other works: the power of the church and the power of music. The opening stage directions construct in rich symbolism of place and space the major forces of the main dramatic conflict: "Before the curtain rises, we hear street sounds, laughter, cursing, snatches of

someone's radio; and under everything, the piano, which David is playing in the church. . . . The church is on a level above the apartment and
should give the impression of dominating the family's living quarters"
(5). While David's piano is "under everything," the church "should give
the impression" of dominating the lives of the major characters.
Throughout the play, we gradually become aware of a crucial dramatic
irony: What is "under everything," namely music, is what actually dominates and influences the real life of the individuals, whether musicians
or not. To further emphasize the role of music in the fate of these characters, Baldwin ends the opening stage directions with:

> At rise, there is a kind of subdued roar and humming, out of which is
> heard the music prologue, "The Blues Is Man," which segues into a
> steady rollicking beat, and we see the congregation singing. (6)

The general image that emerges from the stage directions is that
music—the undercurrent and more genuine life of the characters—is
in constant conflict with the powers of religion symbolized by a dominating "pulpit" with an "immense open Bible" (5) and "the congregation singing" (6). Significantly, the pulpit, the Bible, and the singing are
all various tools for religious discourse. Of course, of the three, the
least discursive and most musical is church singing. In the last section
of this chapter, I will examine the expedient, yet uneasy, suspect, and
problematic presence of music in the church, as it is dramatically
embodied in the character of David.

In *The Amen Corner* there are two major musicians: Luke and his
son, David. Luke plays the blues, of course outside the church. Young
David plays music in the church under the fanatical instruction of his
mother, Sister Margaret, the minister in a Harlem storefront church.
After a miscarriage due to malnutrition, Margaret turns to religion and
absolutely rejects all worldly desires, especially sexual love. Losing her
love, Luke starts to go under, leaving home and immersing himself in
drinking. As a homeless vagabond, he plays jazz both to make a living
and to sustain his sanity, as he later tells his son. Typical of Baldwin's
figure of the artist, Luke is both a powerful jazz musician and an iconoclast, especially against established religion. In his battle against the
establishment, his weapon is music and his ultimate desire is love: not
Christian love, but unlimited humanistic love. When Luke suddenly
reappears after a ten-year absence in downtown New York, his jazz, like
a Biblical serpent, starts to penetrate Margaret's religious and ascetic
defenses. Despite years of religious instruction against his father's music

and worldliness and against the satanic white world full of movies, alcohol, drugs, and jazz, David is attracted by Luke's music. It emboldens his individuality and rebellion. Like John Grimes in *Go Tell It on the Mountain,* who, according to his tyrannical father, is secretly fascinated with the "pleasures" and "sins" of the white world, David starts to visit clandestinely the bar where his father plays jazz with white musicians:

> BROTHER BOXER: I got news for you, Sister Odessa, Little David ain't so little no more. I stood right in this very room last Sunday when we found out that boy had been lying to his mother. That's right. He been going out to bars. And just this very evening, not five minutes ago, I seen him down on 125th Street with some white horn-player—the one he say he go to school with—and two other boys and three girls. (*The Amen Corner* 37–38)

After years of absence, Luke comes back to the storefront church to retrieve his wife who has been, according to him, kidnapped by the Lord: She gives all her love to the Lord, not to humans, not even to herself. Like Elisha, the musician in *Go Tell It on the Mountain,* the congregation and even his mother view David as vulnerable, a possible backslider, and suspect (23, 38). Actually, it is through David, the weakest member of the church, that Luke comes to invade the church with his jazz and ultimately overcomes the Lord in Margaret's heart. Although he is dying, Luke wins the battle against Margaret's God, shattering the house that she thought for years she had put in order: her favorite Biblical text obsessively has been, "Set thine house in order, for thou shalt die and not live" (8). Ironically, once she rediscovers love, she loses the power to preach. Similarly, when Luke regains love, he dies and all that jazz is stopped. Metaphorically speaking, once his love is requited, Luke the musician dies, for there seems to be no need for music anymore. Actually Luke (or Baldwin) is quite aware of the connection between music and suffering in the hell of the absence of love:[7]

> LUKE: When you seen me. And you go to wondering all over again if you wanted to be like your daddy and end up like your daddy. Ain't that right?
>
> DAVID: Yeah, I guess that's right.
>
> LUKE: Well, son, tell you one thing. Wasn't music put me here. The most terrible time in a man's life, David, is when he's done lost everything that held him together—it's just gone and he can't find it. The

whole world just get to be a great big empty basin. And it just as hollow as a basin when you strike it with your fist. Then that man start going down. If don't no hand reach out to help him, that man goes under . . . and, son, I don't believe no man ever got to that without somebody loved him.

DAVID: Daddy—weren't the music enough?

LUKE: The music. The music. Music is a moment. But life's a long time. In that moment, when it's good, when you really swinging— then you joined to everything, to everybody, to skies and stars and every living thing. But music ain't kissing. Kissing's what you want to do. Music's what you got to do, if you got to do it. Question is how long you can keep up with music when you ain't got nobody to kiss. You know, the music don't come out of the air, baby. It comes out of the man who's blowing it. (43–44)

But love, as Baldwin seems to suggest through Luke and Sister Margaret, is the end of suffering and of music and of religion. For it is in the absence of love, when "the whole world just get to be a great big empty basin," that music and religion seem to be needed most. This absolute emptiness threatens Luke with frightening silence and looming death. Thus, sonority, or just noisemaking, as both Theodor Adorno and Gilles Deleuze expound, negates silence; and music, or human sound in turn, not only negates death but also affirms and celebrates life. In this sense the musician such as Luke, consciously or not, plays to avow life in the face of silence and death. "The song is like a rough sketch of a calming and stabilizing, calm and stable, center in the heart of chaos" (Deleuze 201). To Luke, "music's what you got to do, if you got to do it" primarily because he, lonely in an empty universe, is frightened by the silence, the sure archetypal image of death, and has to play to join, at least momentarily, "to everything, to everybody, to skies and stars and every living thing." From an existential point of view, Adorno seems to articulate Luke's intuition that human exigencies such as fear, loneliness, and absence of love or meaning compel the musician to play and the listeners to relate:

By circling people, by enveloping them—as inherent in the acoustical phenomenon—and turning them as listeners into participants [and vice versa, by extension], it [music] contributes ideologically to the integration which modern society never tires of achieving in reality. It leaves no room for conceptual reflection between itself and the subject, and so it creates an illusion of immediacy in the totally mediated world, of proximity between strangers, of warmth for those who come to feel the chill of the unmitigated struggle of all against all. (Adorno 46)

As a musician, Luke, like Adorno, is aware that "music is a moment" of integration, and that life requires more than just music in order to be a happy one. Experience has taught Luke that love does not need music. Rather, music, coming out of that "empty basin," is a cry for love, and that is what actually happens when the estranged lovers, Luke and Margaret—who took refuge in music and religion, respectively—rediscover that they still love each other: They immediately lose their powers of playing and preaching.

In *The Amen Corner,* the traditional quarrel between music and religion (or the musician and the preacher) is dramatically delineated. Here, more emphatically than in *Go Tell It on the Mountain,* the worldly musician is able not only to effectively preach human love and sexuality, but also to ultimately seduce and convert the pastor to the world. Not only an apostle of human love, Luke as a jazz musician, even while dying, teaches his son, like Nietzsche's Dionysian musician, to dance in the face of the hostile world. Luke tells David: "Son—don't try to get away from the things that hurt you—sometimes that's all you got. You got to learn to live with those things—and—use them. I've seen people—put themselves through terrible torture—and die—because they was afraid of getting hurt" (41–42).

In the context of the play, Luke here clearly alludes to his wife, Sister Margaret, who—out of fear of the hostile outside world, with its racism, poverty, sex, drugs, and crime—has for ten years repressed her own worldly desires, denied her husband love when he most needed it, forced her son to play religious music against his will, and enslaved and alienated her congregation. While Luke inspires his son to face up to the hostile world outside the church and to try to make the best out of it by means of will power and music, he forces Sister Margaret, as Darwin Turner observes, to "recall the past and to perceive the truth that her venture into religion was not a response to a call from God but a flight motivated by her own fear of life" (193). In that confessional scene, Luke not only succeeds in making his wife reconcile life and human reality within her and without, he even inspires her to utter the play's most important passage, as identified by Baldwin in his introduction (xv):

MARGARET: All these years I prayed as hard as I knowed how. I tried to put my treasure in heaven where couldn't nothing get at it and take it away from me and leave me alone. I asked the Lord to hold my hand. I didn't expect that none of this would ever rise to hurt me no more. And all these years it just been waiting for me, waiting for me to turn a corner. And there it stands, my whole life, just like I hadn't never gone nowhere. *It's an awful thing to think about, the way love never dies!* (81, italics added)

The ending demonstrates the musician's power to bring the idea of love down to earth, where it is most needed, like Prometheus stealing the fire from the gods. Symbolically significant, Sister Margaret gets confused in the middle of her final sermon, immediately after Luke's death in her arms, when she notices his trombone mouthpiece "clenched against her breast" (87). Her newly acquired sense of herself as an individual in need of human love not only costs her the gift to deliver the traditional sermon of abstract divine love, but it also reveals her unconscious yearning for jazz. And for the first and last time, since the elders have decided to dismiss her as a pastor, Margaret uses no text, speaking spontaneously from the heart like a jazz musician improvising:

MARGARET: Children. I'm just now finding out what it means to love the Lord. It ain't all in the singing and the shouting. It ain't all in the reading of the Bible (She unclenches her fist a little). It ain't even—it ain't even—in running all over everybody trying to get to heaven. To love the Lord is to love all His children—all of them, every one!—and suffer with them and rejoice with them and never count the cost! (88)

This dramatic epiphany profoundly not only shatters "the house" that for many years Margaret thought she had kept in order, but it also undermines the symbolic order of the church as an ideological construction that thrives on self- and world-denial. The "singing and the shouting," "the reading of the Bible," and the "running all over everybody trying to get to heaven," according to the disillusioned Margaret (and, of course, to Baldwin), do not lead to honest and happy life. Judged by the moral scales implicit in the play, Luke the jazz musician is more honest, more life-affirming, and more spiritual than Margaret the pastor. Similarly, David discovers, thanks to his musical talent and to his father, that the church has turned his mother into a hypocrite and a liar. Outside the church he recognizes the purity of his music, his liberated individuality, and a larger consciousness of the human condition.

But what is there in the nature of sound that makes music, as the play seems to advocate, the sole arbiter of truth, honesty, and freedom? And what specifically prevents music in the church from functioning in the same manner as secular music?

"TO THE RIGHT OF THE PULPIT, THE PIANO, THE TOP OF WHICH IS CLUTTERED WITH HYMNBOOKS"

Because *The Amen Corner* is a tragedy in the Aristotelian sense with powerful irony, reversal, and recognition, it begins by underscoring the pride and dignity of the dominant dramatic characters, who are unaware of their fatal tragic flaws. In the opening, we hear powerful singing, whose lyrics run for almost the first two pages. The content of the spirituals is love of the Lord, of His miracles, and of abstract love of His creation. The implicit dramatic and tragic irony, which, of course, becomes more poignant on a second reading or viewing of the play, lies in the fact that the singing, while releasing genuine yearning for love, mystifies the real object and subject of love: the human. By privileging the words and the Word over music and desire, the singing becomes, like the singers, a suppressed music of suppressed individuals. Yet even in this form of ideology-controlled music, the church elders—and the religious in general, historically speaking—have mixed feelings toward music's ultimate impact on worshippers. The relationship between the Word and music always has been acrimonious, at least since Plato and Saint Augustine, as many historians of music and the church have revealed. In his *Republic,* Plato grudgingly recognizes music's unlimited power over the soul. But in order to engage that power in his ideological and moral vision, he mandates that music must be accompanied by words (77–78). More specifically, Saint Augustine, the great founder of Western Christianity, in his *Confessions* expresses the traditional ambivalence of religious leaders toward even church singing:

> But when I remember the tears that I shed on hearing the songs of the church in the early days, soon after I recovered my faith, and when I realize that nowadays it is not the singing that moves me but the meaning of the words when they are sung in a clear voice to the appropriate tune, I again acknowledge the great value of this practice. So I waver between the danger that lies in gratifying the senses and the benefits which, as I know from experience, can accrue from singing. Without committing myself to an irrevocable opinion, I am inclined to approve

of the custom of singing in church, in order that by indulging the ears, weaker spirits may be inspired with feelings of devotion. Yet, when I find the singing itself more moving than the truth which it conveys, I confess that this is a grievous sin, and at those times, I would prefer not to hear the singer. (239)

Sister Margaret and other saints in *The Amen Corner* echo Saint Augustine's anxiety over music in the church. This ambivalence suggests that the words in singing, no matter how religious they are, and even the Word itself, fail to obliterate the sensual element that music, even church singing, is capable of evoking. In this context, Kierkegaard's concept of music in "The Immediate Erotic Stages or The Musical-Erotic" as the ideal medium of the sensual seems relevant (*Either/Or* 71). In *The Amen Corner*, Margaret, like Plato, Saint Augustine, and the traditional moral philosopher in general, is poignantly aware of music's powerful impact in making her aware of her sexuality. In order to protect her "House" or her "Republic" against worldliness and the world, she must employ the words or the Word as a shield when using music in church.

But if music is so unruly and perfidious, why is it needed in church? According to *The Amen Corner*, music and singing usually make a better service. The pastor, the church elders, and the congregation indicate that there is good and bad music. The good music is that which is used in the hymns. But the music that does not serve that purpose is evil, confusing, or at the least frivolous. In his careful assessment of music and religion, Kierkegaard offers an interesting summary of that vying relationship:

It is well known that music has always been the object of suspicious attention on the part of religious fervor. Whether it is right in this or not does not concern us here, for that would indeed have only religious interest. It is not however without importance to consider what has led to this. If I trace religious fervor on this point, I can broadly define the movement as follows: *the more rigorous the religiousness, the more music is given up and words are emphasized. The different stages in this regard are represented in world history. The last stage* [Puritanism and Calvinism] *excludes music altogether and adheres to words alone.* (72, italics added)

This intense rivalry between music and words or the Word operates in *The Amen Corner* as one level of the essential dramatic conflict between human desire and the human condition. More than anywhere in the play, the fierce competition between music and God is articulated by

David, who has been trapped in a church that requires him to play according to strict rules:

> DAVID: A few months ago some guys come in the church and they heard me playing piano and they kept coming back all the time. Mama said it was the Holy Ghost drawing them in. But it wasn't.
>
> LUKE: It was your piano.
>
> DAVID: Yes. And I didn't draw them in. They draw me out. They setting up a combo and they want me to come in with them. That's when I stopped praying. (42)

To David and Luke, praying, in its conventional sense, and playing cannot coexist. In contrast, the faithful seem to believe that playing outside the church necessarily compromises faith, if not outright blasphemes it. Significantly, the elders' main charge against Sister Margaret—a charge that ironically helps Luke and David in undermining her faith—is her biological connection with music and lust as they are embodied in her husband and son. When Sister Odessa, Margaret's sister, challenges the elders, who now are determined to dismiss Sister Margaret, to define her sin: "I want to know what is she *done*?" Sisters Boxer and Moore cite Margaret's failure to save her husband and son from the sins of music and lust (72–73).

Although music constantly is linked with sex or lust throughout the play, the church members all agree on its importance in the service. In each singing scene, the congregation's need to heighten emotional conviction against real or imaginary threats is evident. Sister Margaret believes singing in church is inspired by the Holy Ghost, but that is a religious interpretation with which David and Luke cannot agree. A more plausible interpretation is Schopenhauer's notion that music has the galvanizing power of intensifying any situation. Because music, unlike other arts, does not imitate human desire or will, but becomes human desire and will, it is capable of

> exhibit[ing] itself as the metaphysical to everything physical in the world, and as the thing-in-itself to every phenomenon. We might, therefore, just as well call the world embodied music as embodied will; and this is the reason why music makes every picture, and indeed every scene of real life and of the world, at once appear with higher significance, certainly all the more in proportion as its melody is analogous to the spirit of the given phenomenon. (329–30)

But this bolstering power of music cannot be limited to religious or ideological purposes; it constantly leaks in all kinds of unwanted directions. And this fluidity is precisely what makes the religious person and the ideologue in general distrustful of music's unpredictable effect.

At the climax, near the end of act 2, the moment of the reversal dramatically coincides with the moment of recognition. Almost like Agave in Euripides's *The Bacchae* realizing with horror that she is holding her son's bleeding head after she unwittingly has severed it, Sister Margaret hears the *"sound of Luke's trombone fill"* (55) the sanctified air of the church:

ODESSA: We better all fall on our knees and pray.

MAGARET: Amen.

(DAVID *has turned on the record, watching* LUKE. *The sound of LUKE's trombone fills the air.*)

SISTER MOORE: Where's that music coming from?

ODESSA: It must be coming from down the street.

MAGARET: *(Recognition)* Oh, my God.

SISTER MOORE: It coming from your house, Sister Margaret.

MAGARET: Kneel down. *(They watch her)* Kneel *down*, I say! (55)

The conjunction of the dramatic irony and the tragic irony in this climax points to the complexity of the character of Sister Margaret and ultimately to the complexity of Baldwin's vision of humanity and humanism. One wonders whether Sister Margaret's awful cry "Kneel *down*" at her encounter with the forbidden music signifies her surrender to music or to the Lord, or to both. The close of the play suggests that she realizes the importance of music in defining a more humanistic God.

In *The Amen Corner* the tension between music and established religion (or the musician and the preacher) is dramatically delineated in the context of a racially and economically segregated African American community in the Harlem of the 1950s. Here the musician is able, as always, to preach unrestricted human love and sexuality, and even to seduce the minister or the religious person. Since music ineluctably dilutes faith, David, the young religiously trained pianist, is naturally the first to be seduced by his father, the jazz musician. Yet, being a musician and hence iconoclast, David naturally ruptures his father's image and his music. David lights out into the world determined to fight the root causes of African American poverty that makes love impossible by using a music distinct from his mother's and his father's. In this play, Baldwin equates music with the eternal yearning for freedom and for the absolute humanism in which individuals are capable of loving themselves and others more than abstract values or missions that do not enrich and expand their humanity. To Baldwin, who is naturally allergic to ideologies, music in *The Amen Corner* becomes the only religion worth practicing, primarily because it lends full expression to the deepest human desire and feeling. At the end, Luke, David, and Margaret—and Baldwin, too, who has divided himself between Luke and David—redefine their humanity and selfhood in terms of their attitudes toward music—music that celebrates their minds and their bodies. Yet despite the spiritual power Baldwin perceives in music as antidote to suffering in a hostile or indifferent universe, he is aware that music does not supersede human love. In a world without love and safety like the world in *The Amen Corner,* music becomes both a shield against annihilation and self-destruction and a cry for love.

NOTES

Epigraphs: James Baldwin, "As Much Truth as One Can Bear," sec. 7, part 1, p. 1; James Baldwin from a 1965 speech quoted in Fern Marja Eckman, *The Furious Passage of James Baldwin* (New York: M. Evans & Co.), 1966, 242.

1. An early version of this chapter was presented as a paper at the annual convention of the College Language Association, Baton Rouge, La., April 1994.

2. I am aware that religion and ideology are distinct phenomena that constantly overlap and diverge depending on the situation. Because this is not the place to articulate fully the differences between ideology and religion, I will use Bruce B. Lawrence's helpful distinction in his *Defenders of God: The Fundamentalist Revolt Against The Modern Age.* Lawrence argues that ideology, unlike religion, is "explicit not implicit. It is conscious and volitional, while religion may be subconscious or determined" (78). More importantly, "ideology is motivational to this world, not cognizant or reflective of the other world" (79). "It is on this point that the content of ideology and religion diverge most widely. Religions are marked by rites of passage for the individual, while ideologies aim to mobilize energies toward achieving corporate goals" (79). According to Lawrence's argument, which is germane to Sister Margaret's fundamentalism, individuals may be religious without being ideological, but they become religious ideologues when they turn one aspect of the Scripture into zealous missionary work aimed at changing the existing social order. While ideologues

may not be necessarily religious, even secular ideologues tend to be quasi-religious in their belief that they work in order to "show others what they need to do, to correct and help them to that end." In general, "ideologies are not merely world-reflecting but world-constituting" (80).

3. See Julius Portnoy, *The Philosopher and Music: An Historical Outline.* See also the chapter on music in Allan D. Bloom, *The Closing of the American Mind,* 70–73.

4. Nietzsche's well-known concept of the Dionysian music and musician as articulated in his *The Birth of Tragedy* is defined by the following attributes: a) Dionysian music makes possible the truer yet tragic vision of human reality. It undermines the ideological illusion embodied in what Nietzsche calls the "theatrical man" or Socrates (94); b) Dionysian music, in contrast to plastic art and Apollinian music, tends to systematically subvert the artificial principle of individuation in an effort to restore humanity to its pristine oneness in the face of the eternal tragedy, which is the essence of human life. "Apollo [the founder of plastic arts, including Apollinian music] overcomes the suffering of the individual by the radiant glorification of the *eternity of the phenomenon:* here beauty triumphs over the suffering inherent in life; pain is obliterated by lies from the features of nature" (104); c) Dionysian music, like the blues and jazz as Baldwin understands them, provides what Nietzsche calls "metaphysical comfort," that empowers humans in their struggle against a hostile universe. "I believe, the Greek man of culture felt himself nullified [as an individual by merging in the oneness of humanity] in the presence of the satyric chorus; and this is the most immediate effect of the Dionysian tragedy, that the state and society and, quite generally, the gulf between man and man give way to an overwhelming feeling of unity leading back to the very heart of nature. The metaphysical comfort—with which, I am suggesting even now, every tragedy leaves us—that life is at the bottom of things, despite all the changes of appearances, indestructibly powerful and pleasurable" (59). Although the similarity between Baldwin's and Nietzsche's views on the subversive and emancipative power of music is striking, I am not aware of any evidence that Baldwin was familiar with Nietzsche's views on music.

5. Music, according to Hegel, affects the individual so deeply and so immediately due to the ideal similarity between the simple, empty self—that is, the self before reflection—and the immediacy of time, that is, "now." The "now" and the empty self coincide perfectly through the medium of music, where the subjective and the objective ideally merge and become one. See G.W.F. Hegel, *Aesthetics: Lectures on Fine Art,* vol. II, 907–8.

6. "Music always expresses the immediate in its immediacy. This is also the reason that in relation to language music appears first and last. . . . Reflection is implicit in language, and therefore language cannot express the immediate. Reflection is fatal to the immediate, and therefore it is impossible for language to express the musical." Soren Kierkegaard, "The Immediate Erotic Stages or the Musical-Erotic," 70.

7. Baldwin probably was aware of the well-known statement on the absence of love as the real hell on this earth declared by Father Zosima in Dos-

toevsky's *The Brothers Karamazov.* Luke's cry for love seems to echo Father Zosima's: "Fathers and Teachers, I ponder 'What is hell?' I maintain that it is the suffering of no longer being able to love" (301). Yet, in Baldwin's vision in *The Amen Corner* Margaret's inability to love sends not only Luke into hell, but herself, too. In this sense Baldwin seems to suggest that hell can be created by both inability to love and the inability of being loved.

Works Cited

Adorno, Theodor W. Introduction to the *Sociology of Music.* Trans. E. B. Ashton. New York: Continuum, 1976.

Aristotle. *Politics.* In *The Basic Works of Aristotle.* Ed. Richard McKeon. 1941. Reprint, New York: Random House, 1966.

Baldwin, James. *The Amen Corner.* New York: Dial, 1968.

———. "The Uses of the Blues: How Uniquely American Art Form Relates to the Negro's Fight for His Rights." *Playboy,* January 1964.

———. "Many Thousands Gone." In *The Price of the Ticket: Collected Nonfiction, 1948–1985.* New York: St. Martin's, 1985, 65–78.

———. "The Creative Process." In *The Price of the Ticket: Collected Nonfiction, 1948–1985.* New York: St. Martin's, 1985, 315–18.

———. "As Much Truth as One Can Bear." *New York Times Book Review,* 14 January 1962, sec. 7, part 1, 1.

Bloom, Allan D. *The Closing of the American Mind: How Higher Education Has Failed Democracy and Impoverished the Souls of Today's Students.* New York: Simon & Schuster, 1987.

Campbell, James. *Talking at the Gates: A Life of James Baldwin.* New York: Viking, 1991.

Dostoevsky, Fyodor. *The Brothers Karamazov.* Trans. Constance Garnett, rev. and ed. Ralph E. Matlaw. New York: Norton, 1976.

Deleuze, Gilles. "Music and Rifornello." In *The Deleuze Reader,* ed. Constantin V. Boundas. New York: Columbia University Press, 1993, 201–3.

Ellison, Ralph. *Shadow and Act.* New York: Vintage Books, 1972.

Eckman, Fern Marja. *The Furious Passage of James Baldwin.* New York: M. Evans & Co., 1966.

Giovanni, Nikki, and James Baldwin. *James Baldwin and Nikki Giovanni: A Dialogue.* Philadelphia: J. B. Lippincott, 1973.

Hegel, G.W.F. *Aesthetics: Lectures on Fine Art.* Trans. T. M. Knox. Oxford: Clarendon Press, 1975.

Kierkegaard, Soren. "The Immediate Erotic Stages or the Musical Erotic." In *Either/Or.* Vol. I, trans. Howard V. Hong and Edna H. Hong, 46–135. Princeton, N.J.: Princeton University Press, 1987.

Lawrence, Bruce B. *Defenders of God: The Fundamentalist Revolt Against the Modern Age.* Columbia: University of South Carolina Press, 1989.

Leeming, David A. *James Baldwin: A Biography.* New York: Knopf, 1994.

Nietzsche, Friedrich. *The Birth of Tragedy and the Case of Wagner.* Trans. Walter Kaufman. New York: Vintage Books, 1967.

Plato. *The Republic.* Trans. Allan D. Bloom. New York: Basic Books, 1968.

Portnoy, Julius. *The Philosopher and Music: A Historical Outline.* New York: Humanities Press, 1954.

Schopenhauer, Arthur. *The World as Will and Idea.* Vol. 3. Trans. R. B. Haldane and J. Kemp. 1957. Reprint, London: Routledge and Kegan Paul, 1983.

Standley, Fred L., and Louis H. Pratt. *Conversations with James Baldwin.* Jackson: University Press of Mississippi, 1989.

St. Augustine. *Confessions.* Trans. R. S. Pine-Coffin. 1961. Reprint, London: Penguin Books, 1978.

Turner, Darwin T. "James Baldwin in the Dilemma of the Black Dramatist." In *James Baldwin: A Critical Evaluation,* ed. Therman B. O'Daniel, 189–94. Washington, D.C.: Howard University Press, 1977.

Weatherby, W. J. *James Baldwin, Artist on Fire.* New York: Donald I. Fine, 1989.

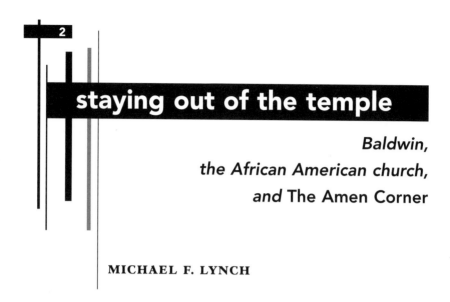

staying out of the temple

Baldwin,
the African American church,
and The Amen Corner

MICHAEL F. LYNCH

So, in my case, in order to become a moral human being, whatever that may be, I have to hang out with the publicans and sinners, whores and junkies, and stay out of the temple where they told us nothing but lies anyway. —*James Baldwin*

I

In his memoir about James Baldwin's tenure as a visiting professor at Bowling Green State University in the late 1970s, Ernest Champion relates an incident that suggests the intensity and durability of Baldwin's feelings about his formation as a youth in the black fundamentalist church. One evening, Baldwin attended a university choir concert dedicated to him, and while the choir was singing "some very moving and emotional lyrics" (99), suddenly he left his seat in the front row of five hundred people, asking Champion to accompany him:

> Baldwin said he wanted to use the restroom. . . . As I was standing outside, I thought I heard sounds that seemed to come from somebody in some distress. Then he came out and I realized that he had been crying. He dabbed his eyes with his handkerchief and said to me, "Ernest, they are singing my life. That is where it all began." . . . He refused to

go back and sit in the front row, preferring instead to stay in the back because he could not trust himself if the whole experience became overpowering again. (100)

As is well known, Baldwin underwent a powerful conversion experience at the age of fourteen, which is reflected in the climax of his first novel, *Go Tell It on the Mountain,* and he served as a young minister or preacher in the church for three years. He left the pulpit and the church at seventeen, no longer able to reconcile the Christian ideals that had affected him so deeply with what he came to see as the clergy's cynicism and negative theology and the congregation's generally unloving attitudes.

The tension and perhaps inevitable severing of Baldwin's relationship with the church were prefigured when he was only twelve, even before his initiation into the church. In the opening paragraph of his "Autobiographical Notes" introducing *Notes of a Native Son,* his first book of essays, Baldwin recalls his "first professional triumph," when the printing of a short story "about the Spanish revolution won some sort of prize in an extremely short-lived church newspaper. I remember the story was censored by the lady editor, though I don't remember why, and I was outraged" (3). Baldwin's early sense of outrage at the institutional church, which was muted during his years in the pulpit, took deep root nonetheless and characterized his attitude toward the church for virtually the rest of his life. But the indignation of the twelve-year-old student and the tears of the distinguished writer and visiting professor, as well as his many works produced in the intervening years, suggest that Baldwin could neither end his argument with the church nor break totally his emotional ties with the faith whose ideals had formed his vision.

Baldwin's first two fictional works, *Go Tell It on the Mountain* and *The Amen Corner,* whose setting and subject is the African American church, offer his most sustained critique of the institution. Because with *Amen* Baldwin pursues many of the implications of *Go Tell It* and extrapolates the likely future of John Grimes, this chapter considers the play as an essential corollary of the novel. The early books of essays *Notes of a Native Son* and *The Fire Next Time* continue the critique with more explicit commentary on the black church's moral and theological inconsistencies that drove Baldwin to seek salvation elsewhere, while they also expand the discussion to the white church. In *The Fire Next Time* he explains in detail the pressures and dangers in his Harlem environment that influenced him to submit to the church's "spiritual seduction" (43) and to accept its apparent safety. But before long he came to view it as one "racket" (43) among, and not unlike, the many on the street. Being a preacher and an insider "was like being in the theater," for he was "behind the scenes and knew how the illusion was worked" (51). Among the other ministers Baldwin observed a "subtle hypocrisy" and learned cynically how to manipulate and "work on a congregation until the last dime was surrendered—it was not very hard to do—and I knew where the money for 'the Lord's work' went" (52). Eventually he lost respect for those nominally serving but actually exploiting the faithful, and he nearly lost respect for himself as well. He found blacks' faith "actually a fairly desperate emotional business" because it was essentially synonymous with fear of the vengeful "God our ancestors gave us and before whom we all tremble yet" (*Notes* 65). In the essay "A Stranger in the Village" he reflects on the terror evoked in him by a European cathedral because of the theology of his upbringing: "and I am terrified by the slippery bottomless well to be found in the crypt, down which heretics were hurled to their death, and by the obscene, inescapable gargoyles jutting out of the stone and seeming to say that God and the devil can never be divorced" (*Notes* 174). Baldwin observes that this theology of fear results in a religion that functions for many African Americans "as a complete and exquisite fantasy revenge" on whites and a source of pervasive bitterness (*Notes* 66). Many years after leaving the church, when he met Elijah Muhammed and was being courted to join the Muslims, Baldwin recalled the similar seductive power of the church, and he linked the Muslims' hatred of whites to the vengeful, fear-ridden theology of the black fundamentalist church (*Fire* 81).

Returning to the topic of his early days in the church in the closing pages of *The Evidence of Things Not Seen*, Baldwin's last book, he reflects deeply on it as a community that often used its considerable potential power for love only to reject and destroy individuals. He tells the story of Buddy, a seventeen-year-old church member who had "backslid" and was ostracized. The fourteen-year-old Jimmy Baldwin disobeyed church orders and spoke to this young man, preferring the Christian injunction to love others over the loveless church directive to avoid the "fallen." Shortly after this conversation Buddy died, and Baldwin was haunted for years by his "unbelievably lonely" face (121) and by the realization that "he had been rejected by the only community he knew, that we had it in our power to bring back the light to his eyes" (122). Clearly scandalized by the church's lack of love and forgiveness, Baldwin echoes a passage published twenty-two years earlier in *The Fire Next Time* and reiterates the central contradiction in the church while underscoring his personal dedication to the principle of universal love: "I was acting, after all, on the moral assumptions I had inherited from the community that had produced me. I had been told to *love everybody*. Whoever else did not believe this, *I* did" (122). It is significant that in the conclusion to his final work Baldwin is again and still "obsessed" (*Rap on Race* 83) with religion and belief, and that he feels the need to explain his decision to leave the church some forty-four years previously. Perhaps most significant is his portrayal of that decision not as one he wished to make, but as one forced on him by the church itself: "it took me many years to realize that the community that had formed me had also brought about that hour and that rupture" (122). This tone of reluctance and regret is unique to Baldwin's frequent discussions of his break with the church, and it provides a hint of the complexity of his attitudes in *Amen*.

In the "Notes for *The Amen Corner*," written for its publication in 1968, Baldwin discusses two intense and conflicting motivations that drove him in 1952 as he considered what kind of work should follow *Go Tell It*, a book that had taken ten years to complete. On one hand, he was a young writer with one novel about to be published, still seeking to establish his reputation and potential. During his early stint as a book reviewer in the 1940s, Baldwin had become frustrated by the preponderance of assignments dealing with "the Negro question," as though he were qualified to deal only with issues relating to black life. Now having written a first novel treating an African American family and church, when he returned from Paris to New York to sell the novel, he felt he "was being corralled into another trap: now I was a writer, a *Negro* writer, and I was expected to write diminishing versions of *Mountain* forever" (xv). Given his fierce desire to defeat such expectations, it would seem logical, if not absolutely necessary, for him to avoid an all-black cast of characters and certainly the black church in his second creative work. (In fact, he would do this, in a sense, for *Amen* would not be published until 1968, and his second novel, *Giovanni's Room*, published in 1956, presents only white characters.)

On the other hand, *Go Tell It* had left Baldwin with a certain amount of unfinished business, both personal and artistic—considerations that overcame his reluctance to revisit familiar territory in his second work. Evidently he needed to return to the environment of a black family in the black church, more specifically to the situation of a young black male (now older) struggling to establish his identity as an artist in a repressive church atmosphere while redefining his relationships with his parents. Baldwin sought to complete his critique of the church

begun in *Go Tell It,* which ends with John Grimes's ambiguous new status as one of the saved who feels profound doubts about his ability to
pursue his artistic vocation in the church. With *Amen,* Baldwin would
account for and depict his own defection from the church through
that of David Alexander, showing it as inevitable, necessary, and salutary. He also would attempt to create a compassionate and loving,
though far from perfect, father figure and an eventually positive father-
son relationship in order to compensate imaginatively for the harshness and emotional pain that characterized his relationship with his
stepfather and to express forgiveness for him, who had been dead for
some eleven years. The least recognized and perhaps most interesting
of Baldwin's motives (though never acknowledged explicitly by him) for
writing *Amen* was his interest in exploring the possibility of an individual's retaining essentially Christian ideals and pursuing one's vocation
outside the church. Nearly two decades after writing *Amen,* as he told
Margaret Meade in a series of uniquely open admissions regarding his
identity as a Christian, Baldwin identifies with Christ and relates his
own need to realize his vocation outside the institutional church: "So,
in my case, in order to become a moral human being, whatever that
may be, I have to hang out with the publicans and sinners, whores and
junkies, and *stay out of the temple* where they told us nothing but lies anyway" (*Rap* 86, italics added). This dialectical companion to Baldwin's
heightened critique of the church is certainly evident though widely
unexamined in *Go Tell It* in John's ecstatic glimpse of the Lord and in
his sense of the Lord's love and guidance.[1] Some form of this implicit
faith is present in varying degrees throughout Baldwin's works.

Conscious, then, that he was expected, and felt virtually required,
to write a second novel rather like *Go Tell It,* and keenly aware that the
subject of the black church exactly reiterated that of his first work,
Baldwin decided to make a fundamental alteration in form:

> I had no idea whether or not I could write a play, but I was absolutely
> determined that I would not, not at that moment in my career, not at
> that moment in my life, write another novel. I did not trust myself to
> do it. I was really terrified that I would, without even knowing that I
> was doing it, try to repeat my first success and begin to imitate myself.
> I knew that I had much more to say and much, much more to discover
> than I had been able to indicate in *Mountain.* ("Notes for *Amen*" xv)

If he could not resist the various reasons impelling him to treat the
black church again, he could avoid the danger of imitating himself only

by the "desperate and even irresponsible act" (ix) of writing a work for the theater that might never be produced. For Baldwin, being a writer and being a person have nothing to do with the folly of "trying to be safe" (xiii), and his frequent theme of the necessity of avoiding ostensible safety appears first, appropriately, in *Amen*, whose very writing involved significant professional risk.

In the "Notes for *Amen*," Baldwin states that when he returned to the United States in the summer of 1952 in order to sell his novel, "It may have been the emotional climate and the events of that summer which caused me to write *The Amen Corner*" (xii). The only event he describes in memorable detail in the Notes involved his first meeting with the editor for *Go Tell It*, who asked him, "What about all that come-to-Jesus stuff? Don't you think you ought to take it out?" (xiv). Horrified by the cultural arrogance as well as the critical insensitivity of such a suggestion—which in his view would amount to the destruction of the book—Baldwin fled the office but returned to insist on the absolute need for that particular idiom. The apparent apostate's defense of such material in *Go Tell It* may have proceeded not just from his artistic judgment, but partially also from his memories and associations as a saved member of the church, who once had venerated and found rich emotional satisfaction and spiritual life within that idiom. Baldwin's inclusion of this story in the prelude to *Amen* suggests that he wrote the play, begun shortly after this incident, partially as a defense of the idiom and subject matter of *Go Tell It*, and also as a challenge to his own self-interest and to the publishing world.[2]

In describing his nightlong conversion experience of "unspeakable pain" (*Fire* 44) on the church floor that led to his becoming one of the saved in the church, Baldwin reflects that the religious conversions of many poor blacks can be ascribed largely to the supreme difficulty of their achieving communion in human relationships:

> You very soon, without knowing it, give up all hope of communion. Black people, mainly, look down or look up but do not look at each other, not at you, and white people, mainly, look away. . . . There is no way, no way whatever, so it seemed then and has sometimes seemed since, to get through a life, to love your wife and children, or your friends, or your mother and father, or to be loved. . . . And if one despairs—as who has not?—of human love, God's love alone is left. (*Fire* 44)

In *Go Tell It*, John Grimes's being saved and his new sense of communion with the Lord, although treated without irony by Baldwin, are shown to be virtually necessary for John's psychological survival in his family and social environment. Baldwin testifies to the powerful sense of drama, excitement, and fulfillment he experienced in communion with the congregation during their worship:

> The church was very exciting. It took a long time for me to disengage myself from this excitement, and on the blindest, most visceral level, I never really have, and never will. There is no music like that music, no drama like the drama of the saints rejoicing, the sinners moaning, the tambourines racing, and all those voices coming together and crying holy unto the Lord. There is still, for me, no pathos quite like the pathos of those multi-colored, worn, somehow triumphant and transfigured faces, speaking from the depths of a visible, tangible, continuing despair of the goodness of the Lord. (*Fire* 47)

Especially significant here are Baldwin's certain knowledge that never again will he achieve any such intense transcendence, and his joyful feeling of oneness with the entire church:

> I have never seen anything to equal the fire and excitement that some-times, without warning, fill a church. . . . Nothing that has happened to me since equals the power and the glory that I sometimes felt when, in the middle of a sermon, I knew that I was somehow, by some miracle, really carrying, as they said, "the Word"—when the church and I were one. Their pain and joy were mine, and mine were theirs . . . and their cries of "Amen!" and "Hallelujah!" and "Yes, Lord!" and "Praise His name!" and "Preach it, brother!" sustained and whipped on my solos until we all became equal, wringing wet, singing and dancing, in anguish and rejoicing, at the foot of the altar. (47)

Although *Amen* offers a predominantly negative presentation of the church, it also conveys, perhaps in spite of itself, something of its author's fascination with and onetime reverence for its potential for communion. Carlton Molette finds the play successful in performance because the audience is so powerfully drawn into and affected by the church ritual, which creates a strong "sense of belonging, of commu-nity, of togetherness within the congregation" (184). While Baldwin does evoke for the audience that joyous togetherness possible in the black fundamentalist church, his more basic purpose is to create the communion of the theater as a means to change people, in much the same way a preacher would attempt to inspire his congregation:

> I was armed, I knew, in attempting to write the play, by the fact that I
> was born in the church. I knew that out of the ritual of the church, his-
> torically speaking, comes the act of the theater, the *communion* which is
> the theater. And I knew that what I wanted to do in the theater was to
> recreate moments I remembered as a boy preacher, to involve the peo-
> ple, even against their will, to shake them up, and, hopefully, to change
> them. ("Notes for *Amen*" xviii)

Thus, Baldwin speaks as a virtual secular minister, using his art to serve people just as he once delivered sermons crafted by his literary and rhetorical skills that sought to lead the congregation toward salvation.

Although before his defection from the church Baldwin saw preaching and writing in dichotomous terms, largely because of the church's insistence on the dualism of the sacred versus the secular, afterward he discovered the potential compatibility of delivering the Word and crafting words in art. In *Notes of a Native Son* Baldwin recalls the one time when he and his stepfather really spoke to each other. During his latter high school days, when James's growing passion for writing was overshadowing his waning love of preaching, his stepfather one day asked him abruptly and with evident resentment, "You'd rather write than preach, wouldn't you?" James, astonished at the question "because it was a real question" (108), answered yes. Although his step-father's question presented Baldwin's interests as dichotomous, and although young James indeed would reject preaching and the church before long in favor of a career as a writer, evidence suggests that Bald-win would come to believe that the essence of preaching (i.e., deliver-ing the Christian message of love for all people) was compatible with the work of a writer. He would reject the external form of that preach-ing, the institution, but not its interior purpose and content. As David Leeming notes in his biography, "Baldwin often said that he left the pul-pit to 'preach the gospel'" (102), a strikingly explicit statement of Bald-win's sense of religious vocation and of the relevance of Christian belief to his life. Sondra O'Neale, echoing Baldwin's comment while identi-fying his dialectical attitude toward professed Christians, states that he "searched for a medium other than the pulpit in order to work out and affirm both a proper communal response for those who had valid spir-itual experience and a proper holocaust judgment for those who pro-fess salvation without manifesting universal love" (135).

II

In order to discuss the critical treatment of *Amen,* it is helpful to consider first the Western critical tendency to attempt to separate the aesthetic/spiritual from the political/social aspects of art. Joyce Ann Joyce points out that the African American literary tradition is founded on and sustained by the understanding that the aesthetic and the political comprise a unity rather than separable elements. She finds that "the post-modern tendency to divorce the aesthetic dimension of art from the moral reflects the effete nature of Western thought" (17), resulting in "the nihilism that now characterizes a lack of a political component in Euro-American literary theory" (20). Joyce argues that "too many Black literary critics have adopted the Euro-Americans' impossible task of attempting to separate art from politics" (21), creating an "imaginary dichotomy between art and function" (29) which can be countered only with "a critical methodology that attempts a synthesis between ethics and aesthetics" (32). While Joyce's argument is cogent and useful in its insistence on the synthesis or dialectic, it may place too much emphasis on art's political aspect, which always has attracted far more attention than aesthetics, craft, or subjectivity from black and white scholars of African American literature. Baldwin's output in particular has suffered greatly from almost exclusively social/political, and frequently heavy-handed, analysis.

In *Psychoanalysis and Black Novels,* Claudia Tate shows that the critical tendency to focus predominantly on the social aspects of black literature, including matters of race, class, and gender, often has resulted in readings of texts that are not as rich and as complex as is possible, and in the inevitable exclusion from the canon (and from print) of texts that do not offer what is judged to be sufficient or satisfactory treatment of racist perspectives and racial oppression. Tate demonstrates that many African American texts, even some by renowned authors such as Richard Wright and Zora Neale Hurston, have been marginalized and suppressed because they do not conform to the "materialist or sociological analyses that constitute the familiar racial paradigm" (9). Citing the dangers of "reductively defining black subjectivity as political agency," she argues for, if not a depoliticization of literary analysis, at least an expansion of it to include complex considerations of conscious and unconscious subjectivity, desire (not just sexual desire, but all kinds of wanting, wishing, and striving—not just the desire for civil rights and justice), and existential freedom (10). Although Tate differs from Joyce by stressing the personal more than the social, she agrees with Joyce's call for a synthesis, attempting to analyze texts' "dialectical engagement of the material and the psychical" (15).

Most of Baldwin's critically valued texts have been appreciated mainly for their perceived content of social criticism. Although *Go Tell It* is well regarded in spite of its relative lack of elements of racial conflict and oppression, the other successes are praised primarily for their social/political "message": *Giovanni's Room* and *Another Country* for attacking homophobia and discrimination against homosexuals, and *Notes of a Native Son* and *The Fire Next Time* for their analyses of racism and for the prophetic tone of judgment on American society. These critical estimations may identify and laud significant elements of these texts, but they tend to ignore deeper insights and meanings as well as accomplishments of craft. Baldwin's works that are deemed unsuccessful also are seen, not surprisingly, through the confining prism of social analysis. The complaint that the later Baldwin often becomes too political, too angry, or just redundant fails to realize how its own narrow focus prevents the discovery, in Tate's terms, of great(er) subjectivity, desire, and meaning in these texts (as well as in the better received ones). In Baldwin's works generally, the social/political content often masks more subtle, more complex, and more paradoxical concerns such as human responsibility and freedom, love and betrayal, and the spiritual nature of identity and personality. With respect to Baldwin's exploration of religious or spiritual subjectivity, the critical response for the most part might be said to exhibit the "come-to-Jesus stuff" syndrome documented in his Notes for *Amen,* that is, the refusal to take seriously or to examine his obvious and admitted obsession with religion. Rosa Bobia's recent study of Baldwin's critical reception in France documents a situation parallel to the American critical failure to understand and appreciate those aspects of his work that transcend sociopolitical concerns. Bobia demonstrates that French critics, often puzzled by the lack of social commentary in such works as *Go Tell It, Giovanni's Room,* and *Amen,* have tended to dismiss them (43) or to offer merely stereotypical comparisons to black music (19).

The Amen Corner has not been a popular object of critical inquiry. Essays examining this work are rare, and four of the seven full-length studies of Baldwin do not even mention the play, with the remaining three devoting only a few pages to it.[3] In the context of the general critical failure to apprehend the dialectical nature of Baldwin's texts and the concomitant preoccupation with finding only social analysis therein, *Amen* is most often interpreted superficially, as merely intensifying the critique of the black fundamentalist church found in *Go Tell*

It. Those looking for racial or social content find little that is new or provocative in Baldwin's second work, which was not published until 1968, fifteen years after he had written it, and a time when politics and polemics ruled American discourse and much of African American literature. Stanley Macebuh's study purports to analyze what he sees as the "theological terror" (46) or dread of God and hell at the root of Baldwin's world view. But after the promising first chapter on *Go Tell It,* in the only book that treats the relevance of theology to Baldwin's texts, the chapter titled "The Amen Corner" amazingly never mentions *The Amen Corner* and provides no analysis of Baldwin's second and last work dealing wholly and explicitly with the black church. This mystifying omission contributes to the rapid degeneration of Macebuh's thesis in favor of sociological commentary. In a similar vein, Heather Mayne in an unpublished dissertation notes the dearth of research on black Christianity's influence on black literature, and she proposes to show that African American novelists including Baldwin, to whom she devotes a chapter, develop their own liberation theology and "revise traditional notions of God" (19). Her thesis likewise founders, however, limiting itself to social and political implications of the apocalyptic theme in *Go Tell It.* Mayne's proposal might have yielded some intriguing results if applied with the proposed theological focus to *Go Tell It* and *Amen* in particular. Patricia Schnapp demonstrates that Baldwin's early work anticipates and is quite compatible with black liberation theology, and she argues the centrality of theology to Baldwin's vision (48). Her dissertation offers analysis of his sociopolitical content that is excellent because of its substance and specificity, which are rare qualities in the published research. Her thesis extends beyond the usual attention to social matters, recognizing that Baldwin is very concerned also with the interior, personal aspect of freedom. But her chapter promising substantial examination of his treatment of this theme offers little analysis and returns to the common critical ground of commentary based on race and society. Jean-François Gounard's book on Wright and Baldwin claims that *Amen* is "a logical continuation of the author's religious thought" (179) but does not elaborate, offering only such simplistic social commentary as "the main goal of this play is to show that religion is often a simple refuge for blacks" (180). Carol Sylvander correctly points out that the depiction of the church is much less balanced in *Amen* than in *Go Tell It,* but her assertion that "the church, even as protection from the streets, is not given any positive characteristics" (96) in *Amen* is inaccurate because it ignores some ameliorating elements. Aside from the prevalent plot summary, her book offers little analysis of the play. Carlton Molette's praise for the strong sense of community created among the audience by the church ritual (184) may report accurately one aspect of the play's reception, but he misses both the joylessness of the congregation and their indifference and even contributions to the sufferings of the Alexander family. Molette's article greatly exaggerates the family love evident in the play, and he gushes over "an extended-family love that surrounds the congregation on the stage (the actors) and the congregation in the auditorium (the audience)" (184). His appreciation of the play as a performance distracts him from grasping Baldwin's central critique, that the church as a whole, or at least many of its members, sin grievously against the ideal of community by their pettiness, selfishness, and refusal to include everyone in the fold of the saved. In the few pages dealing with *Amen* in Louis Pratt's full-length study, the author rejects any possible religious significance, adding that some critics "have fallen victim to the idea that the black man's world is a sphere of religious and racial consciousness, and therefore it is expected that the theme of religion should dominate his writings in the instances where race has *failed to prevail*" (84, italics added). Pratt's phrase about race failing to prevail in some works illustrates Tate's assertion that critics often privilege and judge worthy of analysis only those works of African American literature that include content of racial discrimination and protest. Not finding the usual and expected racial content, and denying the presence of religious content, Pratt merely makes some generalized remarks about the play's social meaning, coming to the standard conclusion that "the social significance of the play . . . is paramount" (85).

As suggested above, the most common and fundamental flaw in Baldwin criticism is the tendency to see his work only in binary terms, especially his relationship to Christianity and the black and white churches. One explicit expression of his dialectical thinking illustrates the seeming contradiction of transcending social and political concerns while also committing to resist all forms of injustice:

> It began to seem that one would have to hold in the mind forever two ideas which seemed to be in opposition. The first idea was acceptance, the acceptance, totally without rancor, of life as it is, and men as they are: in the light of this idea, it goes without saying that injustice is a commonplace. But this did not mean that one could be complacent, for the second idea was of equal power: that one must never, in one's own life, accept these injustices as commonplace but must fight them with all one's strength. (*Notes of a Native Son* 113–14)

Yet Baldwin knew that in the United States, "this country devoted to the death of the paradox" (*Notes* 22), an approach such as his that sought to mediate contradictory positions would not be understood. Only a few scholars have recognized and written in detail on Baldwin's religious dialectic or his serious treatment of the search for faith and God.[4] Even *Go Tell It*, his most acclaimed novel, has attracted little criticism that examines this key component of his thought. Shirley Allen's two articles demonstrate the novel's "serious attitude toward religious faith" ("Ironic Voice" 36) and its theological significance as an affirmation of Christian belief. Rolf Lunden, although he asserts without any evidence or argument that Baldwin is "an unbeliever" (115), shows that the critics who interpret *Go Tell It* as a nonreligious or antireligious novel tend to do so because they begin with and base their conclusions on the much later *The Fire Next Time*, with little support offered from the novel's text (114). Noting that Baldwin is "concerned with an exposition of false and true Christianity" (115) in *Go Tell It*, Lunden finds "no irony whatever" (126) in the account of John's deliverance. O'Neale, discussing Baldwin's theology generally, makes a brief but insightful reference to *Amen* and identifies the ambivalence Baldwin experienced over leaving the church and also during his lifelong conflicted relationship to Christianity:

> He realizes that he is attempting to "marry" incompatible elements in agnostic art and traditional black Christian faith. His conflicting emotions when in late adolescence he moved away from the church and his ministerial calling are . . . perhaps most eloquently expressed in both Sonny's ("Sonny's Blues") and David's *(The Amen Corner)* experiences when they suffer parental rejection because they must steal away to discover nonecclesiastical epiphanies in the ethereal grasp of black music. (138)

O'Neale argues the relevance of "close critical and theological exegesis" of Baldwin's texts, concluding that "more than the heritage of any other black American writer, Baldwin's works illustrate the schizophrenia of the black American experience with Christianity" (127). In an important summary of his religious dialectic she refers to the conflict between his early religious experience and his rejection of the church, noting that "the divisiveness of this apparently irreconcilable dichotomy . . . dominated his worldview, his theology, and his writing" (127).

Jon Michael Spencer asserts that several of the most famous writers of the Harlem Renaissance, whose critical images entail strong atheistic impressions, in fact maintained an implicitly dialectical relationship with Christian belief. Nella Larsen, Alain Locke, Langston Hughes, James Weldon Johnson, and Zora Neale Hurston all sharply criticized Christianity and the church, but the work of each also reveals a spirituality and an openness to certain aspects of Christian theology. Several quotations cited by Spencer to convey Locke's compatibility with Christianity sound remarkably like Baldwin, with their emphasis on the rediscovery of God being contingent on the creation of a more loving society: "In some very vital respects God will be rediscovered to our age if we succeed in discovering the common denominator of humanity and living in terms of it. . . . The word of God is still insistent and more emphatic as the human redemption delays and becomes more crucial" (Spencer 457). Although Spencer's article does not mention Baldwin, it establishes that the Renaissance, the context in which Baldwin matured, was not so monolithically atheistic as is commonly supposed, and one might infer that Baldwin was influenced to some degree by the complexity of these writers' attitudes. Spencer argues that the refusal to investigate writers' possible religious themes and influences is often based on critics' choice "to exclude the consideration of religion based on their own secular hermeneutics" (459). The possibility of Baldwin's having some "religious" intent even in the early works, *Go Tell It* and *Amen,* which are saturated with the experience of the black church, is not even considered by most scholars, many of whom "have fallen victim to their own reluctance to believe that a writer of Baldwin's caliber could write seriously about religion" (Lunden 114).

III

Go Tell It concludes with John Grimes's incorporation into the company of the saved. His glimpse of the Lord after the night on the threshing floor fires John with an intense feeling of God's love and a purifying experience of salvation that transcends his church and its often harsh, limiting theology. Suddenly he has gained new strength, confidence, and resolution to confront and possibly even defy his stepfather, Gabriel, and to develop his emerging identity as an artist. Yet the novel's ending is fraught with ambivalence regarding John's future. For the church, which suddenly has embraced John as one of its community and has become a protective haven and shield from Gabriel's attacks on his dignity, also will place an increased burden on John in the form of greater repression of all "secular" interests and joys, including sexual development and artistic aspiration, while it will insist on a loveless, self-righteous attitude of exclusion toward those who are not deemed "saved." The implication is that John will attempt to work out his salvation within the church and will make good use of the benefits of his new status, but that the restrictions on his identity as an intelligent, talented young man inevitably will prove too strong for him to remain.

Although this implication can be supported by the text, Baldwin apparently was concerned that John's conversion, while genuine and treated without irony, might overshadow the depiction of the church's negative aspects. In fact, as Lunden points out, critics did not "discover" the supposed irony in John's conversion or begin to accentuate the novel's critique until the appearance of *The Fire Next Time* some ten years later (114). When Baldwin began writing *Amen* in 1952, before the publication of *Go Tell It,* he decided to project John's fate as a young church member, to extrapolate his likely chances for both salvation and personal fulfillment within the church's structure. Baldwin seems to have believed that the novel's conclusion, while artistically appropriate with its complexity and subtlety, might leave the impression, as it evidently did to many, that John would be able or willing to remain committed to such a stifling regime. Baldwin knew that John would not be able to remain in the church indefinitely any more than he would be able to stay for long in his stepfather's house after acquiring a fundamental affirmation of his worth and identity from the Lord. With the play, Baldwin saw his opportunity to demonstrate why within a few years fourteen-year-old John, now in the person of eighteen-year-old David, would have to revolt. That which only was implied in *Go Tell It* becomes explicit in *Amen,* as John's serious doubts about the church have escalated into David's irresolvable conflicts. With David, Baldwin attempts both to approximate his own situation at age seventeen and to project that of John several years after his conversion on the verge of his necessary divorce from the church. The play's critique of the church is more strident than the novel's because of Baldwin's need to account for, though he does so perhaps a bit polemically, his protagonist's difficult but clear choice to leave. In this sense, *Amen* completes *Go Tell It,* and the works should be considered together because they complement each other and are two parts of essentially the same story.

When Baldwin began *Amen,* he had not yet written the famous essay *The Fire Next Time,* which would delineate his personal conflict between the roles of adolescent minister and aspiring artist as well as his choice to abandon the former for the latter. Aside from his desire to project John Grimes's probable development in the church, *Amen* also met Baldwin's need to represent his own defection from it. In the

well-known essay "Everybody's Protest Novel," in which Baldwin crit-
icizes Wright's *Native Son* for its narrowness as social protest, he states
that Bigger Thomas's tragedy is "that he has accepted a theology that
denies him life" (*Notes* 23), referring primarily to society's racist definition of Bigger as subhuman. Although the theology of Baldwin's
church did not entail racism against blacks, he rejected what he saw as
its denial of his life. *Amen* continues the critique begun in *Go Tell It* of
the theology of the vengeful God, and it demonstrates even more clearly
that Baldwin felt forced to repudiate that theology in order for him to
live as he felt called. Despite his correct estimation that *Amen* would
not be published for some time after its composition and might never
be appreciated, its portrayal of his leaving the church was important
enough to Baldwin for him to risk failure. *Amen* has been one of the
most neglected Baldwin texts, but among the reasons it deserves more
examination is its largely autobiographical account of a young man's
difficult but necessary break with his family and his church.

As discussed above, *Amen* has attracted little critical attention
mostly because scholars who tend to look only for racial or political
material find none and because its commentary on the black church
seems a less interesting restatement of that in *Go Tell It*. Perhaps because
the play does indeed offer a less complex, somewhat more strident, and
decidedly more one-sided view of the church and of theological experience, its apparently simplistic and polemical intent obscures for many
its dialectical dimension of considering the possibilities of a secular
faith and vocation outside the church.

As seen in *The Fire Next Time*, Baldwin's conversion experience at
age fourteen closely parallels that of John in *Go Tell It*. But as Baldwin
also carefully points out in his autobiographical essay, the seeds of his
defection were sown quite early, both in his own mixed motives for
joining the church, including fear and self-interest, and in his growing
realization of the corrupt practices of many of its ministers. John, like
the young James, searches desperately for and finally discovers a glimpse
of the loving God, which imparts a deep faith and inspires hopes of personal integration and fulfillment. David of *Amen*, age eighteen, presumably has undergone an ecstatic, transforming moment similar to
John's years earlier. If so, the euphoria and inspiration of the encounter
have faded in the years since his early adolescence under the weight of
disillusionment such as Baldwin underwent and such as John is certain to undergo. David still seeks the Lord in his way, though dimly and
indirectly, no longer through the "acceptable" medium of the church
because he has concluded that the Lord cannot be realized within its

structure. Perhaps he understands that he, like his mother, actually has had no authentic glimpse or vision of God and that any such apprehension, if possible at all, must be pursued in the outside world. The church's hopeless duality of the sacred versus the secular forbids David's growing belief in his musical heritage and talent as a source of "sacred" experience and communality. But David has chosen devotion to his creative art and sharing it with others over joyless obedience to his mother's severe God.

Baldwin's characterization of David is, if not quite simplistic compared to John's, at least much less complex and conflicted, due to his overriding purpose of demonstrating David's compelling need to leave the church. Although David is in a sense a far less interesting character, especially from a theological point of view, his relative lack of depth is a byproduct of Baldwin's attempt to create a more explicitly heroic character who will challenge and reject his dominant parent and the church.[5] In addition to possessing the greater confidence of an eighteen-year-old, David has enjoyed the nurturing acceptance of the church community for years, even contributing to worship services with his piano playing. John's vague hopes of literary accomplishment have become David's burgeoning plans for a musical career. John's intense guilt over sex and his terror of God's punishment have dissipated, as David engages in sexual activity without remorse and is not ruled by the wrathful God. Though in rebellion against his mother, he seems to appreciate her care and to love her. And, quite unlike John, he has a father who imperfectly but clearly loves him and who exerts a positive influence on his life. Although these various strengths and "improvements" in David's character and situation enable him to achieve a new maturity and freedom by the play's end, the effect is more ideologically pointed than psychologically profound or artistically convincing because Baldwin neglects to depict with much detail, tension, or interest either David's earlier faith or his recent crisis and loss of faith. While the various evidence adduced in the play argues in favor of David's revolt, *Amen* would be a more powerful human drama if it dealt in a more complex way with its young protagonist's interior struggle.

David has grown up under the sole care and control of his mother, immersed in the harsh, self-serving theology with which she rules her church. In one of Baldwin's rare indirect endorsements of Christianity, he draws a basic distinction between Christ and "the real architect of the Christian church, . . . the mercilessly fanatical and self-righteous St. Paul" (*Fire* 58). Both Gabriel of *Go Tell It* and Margaret are seen as ministers who embody the negative spirit of St. Paul and thus poison the spirit of Christianity. Their shared choice of a favorite biblical text, "Set thine house in order, for thou shalt die and not live" (*Amen* 7), reveals their presumption of holiness and salvation, their judgment of all others without love or compassion, and their blindness to the massive disorder in each of their houses. Gabriel, whose church career has deteriorated from a brilliant beginning to a lowly part-time status performing mostly menial tasks, perverts Christian theology by transforming his frustration and bitterness into a supposedly divinely sanctioned wrath against the world's evil, which only creates misery for his entire family and especially John. Margaret, with a far superior position as pastor of a congregation for ten years, is, unlike Gabriel, privileged and protected from the often humiliating demands on an African American of making a living in the outside world. She is consumed not so much by anger but by the desire to perpetuate her control of others, which she accomplishes not by leading and ministering but by commanding and bullying. Her theology consists of a series of prohibitions that dominate her opening sermon, as she defines sanctity not by any positive activity of love but only by a list of forbidden indulgences.

David's faith as a young church member, tested and demoralized over the years by his mother's acrid example as leader of the Christian community, is undone by her unconscionable treatment of her husband and by her demonization of her son's vocation. As the context in which David's overt revolt will take place, Baldwin depicts the history of Margaret's insincere religiosity and suggests its effects on her family. When Margaret and Luke's baby girl died, she sought safety from suffering in a spurious, self-ordained holiness induced, as in the case of Baldwin's stepfather, by a form of self-hatred (*Fire* 18). Baldwin admits that as a fourteen-year-old he, like Margaret, "supposed that God and safety were synonymous. The word 'safety' brings us to the real meaning of the word 'religious' as we use it" (*Fire* 30). But Margaret somehow contradictorily views the same God who is the source of safety as a heartless killer who takes revenge not only on the disobedient but also on the simply happy. She fled into the church after her daughter's death out of a bizarre guilt based on an image of an inhuman, cruel God: "In my heart, I always knew we couldn't go on like that—we was too happy— ... He weren't going to have no mercy on neither one of us" (87, 88). Now Margaret, seeking to justify her abandonment of her husband ten years earlier, interprets Ida Jackson's loss of a child as the Lord's action and suggests that he will take her other child if Ida does not leave her supposedly ungodly husband. Margaret's response to Ida's troubles represents her fear that God would have killed another child had she and Luke stayed together and pursued the happiness that in her mind invited divine censure. Late in the play Margaret realizes that at the time of her daughter's death, in clear contrast to John Grimes's life-transforming glimpse of the Lord, she never had an authentic vision that inaugurated her pastorship. Instead, she remembers only wanting her husband and hearing a voice tell her to find a hiding place from all the pain and from the judgment of the terrible God. Her previous absolute certitude about her anointing and calling by the Lord, very similar to Gabriel's, thus is finally shattered, her false vocation exposed as merely a career of self-delusion, self-promotion, and power.

Margaret compounds the sin of breaking her vows to her husband when she responds with utter heartlessness in their first meeting in ten years. Lacking, or perhaps repressing, any sense of guilt toward or compassion for a man whom she wronged and to whose decline she has contributed, she shows no sign of humanity when Luke, broken and dying, finds and tries to make a connection with his wife and son. Margaret denies their previously happy married life and reenacts her earlier betrayal of Luke by leaving the obviously moribund man again, using the familiar excuse of religious duty. Learning that his mother has lied to him for years about the crucial fact that it was she who left Luke, David finds more hypocrisies in his mother's Christianity: "Mama—you just said—God don't like liars" (41). Repulsed by her behavior as a Christian and as a wife, David becomes increasingly disillusioned, and his tone reflects this loss of respect: "You don't know if he be living, time you get back. But I reckon you don't care, do you?" (44). The play's stage set, where the Alexanders' apartment is virtually a part of and dominated by the church, reinforces the perception that Margaret has sublimated her sexual energy and personal life into the sterile zeal of her authoritarian mission, with Luke and David the casualties of her rectitude.

Amen intensifies the criticism in *Go Tell It* of the church's dichotomizing all experience into the sacred versus the secular and condemning the latter, which includes virtually all behavior and activity not directly involved in worship or prayer. In *Notes of a Native Son* Baldwin relates an interesting anecdote about the perceived evil of secular music in his stepfather's home:

> My father never mentioned Louis Armstrong, except to forbid us to play his records; but there was a picture of him on our wall for a long time. One of my father's strong-willed female relatives had placed it there and

> forbade my father to take it down. He never did, but he eventually
> maneuvered her out of the house and when, some years later, she was
> in trouble and near death, he refused to do anything to help her. (87)

Objecting to his stepfather's narrowness and his resentful, unchristian
treatment of his relative, Baldwin depicts these qualities in both Gabriel
and Margaret. Both of them, motivated largely either by the failure
(Gabriel) or the falsity (Margaret) of their vocations, transform the
church's theologically questionable tendency to demonize the secular
into an obsession with preventing any sort of natural enjoyment or personal growth. Margaret, who as pastor has experienced the luxury of
being shielded from the vicissitudes of making a living, does not wish
to understand the compromises required of her parishioners in the
working world. She unfairly condemns Brother Boxer for pursuing a
job driving a liquor truck, an attitude that epitomizes Margaret's sense
of moral and religious superiority and her failure to minister compas-
sionately and wisely to her people. Her disapproval of Luke's musical
career, which preceded her conversion but acquired a veneer of religious force afterwards, has inflated to a contempt that transcends theology as she attempts to compensate for her repressed guilt toward him.
David, inspired by his father's true vocation and gift to others, has chosen or acknowledged musical art as his calling as well. But his mother's
increasingly rigid and sanctimonious denial of popular music as a possible means of worshiping God and ministering to others finally drives
David toward his irrevocable choice to pursue his only possible sanctity outside the church. As Baldwin demonstrates, Margaret, whose
vocation disguises an egoistical career about to implode, ironically
decries the genuine vocations of Luke and David merely because they
acquire meaning beyond the artificial border between the sacred and
the secular, beyond her realm of control.

But the problem is much deeper than Margaret. One might say that
this church, representing for Baldwin the black fundamentalist church
in which he grew up, has constructed a God in its own image—mean,
vengeful, unloving, pitiless; or, more charitably and perhaps more accurately, that these people have modeled their behavior on the image of
God fostered by their past leaders as well as their present pastor. They
cower before the God of retribution while they delight in wishing for
the destruction of their enemies and of those among themselves whom
they presume to judge. Baldwin uses religious songs in the play frequently as an ironic chorus and commentary on the congregation's
meanness of spirit, as when Sister Moore sings, "You can run on for a

long time, / I tell you the great God Almighty gonna cut you down" (73). The "amen corner" of the play's title, which is supposed to designate the place where the saved express their enthusiastic response to and support of the minister's sermon, becomes here a dark locus of revenge and sin. Identifying Margaret's failure to serve them due to her arrogance and lack of love, the so-called "saints" of the church object appropriately to her smug sense of superiority, "like she way up above all human trouble" (49). But they share most of her negative qualities, and their other criticisms of her are unjust, motivated by their desire to humiliate and topple her. Their wish to damage her position by any means possible leads them to condemn her husband, whom they see as "dying in his sins" (53) by divine will, and her son, who has dared to venture outside their circumscribed little world to explore the forbidden fruits of dating and music. As with virtually all the characters in Go Tell It, these people obsess on the idea of the sinner's falling to perdition, reflecting both their image of a punishing God and their passion for others' unhappiness and destruction.

Sister Moore, because she emulates Margaret's hypocrisy and ruthlessness and because she has lived an even more empty, loveless personal life, qualifies as her successor; indeed, she seizes power in the same malevolent way Margaret did from Elder King ten years earlier. After lying about her clear intention from the play's outset to oust the minister, Moore conducts a secret campaign of slander based on Margaret's inability to control the men in her home. The culminating charge against Margaret, that she "ain't been leading the life of a holy woman, especially a holy woman in her position" (108), is true only in the sense that she ministers without love. The accusations of her immorality are groundless and even ironic, for while she is accused of being lustful and "double-minded" (112) and failing to love the Lord, Margaret is only just beginning to accept and to love her husband again, a change that creates the possibility of her real sanctification and relationship with the Lord. Ironically, it is her sudden growth in compassion and her acknowledgment of responsibility toward Luke that give her enemies, i.e., most of her congregation, the opportunity and the excuse to finally bring her low and dismiss her. Baldwin seems to suggest that with the impending installation of Sister Moore as pastor, the church gets if not what it deserves, then at least what it chooses. His vision of the church here is very dark indeed, much more bitter and ominous than in Go Tell It.

One significant subtext of Baldwin's portrayal of the church in Amen, which relates to his career-long examination of the meaning of sex as it affects human love and growth, is the debate on the place of sex in the "holy" or happy life. An entire chapter would be needed to address the complexity of this issue and its connection to issues of sexism and gender relations in *Amen,* and a book could be devoted to the topic for Baldwin's entire corpus. This play is, like several other Baldwin texts, including *Giovanni's Room, Another Country,* "Going to Meet the Man," *Tell Me How Long the Train's Been Gone,* and *Just Above My Head,* a study of the terrible human consequences of sexual repression and denial. For Baldwin, people who do not love sexually lose their opportunity and betray their responsibility to connect with and enrich another's life and possibly to save that person as well as themselves from despair or meaninglessness. However, the church in *Go Tell It* and *Amen* derogates virtually all sexual feelings and activity, even that between spouses, as in some way impure and wrong, and it instills in most members a deep sense of guilt and shame. Perhaps influenced by St. Paul's rather negative view of married love and sexuality generally in his advice that it is better to marry than to burn, the church perpetuates the pathological attitude that sexlessness is equivalent to, and the only requirement for purity. Early in their marriage Margaret and Luke experienced a healthy sexual love as an integral component of their union. After the death of their daughter, however, Margaret, influenced by church teaching, reinterpreted that facet and source of their happiness as an offense against God, a diabolical weakness to which only the weak surrender. In fact, she has perverted the meaning of sexual love, which creates life, into something that literally brings about death. Like David of *Giovanni's Room,* she denies her sexuality and thereby causes great suffering for herself and others close to her. Both she and Sister Moore, who is more like Margaret than the latter would like to acknowledge, sublimate their sexual energies into aggressive, self-righteous actions designed either to usurp or to maintain power in the church. Sister Moore displays fierce pride in her lifelong abstinence, which she thinks makes her uniquely pure and morally superior even to anyone who has known a committed and sanctioned carnal relationship. Baldwin exposes her supposed purity as a shriveled spirituality, her arrogant sexlessness as a life-denying failure to love any other person. The church elders, who gossip about Margaret's supposedly evil "lust" (111) for her own husband, also demonstrate that it is not the sexually active or involved but the repressed prohibitionists who actually harbor an obsession with sex.

Several characters in the play rebel against the church's view and represent Baldwin's thesis about the positive, potentially sanctifying role of sex in human relations. Luke always had understood, and still maintains despite his wife's objections, that his erotic desire for her was a key ingredient in their emotional intimacy and happiness. His reminding her of that happiness is one of the factors that lead to her spiritual awakening near the play's end. David's normal curiosity about the opposite sex and his possible sexual activity indicate not an incipient libertinism but a salutary potential for loving relationship. After Ida Jackson rejects Margaret's self-absorbed advice to leave her husband after their child dies, she revolts against a God who would kill a second child merely because the parents love each other. The happily married Sister Boxer objects to Margaret's self-image as an abstinent and therefore necessarily holy woman, and she correctly identifies the hatred of men that underlies Margaret's chastity as well as the sexual sublimation that results in her vehement performances in the pulpit. Appreciating the beauty of the sexual love that enriches her marriage, Sister Boxer humbly celebrates that "the Lord done blessed me with a real womanly nature" (51). Although Margaret's sister, Odessa, may be a virgin like Sister Moore, she does not claim that she is especially pure or "that the Lord had such special plans for me that I couldn't have nothing to do with men" (114). Her modesty, gentle humor, and wisdom about the sexual aspect of relationships leaven somewhat the harshness and the suffering surrounding this issue in the play.

In spite of the preponderance of harsh criticism of the church in *Amen,* the character of Odessa saves the play from being a totally one-sided assault. The depiction of the church is, as Carolyn Sylvander suggests, "much less balanced than in *Go Tell It,*" and this unbalanced view may be "the greatest weakness in the play" (96). But Sylvander's assertion that "no member of the church is admirable for any reason" (96) ignores the ameliorating figure of Margaret's sister. In powerful contrast to Margaret as well as to Florence of *Go Tell It,* Odessa resembles in some ways the novel's Deborah and Elizabeth, with her sincere faith in a loving God, her refusal to judge others, her compassion for Luke's suffering, and her loyalty to her sister and her family through their trials. At the crucial moment when Margaret is about to leave the dying Luke for a pastoral mission, claiming that she cannot save him, Odessa succinctly states the essence of Margaret's responsibility to Luke both as a wife and as a Christian: "But you might be able to help him, Maggie—if you was here" (44).

David is influenced not just by the scandal of the saints' and especially his mother's failures to embody the basic Christian virtues, but also by his father's rebellion against her God and her church. Years ago Luke repudiated the spiteful God that supposedly took their baby, as he now denies Margaret's idea that they were the objects of a divine curse: "Then that God you found—He just curse the poor? . . . All we'd done to be cursed was to be *poor,* that's all" (88, 89). In the midst of her patronizing lecture and sham concern over the state of his soul, Luke offers a startling insight about which of them is the real spiritual refugee: "I guess I could have told you—it weren't *my* soul we been trying to save" (91), predicting the great spiritual struggle ahead for her. Early in the play, just after Margaret displays her style of ministry by quashing all dissent over the issue of Brother Boxer's employment, Luke appears and asks, "You a good pastor?" (39). Speaking as an outsider, he unconsciously voices the disaffection of the congregation and conveys to David the need for challenging all figures of authority. When Luke then asks for his son's estimation of Margaret's pastorship, David is notably silent because he cannot answer affirmatively. As Luke's death draws near, he, like many of Baldwin's characters who defy the God they have been taught, declines repentance before Margaret's God and the surrender of his self-respect because it "would make *you* right" (90). Although David is not present, he understands and approves of his father's choice of personal integrity over a fawning, insincere repentance.

Before David's first appearance in the play, Margaret indicates her ignorance of her son's extracurricular musical and social activities and her presumption that he will remain in the church: "David's got his first time to disobey me. The Word say, Bring up a child in the way he should go, and when he is old he will not depart from it" (21). But David has disobeyed her and will depart from her negative example and from the church. Aside from their irony, however, these words acquire another meaning at the play's conclusion in the implication that David will carry the original ideals of the church into his future life. In a conversation with Luke, David confides his doubt about whether his mother ever truly found the Lord, and he reveals his own recent crisis of faith marked by his inability to pray, which occurred after some musicians invited him to join their group. After this sudden enlargement of his world has given David the confidence and critical perspective to consider leaving the church, Luke's return and serious illness confirm David's urgent need to proceed toward the inevitable break. The gravest risk to David comes not from the sinful, dangerous world outside but from the false safety his mother thinks the church offers, which in David's case entails the prospect of deepening inner conflict, loss of self-respect, and eventual self-destruction. David cannot afford to replicate his mother's long-term escape into the church, for he acknowledges that such a course for him would incite the urge to hide and the self-hatred that would ruin him. When Margaret leaves Luke for her church business in Philadelphia, David acts with a new decisiveness and maturity in electing to stay with his ailing father. Moments later, he responds to Margaret's command that the faithful praise the Lord by refusing to kneel, an act of defiance analogous to John Grimes's near-curse of God at the altar just before he undergoes his night of pain and desolation. Although David tells his mother that he will see her before he leaves her house forever, he departs before her deposal without a farewell, further conveying his lack of respect for her and the finality of his decision for independence. In *Notes of a Native Son,* Baldwin recalls a favorite biblical text of his stepfather's, which resonates in relation to David's choice: "And if it seem evil unto you to serve the Lord, choose you this day whom you will serve; whether the gods which your fathers served that were on the other side of the flood, or the gods of the Amorites, in whose land ye dwell" (113). These words might be said to provide a theological basis for David's defection, for to him it does seem clearly evil to serve the God whom Margaret and the church have taught him, just as it seems good to refuse such service.

As discussed above, in *The Evidence of Things Not Seen* Baldwin tells of Buddy, the seventeen-year-old boy James knew when he was fourteen, who was previously saved but now was ostracized by the entire church community for having "backslid" and "gone back into the world" (121). Remembering the "lightless and lonely" look on Buddy's face after his rejection and before his death, Baldwin claims that he died because the only community he knew had rejected him (121). David Alexander is, like John Grimes and the teenage James Baldwin, another potential Buddy or victim of the church's judgment, for as the saints learn of his rebellious behavior they begin to censure him as they do his father. But fortunately David preempts their possibly fatal judgment by rejecting their hypocrisy and deciding to live beyond their reach.

IV

The subtle and relatively unexplored dialectic of *Go Tell It* offers not only a critique of the church but also a portrayal of direct religious experience that takes place literally within the church and establishes at least the possibility of some sort of authentic spiritual life therein. Although at the conclusion of the novel John enters the church community as one of the saved, his serious doubts about the freedom to develop his identity and ambitions under the church's strict authority foreshadow his eventual departure. The dialectic of *Amen* presents a sharper critique but also an even more subtle and less examined assertion of the potential for what still might be termed religious experience and some kind of salvation. *Amen* both completes and in a sense reverses the implications of the novel, as David quits the community on the grounds of its own values but also internalizes them as he seeks to make his contribution to the church of the larger world. The autobiographical aspect of *Amen* represents Baldwin's decision to leave the church and his stepfather's home at age seventeen. But it also suggests the beginning of a second, lifelong stage of his relationship with Christianity, marked by his ongoing argument with the church as well as by his implicit investment in its beliefs and the transformation of his calling as a minister into his vocation as a writer. Although Baldwin uses David's development as a completion of *Go Tell It* and as a rationale for Baldwin's personal evolution, he positions Margaret as the protagonist to suggest the possibility of even a spiritually corrupt minister's reformation and discovery of the heart of the gospel. However, as Baldwin himself learned, and as David and Margaret do also, the sanctity and peace promised by the church are attainable only outside it, either through a commitment to the sacred nature of art (David) or through a revised but identifiably Christian dedication to serve others (Margaret).

Carolyn Sylvander makes the point that in *Amen,* as in Baldwin's several "other weighted attacks on the church after *Go Tell It* . . . the very vehemence of Baldwin's assaults undercuts his criticism" (96). Although she overstates the vehemence of *Amen* and misses the dialectic altogether, Sylvander aptly observes that the play "tries to exorcise the power of Baldwin's early religious training" (96). This attempt recurs unsuccessfully throughout Baldwin's career evidently because the intensity and indelibility of his early religious experience ensured his consistently dialectical response. Barbara Olson finds that Baldwin offers the stronger critique of the church in *Amen* because of the supposedly puzzling, unsatisfactory ambiguity of *Go Tell It.* However, although the novel surely presents a rich ambiguity, its critique is straightforward and clear. Olson exaggerates the ambiguity of *Go Tell It* because she does not realize that Baldwin is equally committed to both the critique and the mystery of faith. Instead of apprehending his dialectical approach, she interprets it as a kind of failure of control, stating that "Baldwin's intended denunciation was undermined by the black church idiom he chose to use" (296). She interprets *Amen* as a similar failure on Baldwin's part to convey his supposedly single-minded message of denunciation:

Ironically, however, this second attempt is only slightly more successful than the first, in large part because Baldwin's return to the church
idiom riddled his message more than redeemed it. . . . *The Amen Corner*
then repeats the very problem it was trying to solve. Like *Go Tell It*, its
church idiom renders it as much a vindication of Christianity as an
indictment. And once again Baldwin's plan to lambast the faith is
hoisted with its own petard. (297, 301)

The use of the black church's idiom in both works is only one, and a
rather tangential if not irrelevant, element of their vindicatory content.
Much more significant and relevant are Baldwin's portrayal of the
Christian roots of the major characters' new sense of loving connection with all people and his sympathy with ideas such as charity, sacrifice, and grace. Of course it is possible that Baldwin began writing
Amen with the primary and perhaps sole intention of concentrating on
the iniquities and offenses of the church. But, even granting that possibility, close analysis of the play by itself and in the context of all of
Baldwin's works indicates that he was constitutionally and intellectu-
ally incapable of betraying his dialectical cast of mind and producing a
simplistic broadside (though, ironically, that is exactly the critical consensus on *Amen* and on many of his other works). In spite of Olson's
somewhat limited perspective, somehow treating half of the content of
these two texts as essentially unintentional or accidental, she still presents some excellent analysis of the vindicatory aspect of *Amen*, even if
these findings are not integrated into her argument.

In leaving the church, David rejects the shameful practice of his
mother and most of the congregation, but not the essence of Christian principles, which inform his implicit theology. In *Go Tell It* Baldwin
emphasizes the individual's need to be saved by God over the need to
save oneself. Beginning with *Amen* and extending through the rest of
his texts, however, he shifts the balance toward the ability and responsibility of individuals to save themselves as well as others. Whereas
John Grimes cannot save himself, David Alexander must. David, like
John on a quest for a loving father and a loving God, wants to be
involved in the larger reality of God that he intuits in and through his
music. As Baldwin in *Nobody Knows My Name* refers to the limited, negative conception of God and then to the expansive idea to which John
and David aspire, "from my point of view, this concept is not big
enough. It has got to be made much bigger than it is because God is,
after all, not anybody's toy. To be with God is really to be involved with
some enormous, overwhelming desire, and joy, and power which you

cannot control, which controls you" (113). John, David, and several other Baldwin characters in other works discover God in various senses because of what O'Neale calls their "insistence to forge a 'normal' dependent interaction" with God, establishing various "empirical evidences of God in Baldwin's world" (126).

Consistent with the tradition of the early African American church, which tended to bear "the marks of a holistic community" treating the sacred and the secular as a unified reality rather than as separable entities (Hopkins 1), Baldwin suggests, much more vigorously than in *Go Tell It*, that a person's striving for communication and possibly communion with the world can have quite holy causes and effects. David longs for a musical career not for egotistical or narcissistic gratification but because he feels called to develop the talent he has inherited in the service of other people. In an interview Baldwin explains how the church impressed on him deeply the idea that talent belongs not to the individual but to the community:

> What is important about my work, which I realized when I was a little boy, partly from the Church perhaps, and whatever happened to my mind all those years I was growing up in the shadow of the Holy Ghost, is that nothing belongs to you; it belongs to everybody. My talent does not belong to me, you know, it belongs to you; it belongs to everybody. (Hall, *Conversations* 106)

In his most revealing speech in the play, David echoes Baldwin's fervent dedication to the art that replaced his formal ministry and his attitude of humble responsibility to the world at large:

> If I stayed here—I'd end up worse than Daddy—because I wouldn't be doing what I know I got to do—I *got* to do! I've seen your life—and now I see Daddy—and I love you, I love you both!—but I've got my work to do, something's happening in the world out there, I got to go! ... Every time I play, every time I listen, I see Daddy's face and yours, and so many faces—who's going to speak for all that, Mama? Who's going to speak for all of us? I can't stay home. Maybe I can say something—one day—maybe I can say something in music that's never been said before. (120, 121)

The same Christian roots that inspired Baldwin also influence David to attempt to fulfill his responsibility to himself by connecting with all people. The theological soundness of the decision is implied in the universality of David's intention and in his discovery of the "nonecclesiastical epiphanies" (O'Neale 138) that contribute to the enrichment and healing of the world through the sacred function of art.

A person's willingness to risk self-interest and even survival for personal growth and connection with others is a key determinant of faith in Baldwin's theology. Partly because David realizes the lack of safety in the apparently protective confines of the church, he more readily accepts the risks and dangers of his new life in the world. But with his indulgence in alcohol and casual sex, he shows signs of possibly being unable to bear the very freedom he claims in leaving his mother's house, and he fears that he might duplicate his father's fairly dissolute life in which accomplishment has been overshadowed by lost potential. While David's entry into the world represents for his mother a defeat, a personal loss reminiscent of the death of her baby, and a continual worry, for Luke it is a reason for rejoicing at a new birth: "He's gone into the world. . . . He's living. He's living" (130).

Olson argues convincingly that David's revolt is based on an inner dedication to Christianity that transcends the church and will survive his defection: "while it is true that David Alexander leaves the church, his rejection of Christianity may not be so unequivocal as it seems. Do we have here an irrevocable denunciation or a prophetic challenge? Does David abandon the church or take it with him into the world?" (299). If Margaret had not enforced the sacred-secular dichotomy with such ruthless fervor and not "required such a stark choice between the church and the world" (300), her son would not be going. David's stated grounds for leaving are consistent with Margaret's conversion speech, in which she displays "this same identification with humanity's needs and joys" (299). Because of the integrity and vision of David's choice, Olson declares him "a sort of messiah—the anointed one his mother has been hoping for, a Davidic one, who goes out to the world beyond the closed circle of the church" (299).

By depicting David's warm relationship with his father, Baldwin imaginatively amends both his relationship with his stepfather and John's with Gabriel. In his "Notes for *The Amen Corner*," written for its 1968 publication, Baldwin at age forty-four hints at the play's autobiographical significance and confides that he was moved to write it at twenty-six partly by a need to finally express forgiveness and love for his long-dead stepfather, who had never loved him:

The first line written in *The Amen Corner* is now Margaret's line in the Third Act: "It's a awful thing to think about, the way love never dies!"

> That line, of course, says a great deal about me—the play says a great
> deal about me—but I was thinking not only, not merely, about the ter-
> rifying desolation of my private life but about the great burdens carried
> by my father. I was old enough by now, at last, to recognize the nature
> of the dues he had paid, old enough to wonder if I could possibly have
> paid them, old enough, at last, at last, to know that I had loved him and
> had wanted him to love me. . . . *The Amen Corner* comes somewhere out
> of that. (xvi)

In *Amen* the bitter (step)father-son relationship of *Go Tell It* is replaced
by one involving some resentment on the son's part but also respect
and reconciliation. Baldwin creates Luke as a consoling projection of
the father or stepfather he always wanted, in order to transform more
easily what he saw as his potentially self-destructive hatred of David
Baldwin into forgiveness. John Grimes's quest for the father is ultimately successful in three aspects, as he experiences a direct glimpse
of the Lord, an indirect but powerful connection with his dead father,
Richard, and a confrontation with his stepfather based on a new
strength and ability to love (Lynch, "Quest" 168–72). Similar to John's
case, David's yearning for his father parallels and is closely related to
his desire for some knowledge of a compassionate God. Whereas
Richard, similar to Luke in his ability to love and his defiance of the
church's harsh God, cannot return literally to John, Luke, the semi-
prodigal father, does return to give his son at least a glimpse of him and
a sign of his love before he dies. The encouragement John receives
from the mysterious, ironic voice of his unknown, deceased father is
repeated in Luke's reassurance to David: "That's my son. Go on, boy.
You remember what I told you. . . . Go on, boy. You all right?" (83). The
radically revised portrayal of the father figure from Gabriel of *Go Tell It*
to Luke suggests at least the possibility (as does *Go Tell It,* in John's private religious experience) of a heavenly Father who, in Luke's image, is
compassionate and caring. This implied but significant mitigation of the
church's image of God, following from David's discovery of the truth
about his father, confirms his decision to leave and contributes much
to the hope with which he embarks on his spiritual journey.

Luke, the apparent reprobate who rejects the church's version of
Christianity, contributes more to David's happiness and salvation than
does his mother the minister. Luke's recorded music, which because of
Margaret's ban David just lately has been able to hear, makes David
proud of his legacy and verifies his evolving identity. Although his father's
life has not been a model of fulfillment, David shares with him the open-

hearted response to the calling of the artist, complete with its sacrifices and risks. By reentering the lives of his wife and son, Luke helps them by challenging them to confront the conflicts they avoid. When Margaret grieves that David has gone into the world, Luke expresses confidence in David's well-being and chides her for her lack of faith in the invisible: "Is you got to see your God to know he's living" (130). Ironically, Luke thus approximates St. Paul's definition of faith as the evidence of things not seen, which is the title of Baldwin's last work.

The implication that Luke's suffering serves a redemptive function for Margaret and David represents the first of several instances in Baldwin's plays and fiction—also including *Giovanni's Room, Tell Me How Long the Train's Been Gone, If Beale Street Could Talk,* and *Just Above My Head*—in which one's personal distress has a potentially theological significance in its effect of saving others.[6] Although Luke is perhaps more sinned against than sinning in light of Margaret's abandonment, he bears responsibility for the wasted years and the long separation from his son. However, Baldwin implies that Luke's dissipation, emotional pain, and imminent death have been brought about largely by his choice to bear the suffering from which his wife fled into the church after their baby's death. Luke's unconscious sacrifice for his wife culminates in his death, which in Baldwin's view inspires both Margaret and David to envision and to create a sacred life outside the church. In the "Autobiographical Notes" in *Notes of a Native Son,* Baldwin touches on a theme he would reiterate often in his career, the dialectical unity of suffering and growth: "any writer . . . finds that the things which hurt him and the things which helped him cannot be divorced from each other; he could be helped in a certain way only because he was hurt in a certain way" (5). Luke's paternal advice, which contradicts the lesson of Margaret, also emphasizes the wisdom of confronting and using one's pain for healing: "Son—don't try to get away from the things that hurt you. The things that hurt you—sometimes that's all you got. You got to learn to live with those things—and—use them. I've seen people—put themselves through terrible torture—and die—because they was afraid of getting hurt" (60). David, fortified by his father's assistance and wisdom, both ends and begins his quest for the father at the play's conclusion, having found (and lost) Luke and having put aside his mother's God in place of the God he does not know yet.

Despite the apparent ease and certitude with which Margaret dictates theology and dominates her congregation and her son, the challenges she encounters lay bare the uncertainty of her vocation and the shallowness of her faith while they also prepare her for conversion to the true spirit of Christianity. Not wishing to offer a simplistic indict-ment of the church or Christianity in *Amen,* Baldwin avoids a two-dimensional portrayal of Margaret as a character incapable of change or growth. Her alteration at the play's end may seem at first somewhat sudden and unmotivated, but careful examination shows that Baldwin prepares for it throughout the play. The song that begins the text hints at Margaret's coming desolation as well as her transformation: "One day I walked the lonesome road / The spirit spoke unto me / And filled my heart with love— / Yes, he filled my heart with love, / . . . And he wrote my name above, / And that's why I thank God I'm in His care" (5). The several losses she suffers, including her church and home, her son, and her husband, strip Margaret of her comfortable identity and humble her spirit so that she may acknowledge difficult truths about her life. When she accepts drums and trumpets as appropriate means of worshiping God in church, this surprising reversal of her rigid posi-tion on the secular-sacred dichotomy—although it is used as an excuse to attack her and although it comes ironically too late to halt David's defection—indicates her potential for development. When Ida Jackson returns after her second child has died, Margaret changes her earlier directive and tells her to go home to her husband and to "have another baby right away" (100), implicitly acknowledging her terrible error in leaving Luke years ago and showing a new belief in trusting the Lord even when his ways are inscrutable. Echoing David's and Ida's new inability to pray, Margaret finds that she cannot say amen to the harsh God of her construction, indicating for Baldwin a deepening spiritual-ity. When she thinks back to her entry into the church, Margaret real-izes for the first time that her supposed vision of the Lord, which took place "in a cold, dark place" (122) much like John Grimes's spiritual landscape on the threshing floor, was, unlike John's, something imag-ined or invented out of her terror.

Though Luke's life may seem a ruin, his return and reaffirmation of his love for Margaret contribute to her regeneration. For Baldwin, the committed erotic relationship entails the potential and the respon-sibility to save the other, a duty Margaret abandons but Luke ultimately fulfills. In her first scene with Luke she explicitly denies her responsi-bility to save him, hiding behind the convenient attitude that there "ain't nothing but the Lord can save him!" (44). The congregation accuses her of not saving Luke in the sense of making him subservient to church commands, but her real sin lies in her refusal to cooperate with the divine plan that individuals help to save each other.[7] Sister Moore and the saints accuse her of harboring lustful thoughts for Luke just when Margaret has grown beyond their puritanical obsession with sex and has come to the understanding that married love should include but also transcends physical passion. Margaret realizes that to ascribe the emotional intimacy and happiness of married love to sex alone is to betray the sacred bond:

> I used to know that man, look like, just inside *out,* sometime I knowed what he was going to do before he knowed it himself.... Ain't no man never made me laugh the way Luke could. No, nor cry neither. I ain't never held no man until I felt his pain coming into me like little drops of acid.... Now, you know there's still something left in my heart for that man. (103)

Margaret learns that her flight from suffering into the church, which coincided with her leaving Luke, has only delayed the pain that overtakes her now. But that suffering forces her to understand her life, as her preliminary recognition that "I done something, somewhere, wrong" (121) develops into her clearest and most significant discovery, that she has wasted her life and irreparably harmed her family: "I'm thinking how I throwed away my life.... I'm thinking now—maybe Luke needed it more. Maybe David could of used it better" (125). As she finally reconciles with and embraces Luke just before he dies feeling happy and safe, they illustrate Baldwin's thesis that the only human safety is fragile and provisional, found in contact with and commitment to another.

Deposed and ejected by the church, having lost her temporarily if imperfectly reunited family, Margaret discovers the essence of Christian love, which promises new life for her, like David, outside the structure of the church. Baldwin repeats the pattern of ending/beginning, loss/gain, and death/rebirth with David and Luke and now with Margaret, who may not experience John Grimes's direct vision of the Lord but whose heart has been touched nonetheless. Her glimpse is indirect but intense, purchased in Baldwin's view by her son's courage and especially by her husband's suffering, love, and forgiveness. Because she finally admits her continued love for Luke, her opened heart is susceptible to the fundamentals of her faith, namely humility, universal love, service, and joy:

> Children. I'm just now finding out what it means to love the Lord. It ain't all in the singing and the shouting. It ain't all in the reading of the Bible. It ain't even—it ain't even—in running all over everybody trying

to get to heaven. To love the Lord is to love all His children—all of them, everyone!—and suffer with them and rejoice with them and never count the cost! (134)

As she acknowledges her failings and sins, Margaret emphasizes the universality of Christian love, the absence of which in Baldwin's church prompted his departure. Although she leaves the church unwillingly, in contrast to David's free choice, and although she lacks his invigorating and sacramental pursuit of art, Margaret "has learned what true religion is and, in fact, what true Christianity is" and will be sustained by her faith "without having to abandon God as her reference point or the Bible as her standard" (Olson 300, 299). Her final sermon to the congregation, which is also her first genuinely spiritual one, suggests she not only is a person now capable of giving and receiving love but also a true minister of the Word to the world at large. Clenching Luke's mouthpiece in her fist during her sermon and speaking of accepting suffering and risk, Margaret acknowledges the legitimacy of his and David's vocations as she prepares for her own secular role in salvation. The silence with which the saints respond to her heartfelt address, together with Sister Moore's exultation in Margaret's humiliation and removal, shows that the church either cannot recognize or does not want a sincere servant of the gospel as their leader. Olson finds that Baldwin "has portrayed Christianity as self-corrective" (300), but this assessment appears too optimistic because it ignores the dark implications of the congregation's jubilant choice of a leader such as Sister Moore and the loss of David and Margaret, who were the best hopes for renewal within Christianity's formal structure. Although Margaret's last action in the play is to fall in mourning beside Luke's bed, she is not defeated but rather energized by her "transfiguration" (Olson 301) and thankful for the opportunity to apply the principles she has just come to understand. Still, in her new dependence on God she feels the paradoxical "dreadful weight of hope" that David experiences at the end of *Giovanni's Room:* "I must believe, I must believe, that the heavy grace of God, which has brought me to this place, is all that can carry me out of it" (224).

The experiences of John Grimes, David, Margaret, and even Luke Alexander, as well as Baldwin himself, suggest that only the person with the courage to defy the church and become an outsider can hope for a life of spiritual growth and for knowledge of the loving God. In spite of the gloomy prognosis for the church, Baldwin's first two texts convey an optimistic theology centered on following one's calling wherever it leads and serving others and God even in obscure ways that may seem antithetical to salvation.

Amen was published in 1968, in the middle of Baldwin's alleged period of polemical rhetoric, politicized rage, and even hatred of whites and Christianity. The dismissive charges against *Tell Me How Long the Train's Been Gone* (1968) and other works of these years, which are mostly inaccurate and which betray critics' propensity for restricting their analysis to sociopolitical matters, have prevented much serious treatment. Although *Amen* itself does not deal with whites, Baldwin's Notes for the play reveal a rather temperate position on race, as he qualifies a statement that he felt oppressed by "everyone" when he lived in New Jersey: "I say 'everyone' for the sake of convenience, for there were, indeed exceptions, thank God, and these exceptions helped to save my life and also taught me what I then most bitterly needed to know—i.e., that love and compassion, which always arrive in such unexpected packages, have nothing to do with the color of anybody's skin" (x). Aside from the issue of race, *Amen* clearly refutes the common charge through his middle and later years that Baldwin held nothing but bitterness for the Christian church and faith. His false image as an apostate ignores the dialectic that is so pervasive not just in *Go Tell It,* published in 1953, but also in *Amen,* published in the midst of his supposedly darkest period. Considering the dual significance of the play being written in 1953 and 1954 but not published until 1968, it can be viewed both as the second and last work where Baldwin expresses a qualified but clear hope for Christian faith and as a quite surprising if not shocking reaffirmation of the same during a period of his most intense criticism of the practice of Christianity in white America. Hopefully this study of the play can contribute toward a much-needed reassessment of the complexity and open-mindedness of *Amen* and all of Baldwin's work.

One reason for Baldwin's importance in modern African American literature and culture is his unique position as the last black American writer both "to exploit as a major theme the black man's relationship with Christianity" and "to distance himself from the lone enduring black institution, the black church, not by its notable absence," as in the works of many other writers, "but by his overtly consistent portrayal of its lack of authentic Christian commitment" (O'Neale 140). *Amen* illustrates perhaps the most forcefully of all his works Baldwin's belief that "the black man's experiential condition rendered it impossible for him (Baldwin in particular and the race in general) to find salvation in the black church" (O'Neale 135). But although his position is persistently dialectical, his noted critique of the church has dominated his image and "opened the floodgate for contemporary anti-Christian, non-biblically based black American literature" because "his boldness invited younger writers to complete the schism between black art and black faith" (O'Neale 140). Unfortunately, the dialectic that provides much of his work's tension and energy is generally eviscerated in the scholarship, reduced to nothing but complaint against and rejection of the church and Christianity as part of his drastically oversimplified image as the raging social and political critic/prophet. Yet, as O'Neale notes, Baldwin invariably

> attempts to separate the visible history of black America's experience with Christianity from the spiritual, visionary experience that both he and the race may have internalized. The reality of that unseen spiritual truth, codified in his novels by the suffering blues and tarrying spiritual motifs, enables him to keep advocating that the demonstrable love of Christ will bring to earth that paradise revealed on the threshing floor. . . . Then and only then will his quest end and he can unhesitantly acknowledge oneness with the Christian God, his father. (141)

This first detailed examination of *Amen*'s critique as well as its spirituality and investment in Christian ideals challenges the play's censure and neglect as a simplistic, repetitious diatribe against the African American church and demonstrates its crucial significance as an early work in the context of Baldwin's lifelong search for spiritual fulfillment. It is important to establish that the earnestness of this quest, which a few scholars concede in *Go Tell It* but most deny in every one of his later works, persists in some fashion throughout his texts, up through *The Evidence of Things Not Seen*. Even in that final work, in which Baldwin returns yet again to reflect on his early formation in the church and his consequent sense of community, he discusses "the necessity of attempting to excavate the meaning of the word *community*—which, as I have understood it, simply means our endless connection with, and responsibility for, each other" (122). As quoted above, Baldwin says that in order to become moral and to pursue his vocation he may have to "stay out of the temple" (*Rap* 86) or the church for the rest of his life. But in the introduction to *The Price of The Ticket*, written two years before his death, he concedes that he, presumably like Margaret Alexander in her new life, never really abandoned the pulpit or the message he learned to deliver there: "If I were still in the pulpit which some people (and they may be right) claim I never left, I would counsel my countrymen to the self-confrontation of prayer, the cleansing breaking of the heart which precedes atonement" (xviii).

NOTES

Acknowledgment: Research for this article was assisted by an academic research leave from Kent State University and by a fellowship at the Center for the Study of Literature and Theology at the University of Glasgow.

Epigraph: James Baldwin with Margaret Meade, *A Rap on Race* (Philadelphia: Lippincott), 1971, 86.

1. See also Michael Lynch, "A Glimpse of the Hidden God," 35–37.
2. In the world of drama productions, Baldwin was encouraged by a brief but successful student production of *Amen* at Howard University in 1955, and he sought to have his play produced on Broadway. But it was not until 1965 that he overcame producers' lack of confidence in the subject matter of the black church and enjoyed the satisfaction of a Broadway run. The play was produced very successfully in 1965 throughout Europe and in Israel, and in 1983 a musical version at Ford's Theater in Washington, D.C. was received enthusiastically. Among a flurry of European honors in Baldwin's late years, *Amen* was produced in 1986 in London, where it garnered strong reviews and several months of packed houses.
3. See Jean-François Gounard, *The Racial Problem in the Works of Richard Wright and James Baldwin;* Trudier Harris, *Black Women in the Fiction of James Baldwin;* Stanley Macebuh, *James Baldwin: A Critical Study;* Karin Moller, *The Theme of Identity in the Essays of James Baldwin;* Horace Porter, *Stealing the Fire: the Art and Protest of James Baldwin;* Louis Pratt, *James Baldwin;* and Carol Sylvander, *James Baldwin.*
4. See Lynch, "Just Above My Head," 284–87.
5. John certainly does qualify in a sense as heroic, especially in the mythological sense. See Lynch, "Everlasting Father," 156–75.
6. See Lynch, "Just Above," 295–97, for a general discussion of redemptive suffering and Lynch, "Beyond Guilt and Innocence," 1–18, for a discussion of the theme in *Another Country.*
7. See Lynch, "Just Above," 293–94.

WORKS CITED

Allen, Shirley. "The Ironic Voice in Baldwin's *Go Tell It on the Mountain.*" In *James Baldwin: A Critical Evaluation,* ed. Therman O'Daniel, 30–37. Washington, D.C.: Howard University Press, 1977.
Baldwin, James. *The Amen Corner.* New York: Dial, 1968.

―――. *The Evidence of Things Not Seen.* New York: Holt, Rinehart, and Winston, 1985.

―――. *The Fire Next Time.* New York: Dial, 1963.

―――. *Giovanni's Room.* New York: Dial, 1956.

―――. *Nobody Knows My Name: More Notes of a Native Son.* New York: Dial, 1961.

―――. *Notes of a Native Son.* Boston: Beacon, 1955.

―――. *The Price of the Ticket: Collected Nonfiction, 1948–1985.* New York: St. Martin's, 1985.

Baldwin, James, with Margaret Meade. *A Rap on Race.* Philadelphia: Lippincott, 1971.

Bobia, Rosa. *The Critical Reception of James Baldwin in France.* New York: Peter Lang, 1997.

Champion, Ernest. *Mr. Baldwin, I Presume: James Baldwin—Chinua Achebe: A Meeting of the Minds.* New York: University Press of America, 1995.

Gounard, Jean-François. *The Racial Problem in the Works of Richard Wright and James Baldwin.* Trans. Joseph J. Rodgers, Jr. Westport, Conn.: Greenwood, 1992.

Hall, John. "James Baldwin Interviewed." In *Conversations with James Baldwin,* ed. Fred L. Standley and Louis H. Pratt, 98–107. Jackson: University Press of Mississippi, 1989.

Harris, Trudier. *Black Women in the Fiction of James Baldwin.* Knoxville: University of Tennessee Press, 1985.

Hopkins, Dwight N. *Shoes That Fit Our Feet: Sources for a Constructive Black Theology.* Maryknoll, N.Y.: Orbis, 1993.

Joyce, Joyce Ann. *Warriors, Conjurers, and Priests: Defining African-Centered Literary Criticism.* Chicago: Third World Press, 1994.

Leeming, David A. *James Baldwin: A Biography.* New York: Knopf, 1994.

Lunden, Rolf. "The Progress of a Pilgrim: James Baldwin's *Go Tell It on the Mountain.*" *Studia Neophilologica* 53 (1981): 113–26.

Lynch, Michael F. "Beyond Guilt and Innocence: Redemptive Suffering and Love in Baldwin's *Another Country.*" *Obsidian II* 7 (Spring–Summer 1992): 1–18.

―――. "The Everlasting Father: Mythic Quest and Rebellion in Baldwin's *Go Tell It on the Mountain.*" *CLA Journal* 37 (December 1993): 156–75.

―――. "A Glimpse of the Hidden God: Dialectical Vision in Baldwin's *Go Tell It on the Mountain.*" In *New Essays on Go Tell It on the Mountain,* ed. Trudier Harris, 29–57. New York: Cambridge University Press, 1996.

―――. "Just Above My Head: James Baldwin's Quest for Belief." *Literature and Theology* 11 (September 1997): 284–98.

Macebuh, Stanley. *James Baldwin: A Critical Study.* New York: Third Press, 1973.

Mayne, Heather Joy. "Biblical Paradigms in Four Twentieth Century African American Novels." Ph.D. diss., Stanford University, 1991.

Molette, Carlton W. "James Baldwin as a Playwright." In *James Baldwin: a Critical Evaluation,* ed. Therman B. O'Daniel, 183–88. Washington, D.C.: Howard University Press, 1977.

Moller, Karin. *The Theme of Identity in the Essays of James Baldwin.* Goteborg, Sweden: Acta Universitatis Gothoburgensis, 1975.

Olson, Barbara. "'Come-to-Jesus Stuff' in James Baldwin's *Go Tell It on the Mountain* and *The Amen Corner.*" *African American Review* 31 (Summer 1997): 295–301.

O'Neale, Sondra. "Fathers, Gods, and Religion: Perceptions of Christianity and Ethnic Faith in James Baldwin." In *Critical Essays on James Baldwin,* ed. Fred L. Standley and Nancy V. Burt, 125–43. Boston: G.K. Hall, 1988.

Porter, Horace A. *Stealing the Fire: The Art and Protest of James Baldwin* Middletown, Conn.: Wesleyan University Press, 1989.

Pratt, Louis H. *James Baldwin.* Boston: G.K. Hall, 1978.

Schnapp, Patricia Lorine. "The Liberation Theology of James Baldwin." Ph.D. diss., Bowling Green State University, 1987.

Spencer, Jon Michael. "The Black Church and the Harlem Renaissance." *African American Review* 30 (Fall 1996): 453–60.

Sylvander, Carol W. *James Baldwin.* New York: Frederick Ungar, 1980.

Tate, Claudia. *Psychoanalysis and Black Novels.* New York: Oxford University Press, 1998.

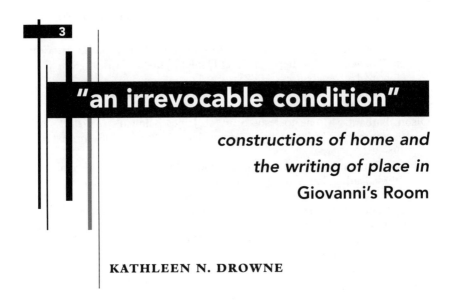

"an irrevocable condition"

constructions of home and
the writing of place in
Giovanni's Room

KATHLEEN N. DROWNE

As a young man in Harlem, James Baldwin earnestly sought to fulfill his potential as a writer of and an honest witness to the painful realities of American culture. But like many African American writers and artists (including his erstwhile mentor Richard Wright), Baldwin found that he could not answer this calling on American soil. Feeling alienated from his homeland and discouraged by the ambiguous but ubiquitous "race problem," he fled to Paris, a city that could and did provide him necessary physical and psychological distance from his turbulent past. Although not without its difficulties,[1] the expatriate lifestyle proved to be a liberating experience for Baldwin. In his 1959 essay "The Discovery of What It Means to Be an American," he writes "in Paris I began to see the sky for what seemed to be the first time" (174). His new city offered him a fresher vision of the problems in American society and in his own life, which created an even more urgent sense of responsibility to address these problems in his writing. When he left for Paris in 1948, Baldwin had been searching for not just a physical but also a spiritual home—a place that would offer him the perspective needed to grapple with the difficult and consuming issues of race, sexuality, nationality, and the meaning and necessity of love. He found this place, for a time, in the French capital.

Baldwin's personal experiences of seeking a "home-away-from-home" and living as an expatriate in Paris (and later in Switzerland and

Turkey) bleed into his fiction in complex ways. Through the elaborate searches that many of his fictional characters undergo to find a home, Baldwin explores issues of nationality, home, and, more specifically, *home place*. And perhaps nowhere is Baldwin's construction of place more important to the moral and psychological struggles the characters undergo than in *Giovanni's Room* (1956). Baldwin sets this novel in his adopted city of Paris, and turns his "American hero" loose to realize, as he himself soon did, that "Paris was no cure for sexual ambivalence" (Leeming 56). Throughout the work David—the self-exiled, self-tortured, and essentially homeless American protagonist—wonders to himself about the nature of home. In time he comes to the startling and significant realization that "perhaps home is not a place but simply an irrevocable condition" (121), finally recognizing the interior, emotional side of home—a condition—as opposed to a simply external, geographical reality. Although David cannot always see it, this dual nature of home surfaces all through the novel and afflicts him as both a physical reality and an emotional wound. His search for a geographical home manifests itself through his nomadic lifestyle, as David moves frequently from place to cheaper place in and around Paris. But apart from this succession of cheap hotels and, of course, Giovanni's room, David's inner sense of homelessness arises in part from his inability to find a sexual identity with which he feels comfortable and secure. This juxtaposition of David's search for a place with his search for an identity exemplifies the way that Baldwin manipulates perceptions of place in order to reveal the psychological struggles of his characters.

Baldwin's tendency to infuse geographical spaces with psychological and moral significance runs throughout his *œuvre*. For Baldwin, geographical reality is often inseparable from both the psychological landscape of his characters *(le paysage intérieur)* and the moral landscape that surrounds their decisions *(le paysage moralisé)*. That is, the ways characters respond to, describe, and imagine the physical places they inhabit reveal intimate details about their own "interior landscapes." This impulse toward *paysage moralisé* emerges early in Baldwin's career. In his first novel, *Go Tell It On the Mountain* (1953), the mountaintop and the threshing-floor become important locations, real and metaphorical, for John and Gabriel Grimes's understanding of themselves and each other. In Baldwin's last book-length essay, *The Evidence of Things Not Seen* (1985), the city of Atlanta becomes a symbolic proving ground for morality and justice after the murders of twenty-eight children. And in many of his works in the intervening three decades, Baldwin's preoccupation with the way that place conveys moral meaning becomes evident in the very titles of essays such as "The Harlem Ghetto" (1948), "Journey to Atlanta" (1948), "The Negro in Paris" (1950), "Stranger in the Village" (1953) "Equal in Paris" (1955), "Fifth Avenue, Uptown: A Letter from Harlem" (1960), and novels such as *Another Country* (1962), *If Beale Street Could Talk* (1974), and *No Name in the Street* (1972).

Often Baldwin constructs place in his writing to emphasize the sense of anonymity, invisibility, and alienation that African Americans feel in a world dominated by whites ("Stranger in the Village" and *No Name in the Street* are just two examples). But particularly in his early fiction, Baldwin's characters' usually intense and often bizarre perceptions of the physical places they inhabit illuminate their moral and psychological struggles between and among forces as strong as hate, sexuality, racism, justice, honor, and love. Leonard Lutwack theorizes that such strong reactions to a place, particularly a familiar place, can expose to the reader details critical to understanding that character's psyche. "A response to a place becomes material for characterization when it is individualized, that is when it does not conform to the customary response and when it cancels or exaggerates the impact place qualities usually have" (71). This idea resonates loudly in *Giovanni's Room,* a work in which Baldwin certainly represents Paris, but hardly with the tone or imagery of familiar, idealized tourist brochures. More importantly, David's unusual and at times virulent response to the legendary city of romance is marked not by tenderness but rather by the terror of impending, inevitable suffocation. His desperate and ultimately fruitless struggle to find happiness takes place in a Paris that explodes conventionally simple, romantic stereotypes by becoming a sinister site full of longing, despair, uncertainty, cruelty, and, at times, utter wretchedness. It is this Paris that reflects David's tortured interior psychological landscape.

Just as place means more than simple geography in Baldwin's fiction, home suggests more than merely the place where one lives. In fact, home for David is perhaps the most ephemeral of places. Unhindered by the sordid details of physical griminess that permeate so many other spaces in the novel, David imagines a homeplace in the most abstract of terms. He feels drawn toward America and "those places, those people which I would always, helplessly, and in whatever bitterness of spirit, love above all else" (84), and laments that "nothing here [in Paris] reminded me of home" (66). Yet his longings for a homeplace in America are not without contradiction; in truth, he fled to Paris to escape this home and its impossible (heterosexual) expectations of him. David tries to convince himself that physically distancing himself from his U.S. birthplace amounts to leaving it behind psychologically. Baldwin himself knew better, writing in the 1951 essay "Many Thousands Gone" that "We cannot escape our origins, however hard we try, those origins which contain the key—could we but find it—to all that we later become" (27). David, however, still tries to escape his white American Protestant bourgeois origins, and as a result feels his alienation from America, his family, and their expectations all the more keenly. The wiser Giovanni already has learned this lesson about the loss of one's home through personal tragedy, and tells David, "You don't have a home until you leave it and then, when you have left it, you can never go back" (154–55).

Despite his professed loyalty to all things American, at several moments David insists on his great love for Paris. Yet his praise often rings hollow; he clings to the worn stereotypes of Paris, and when Giovanni comments on the supposed beauty of New York, David quickly responds that "*no* city is more beautiful than Paris" (46). But precious little about the evocation of Paris suggests that David would feel such strong affinity for the city or its legendary yet strangely absent beauty. Indeed, David seldom notes anything attractive about what Giovanni calls "this old whore, Paris" (61), noting instead more bleak details about Les Halles: "The pavements were slick with leavings . . . and the walls and corners were combed with *pissoirs,* dull-burning, make-shift braziers, cafes, restaurants, and smoky yellow bistros" (65). The details of decay and corruption about Paris that Baldwin offers and David notices offer insight into David's deteriorating inner landscape: David is incapable of playing the role of the transient American enthralled with the glamour of Paris, and the longer he remains, the more dreadful and malevolent a homeplace it becomes.

Along with notions of home, both real and imaginary, the writing of place in *Giovanni's Room* also hinges on the condition of expatriation—a kind of self-imposed exile.[2] An expatriate himself, Baldwin keenly understood the challenges of reckoning with one's American identity while inhabiting a foreign place. Perhaps as a result of this experience, Baldwin paints many of the spaces that David and Giovanni occupy as marginalized, exiled spaces, disconnected from any sense of "mainstream culture," Parisian or otherwise. In *Imagining Paris,* J. Gerald Kennedy explains that one's sense of place often derives from a sense of "insideness" or "outsideness," in relation to the surrounding culture. This may be felt consciously or unconsciously (6–7). As an exiled American, David simultaneously occupies an insider and an outsider position with respect to both America and Paris. Separated by both physical distance and psychological space, he feels outside of American culture. He yearns to lead what he considers a "normal" (that is, heterosexual) American life, thinking to himself, "I wanted to be *inside* again, with my manhood unquestioned, watching my woman put my children to bed" (137, italics added). Yet in the end, he knows that he exists outside this metaphorical "ideal," and that this lifestyle is unavailable to him.

At the same time, an American in Paris is still an American, and David tries to orient himself inside this American label by aligning himself with all he imagines America to represent (including a bitter sense of homophobia). Of course, David is a foreigner, a cultural outsider in Paris, but in spite of his status as interloper he feels safer in France than he does in America, where the pain of his past and the impossible expectations of his future (and his father) await him. But this sense of safety is fleeting. Because David has no real *place*, no sense of home, the expatriate life that Baldwin creates for him in Paris seem to trap him in an identity that he cannot easily accept or reject. By cutting himself off from the "wide open spaces" that characterize America, David essentially has set his own trap. He cannot go back home (as Giovanni makes painfully clear), but he stubbornly resists saying "Yes to life" (10) by refusing to embrace his homosexual life and love in Paris.

In *Ride Out the Wilderness*, Melvin Dixon suggests that Baldwin's construction of place hinges, at least in part, on his protagonists' complicated sexual identities. He explains:

> Baldwin's male protagonists are usually bisexual or homosexual, and as such they are forever outside the realm of redemption offered by the church or by society at large. They must come to different terms as best they can with the spatial and spiritual dimensions sanctioned by church and society.... Within this perspective, the need for alternate space, refuge, or shelter looms paramount. (132)

For more than a year Paris itself functions as David's alternate space, offering him a homeplace that seems preferable to the places he associates with his WASP background. But David's repressed homosexuality won't stay repressed forever, and as his attraction for Giovanni grows and deepens, so too does his need to find other places of refuge that will save him from the sexual longings he most dreads in himself. But this is a fool's errand, as David eventually learns. Paris may be thought of as the city of love, but for David it becomes the city of small, dirty, malevolent places—places that enclose him in an unwanted and uncomfortable, yet strangely irresistible, sexual identity.

For the most part, the physical places described in *Giovanni's Room* are dark and dirty and close; virtually every indoor scene is characterized by a feeling of airlessness, and the characters often seem on the verge of suffocation. David first describes Guillaume's bar, where he initially meets Giovanni, as "a noisy, crowded, ill-lit sort of tunnel" full of smoke and sinister characters (37). When the men leave the bar that night and pile into a taxi, David notes how they were so "unpleasantly crowded together" (61) and then thinks to himself on the way to the café that "I was in a box," unwilling to admit his complicity in the unfolding romantic situation and equally unable to leave it behind (64). Much later, after David abandons Giovanni, Jacques and Giovanni corner him in a bookstore; David recalls leaving the store "as though I were backing out of a cage" (173). Everywhere he turns David feels hemmed in, and it is through this distorted perception of place that Baldwin constructs many of the details of David's tortured inner landscape.

Baldwin's claustrophobic places are not always open to the public; the confined private spaces where the characters engage in sex often are just as frightening. During his demeaning and desperate sexual encounter with Sue, David longs to be free not just of her but of her room; when the sex was over "the dark, tiny room rushed back. And I only wanted to get out of there" (134). And Guillaume's apartment, important despite its small role, becomes a sexual trap twice over for Giovanni. During his first visit to the apartment, he is ambushed by Guillaume, who requires sexual favors in exchange for a job at the bar and a much-needed *carte de travail* (82–83). Later, David imagines Giovanni's last visit to Guillaume's, just before the murder: "He wanted to turn away, to run away. But there is no place to run" (204), and Giovanni (at least in David's imagination) once again is trapped in the suffocating apartment full of silks and perfumes.

The claustrophobic and often sinister places that David occupies throughout his time in Paris pale in comparison to Giovanni's actual room, however. Michael Fabre suggests that Baldwin based his descriptions of it on a room belonging to a friend of his in Paris, though he writes of it "in evocative, rather than realistic, terms" (205). It certainly does evoke strong reactions in David, as no other place carries more symbolic meaning for him than this little room although very little of the novel's action occurs there. David and Giovanni retreat from the larger cage of Paris to the private but even more suffocating air of the room that does serve, for a time, as a refuge from the unfriendly and judgmental forces threatening their already precarious relationship. The room's location on the outskirts of Paris clearly indicates a removal from the center of the dominant Parisian society and, by implication, from society in general. But in spite of the remote location, David perceives the potential danger lying just beyond the walls, and that against the windows "the courtyard malevolently pressed, encroaching day by day" (112). The room shelters David and Giovanni's relationship from the external world's judging eyes, but in doing so effectively traps them in their own internal spaces. These spaces become marked, externally, by confusion and disorder of the room that is almost surreal in its relentlessness.

The prevalence of dirt and confusion in the confining spaces of *Giovanni's Room*, particularly within the room itself, leads to inevitable and necessary connections between the physical dirt of poor housekeeping or urban grime and the metaphorical "dirt" of sexuality, especially homosexual sex. Since the publication of *Giovanni's Room*, critics have debated whether the novel's central concern is in fact David's badly repressed and Giovanni's relatively celebratory homosexuality.[3] Baldwin himself categorically denied that the homosexual affair was at the center of his novel, asserting instead that *Giovanni's Room* "is not about homosexual love, it's about what happens to you if you're afraid to love anybody" (Leeming 125). Nevertheless, the homophobic, confused, and sometimes cruel David is an accepting crucible for the conventional narrow-minded wisdom of his time. He really believes that in spite of the joy he feels with his first male lover, Joey, and later with the exuberant Giovanni, homosexual love and its participants are somehow ineluctably *dirty*. This pervading sense of dirtiness and filth, particularly in association with the spaces that David himself inhabits, forms the foundation of the personal anguish and shame that he experiences throughout much of the novel.

David's belief in the unnatural and therefore "dirty" quality of gay relationships hinges on his corollary belief that homosexuality poses a threat to the established, more "natural" heterosexual order. As he did in his essay "Preservation of Innocence" in 1949, Baldwin takes up this issue in his 1954 essay "The Male Prison," in which he expresses his frustration with André Gide's attempt to decide how "natural" homosexuality is. Baldwin maintains his long-standing position that determining

> whether or not homosexuality is natural seems to me completely pointless—pointless because I really do not see what difference the answer makes. It seems clear, in any case, at least in the world we know, that no matter what encyclopedias of physiological and scientific knowl-

edge are brought to bear the answer never can be Yes. And one of the reasons for this is that it would rob the normal—who are simply the many—of their very necessary sense of security and order. (102)

In *Giovanni's Room,* this violation of "security and order" that the homosexual presence causes becomes doubly painful for David, who both longs for the safety of being one of the "normal—who are simply the many"—but also must recognize himself as one whom society (not least of all his father) would label "deviant." Yet David is not the only character who struggles with the implications of his homosexuality. In spite of the many ways that Giovanni appears to be in direct opposition to David, he too suffers with the conflict between his present gay lifestyle and his former heterosexual existence that was both secure and orderly. The internal struggle within both characters between the homophobe and the homosexual, the orderly and the disorderly, becomes overtly visible in the dirt and clutter that overwhelm the physical spaces they occupy.

Giovanni, of course, recognizes the ironic disarray of his "maid's room," noting ruefully to Jacques that "you could certainly tell that there was no maid if you ever saw my room" (63). This room, covered with the garbage and debris of Giovanni's "regurgitated life" (114), becomes the dumping ground for dirt both literal and metaphoric. More than mere sexual impurity or even "deviance," this cluttered, disorderly, unsanitary room that Giovanni owns and David shares also suggests the profound psychological disorganization and ambivalence that characterize both men's lives. As such, this place becomes much more than merely a site of the story's action; it takes on the role of a mirror, or a gauge, of the hidden aspects of David and Giovanni that manifest themselves in the condition of the room—*le paysage intérieur.* Giovanni's room becomes sinister and unavoidable, stifling yet desirable, both a refuge and a prison. And from the first, David warily recognizes the disorder of Giovanni's room "with the same nervous, calculating extension of the intelligence and of all one's forces which occurs when gauging a mortal and unavoidable danger" (115). At this point David becomes conscious of the threat that Giovanni's room poses to his own sense of personal (sexual) identity. Giovanni's character is instantly complicated by his intimate connection to this horrifying place. David no longer can think of him as a semi-innocent fling, as he tries to believe Joey was. Nor can Giovanni simply be the beautiful, angelic boy with "all of the light of that gloomy tunnel trapped around his head" (59) and his eyes "like morning stars" (79), as David melodramatically describes him. Rather, the state of Giovanni's room forces both the reader and David to recognize that Giovanni is a man who is suffering deeply, and the chaos of his room indicates the depths of his pain. It is this pain that David rightly perceives as dangerous, for it operates as a harbinger for the pain and concomitant disorder that David himself soon will experience.

When David first tries to assess the squalid condition of Giovanni's room, he intuits that "it was not the room's disorder that was frightening; it was the fact that when one began searching for the key to this disorder, it was not to be found in the usual places. For this was not a matter of habit or circumstance or temperament; it was a matter of punishment and grief" (115). That is, Giovanni's room is not a disaster simply because Giovanni is a naturally poor housekeeper. Rather, the disorder is a result of Giovanni's own will (conscious or unconscious); the room serves to remind him of the pain of both his past and his present, but prevents him from living comfortably with either. Haunted by his memories of the past, tormented by the insecurity and humiliation of the present, Giovanni's room symbolizes his lack of control over his life. Thus, Baldwin suggests that Giovanni's character may be far more complex than merely the passionate lover who urges the colder, more brooding David to embrace life and love.

Just as David must reconcile his homosexual desires with his father's expectations of his becoming "a man," rather than a "Sunday school teacher" (24), so too must Giovanni reconcile himself to his own painful heterosexual past. But unlike David, the disorder within Giovanni that manifests itself in the outward conditions of his room does not necessarily result from the prevailing stereotype of homosexuality as "dirty." Rather, the source of the disorder in his life seems to be the combination of his perceived failure to achieve the conventional lifestyle his native Italian village demanded of him and his unwillingness to reckon with that painful past experience. Although he initially embarks on a traditional life of working in the vineyards, marrying "his girl," and raising a family, Giovanni feels compelled to flee his village, his family, his wife, and his religion when his first child is stillborn. The past is so difficult to bear that he seeks escape and relief by entering the homosexual milieu in Paris—an environment with expectations radically different from those Giovanni had fled. Giovanni tries to invent a new life for himself, but his past refuses to disappear, and his resultant emotional confusion manifests itself in the form of his filthy room.

Significantly, both David and Giovanni think themselves capable of saving the other from the disorder of the room and, by implication, the disorder of his life. Critic Stephen Adams suggests that, "Though David, with his economic security, feels the burden of Giovanni's salvation to be on him, it is clear that Giovanni has the more onerous task of rescuing David from the workings of sexual shame" (42). However, Giovanni's financial distress and David's sexual shame are mere fractions of the problem. For even if Giovanni were financially solvent, the heartbreak of his past life in his village would not stay hidden under the surface of his new life forever. And even if David were to accept his homosexual desires gladly and without shame, he would still have to face the father and the past that created him. Ultimately, though, both men attempt to establish new lives without reckoning with their pasts—almost a kind of rebirth inside Giovanni's room. Indeed, David initially (egotistically) believes that he understands Giovanni's motivations for bringing him to the room. He thinks to himself: "I was to destroy this room and give Giovanni a new and better life" (116). Yet this vision of annihilating the old to make way for the new is in no way borne out in the text; David is incapable of destroying or even altering the room, in spite of Giovanni's constant (albeit fruitless) efforts to renovate. In fact, the room only worsens when David moves in. Later, of course, Giovanni's execution dramatically underscores David's inability to fulfill this role of life-giver to Giovanni.

Contrary to David's instinctive belief that Giovanni is the one who needs to be saved, Giovanni assumes that it is David who needs to be rescued from the confusion he feels toward himself, his homosexual longings, and life's "dirt." In a moment of frustration and rage at David's supercilious (but hollow) denial of the importance of their relationship, he screams at David:

> You love your purity, you love your mirror—you are just like a little virgin, you walk around with your hands in front of you as though you had some precious metal, gold, silver, rubies, maybe *diamonds* down there between your legs! You will never give it to anybody, you will never let anybody touch it—man or woman. You want to be clean. You think you came here covered with soap and you think you will go out covered with soap—and you do not want to stink, not even for five minutes, in the meantime. (186–87)

Giovanni recognizes that David's preoccupation with sexual "cleanliness" exists, at bottom, independently from his homophobic anxieties. He attempts to make David understand that to really live is to "stink," to come into contact with the dirt that is necessarily a part of life. He tries to rescue David from the sterility and detachment that he feels certain prevents David from saying "Yes to life" (10), and which traps him in such a relentless state of ambivalence about Giovanni, Hella, his father, his country, everything. Yet in spite of this aggressive denouncement of David and endorsement of the stink of life, ultimately Giovanni is no more successful at rescuing his lover and establishing order than David.

The significance of the room's overwhelming disorder becomes more meaningful as the room resists all human efforts to clean and beautify it. Both David and Giovanni attempt to dispel the dirt and clutter through conventional but ultimately ineffective rituals of cleansing. Significantly, Giovanni begins this attempt at remodeling and reordering the room before he even meets David. When David enters the room for the first time, he immediately notices that "one of the walls was a dirty, streaked white where [Giovanni] had torn off the wallpaper. The wall facing it was destined never to be uncovered, and on this wall a lady in a hoop skirt and a man in knee breeches perpetually walked together, hemmed in by roses. The wallpaper lay on the floor, in great sheets and scrolls, in dust" (113). The wall Giovanni chooses to begin his renovations is not the wall picturing the heterosexual couple in the rose garden—a decision that reinforces David's perception that the room's disorder is at least in part a punishment that Giovanni is willfully inflicting on himself. Ironically, Giovanni also obscures the room's only source of natural light and visual connection to the world outside by painting the windows with cleaning polish. That an item intended only to cleanse is used to obscure the glass further demonstrates the futility of attempting to bring order to this chaos. The dirt in Giovanni's room cannot be cleaned by conventional methods. And when David moves in, bringing his own disordered self to the tiny, claustrophobic space, the confusion and filth only worsen: "On the floor also lay our dirty laundry, along with Giovanni's tools and the paint brushes and the bottles of oil and turpentine. Our suitcases teetered on top of something, so that we dreaded ever having to open them and sometimes went without some minor necessity, such as clean socks, for days" (113). Giovanni's attempt at ordering the disorder of his room fails completely, and the fallout from his efforts only adds to the chaotic mess.

Initially (and naïvely), David believes that he can conquer the power of this physical place by dispelling the frightening mess and thereby preventing any need to escape it. He accepts the formidable task of trying to reorder Giovanni's room through the (gendered) rituals of cleaning. "I invented in myself a kind of pleasure in playing the housewife after Giovanni had gone to work. I threw out the paper, the bottles, the

fantastic accumulation of trash; I examined the contents of the innumerable boxes and suitcases and disposed of them" (116). Eventually,
David realizes that this is no ordinary mess, for in spite of all his
attempts to impose some organization and regularity, the room never
gets any cleaner. And, eventually, David resents the role of "housewife"
that he finds himself unable to perform successfully. The room remains
cluttered, crowded, and untidy for as long as either man is in contact
with it. When David cannot conquer the disorder, he reacts by trying
to distance himself from it. In spite of the fact that he clearly lives in
the room with Giovanni, David never refers to it as "our room" or "my
room," but only as "Giovanni's room," as if to acquit himself of any
responsibility for the defiant mess. Eventually, and eagerly, he begins
to consider abandoning both the room and Giovanni in an attempt to
escape the confusion that he sees around him and, like a mirror of his
inner landscape, feels within him.

Although his remodeling efforts temporarily cease when David
moves in, Giovanni attempts further renovations when he begins to
sense David's impending abandonment. Deeply agitated by David's
aloofness, Giovanni attacks the very walls of the room, ostensibly building a sunken bookcase but in fact merely adding to the clutter that surrounds them. David only partly understands the meaning of Giovanni's
desperate attempt to impose a new order on their little prison room.
He recounts that Giovanni

> had some weird idea that it would be nice to have a bookcase sunk in
> the wall and he chipped through the wall until he came to the brick
> and began pounding away at the brick. It was hard work, it was insane
> work, but I did not have the energy or the heart to stop him. . . . Per-
> haps he was trying, with his own strength, to push back the walls, with-
> out, however, having the walls fall down. (151–52)

In fact, Giovanni was trying to rebuild the room for David, as a gift, a
pledge, a symbol of his love. Meanwhile, pieces of the actual wall literally are falling down, increasing the disorder and representing Giovanni's growing anxiety about the restless David's inevitable escape.

Yet even a physical flight from the room does not allow David to
escape the confusion, for since the disorder characterizes David as much
as it does Giovanni, David unwittingly takes it with him. Living alone
in the south of France, after Hella's departure and just before Giovanni's
execution, David finds that the disorder that suffused Giovanni's room
and came to define it defines his own room. The kitchen and master

bedroom, where David spends almost no time, remain fairly clean. Instead, as if conditioned by all the other small places he has occupied, he gravitates toward the small bedroom, which becomes nearly as filthy and cluttered as Giovanni's. His description of the room attests to his inability to order his own life: "This bedroom, of course, is quite untidy, the light burning, my bathrobe, books, dirty socks, and a couple of dirty glasses, and a coffee cup half full of stale coffee—lying around, all over the place; and the sheets a tangled mess" (94). This room has become another "Giovanni's room," but this time David must accept sole ownership and responsibility for its condition. There is no one else to blame. His description of this room, which, "of course, is quite untidy" acknowledges his inability to order his external environment and thereby to order his inner self. David apologizes to the landlady for the conditions of the rooms, and promises to clean them before he leaves for Paris. "'I should hope so,' she says. 'Everything was clean when you moved in'" (90). But clean things won't stay clean in David's presence. It is David's own disorder, divorced from Giovanni's room, that at this point in the novel indicates that David transforms the places he inhabits into sites of self-punishment and grief just as much as Giovanni did.

Baldwin's suggestive descriptions of each man's living space illustrate both characters' inability to counter the disorder that permeates their lives. That is, their outward places become the vehicle by which Baldwin can reveal their emotional, internal suffering. David and Giovanni are trapped in this disordered room that becomes progressively more malevolent and claustrophobic because they each find themselves unable to come to terms with their inner chaos. Emotionally, disorder rules their lives because they have not faced the implications of the lives they lived before meeting in Paris. In *The Fire Next Time* (1963), Baldwin explains the importance of understanding that "to accept one's past—one's history—is not the same as drowning in it; it is learning how to use it. An invented past can never be used; it cracks and crumbles under the pressures of life like clay in a season of draught" (81). This is a lesson that both David and Giovanni struggle to learn. David denies his past homosexual affair with Joey, never admitting to Giovanni that he once had taken a male lover. Giovanni represses his own traditional, heterosexual life in his Italian village, only sharing with David the story of his wife, his stillborn baby, and his rejection of his religion when the panic of losing David overwhelms him. Both David and Giovanni fail to reckon fully with their histories, and the disorder in which they both live, and which neither can expunge, is a result of conflicting patterns of belief at work within each man. They both are burdened with similar notions of traditional definitions of manhood and masculinity, and the knowledge that their relationship challenges these long-established, dominant social patterns results in their forced existence outside traditional conventions.

Beyond the physical places that Baldwin infuses with moral meaning—dark crowded bars, filthy cramped bedrooms and houses, and Paris itself—he also constructs the body as an important place. Female bodies are portrayed as particularly ghastly and dangerous, and are associated with many of the same confining qualities that color so many other places in the novel. As a young boy, David imagines the body of his dead mother as a site of soft, sucking horror; she appears in his dreams as a "body, so putrescent, so sickening soft, that it opened, as I clawed and cried, into a breach so enormous as to swallow me alive" (17). His heterosexual sex life also is marred by his claustrophobic reactions to women's bodies. David describes Hella's body as a "strong, walled city" (164), and while having sex with her David nearly is overwhelmed by the panicky sense of entering, at great risk, a menacingly small space: "When I entered her I began to feel I would never get out alive" (209). The claustrophobia so evident in other places in the novel is echoed in David's repeated nightmares of being trapped inside the space of women's bodies. The repulsive images that women's bodies conjure up for David indicate at the very least that, for him, heterosexuality is ultimately an untenable lifestyle.

The male body, of course, also functions as an important place in *Giovanni's Room,* for it is both the idea of the body as the location of heterosexual masculinity and his own actual body which defies heterosexual norms that form the core of David's anxieties about his sexuality. From the moment the novel opens, we are faced with David's meditation on his own reflection in a mirror, his own tall body and blond hair that he believes should signify an uncomplicated sort of Anglo-American, heterosexual manhood. But instead he is tormented by his sexual impulses and gazes at his "troubling sex" (223) wondering how he can achieve salvation. As Baldwin maintains in "Preservation of Innocence," there are no simple answers to questions of sexuality and identity. Very early in the narrative, David recounts his first homoerotic experience, with his teen-age friend Joey. He wakes up the next morning thinking that Joey's body "suddenly seemed the black opening of a cavern in which I would be tortured till madness came, in which I would lose my manhood. . . . I thought I saw my future in this cavern" (15). Interestingly, David does not attribute these dark cavernous qualities to Giovanni's body, but instead locates his terror in the cramped and dirty room they share.

Baldwin's construction of place in Paris coalesces for David into a painful lesson, learned too late, about the necessity and the burden of saying yes to life and to love. Sadly, David's inner landscape, manifested in the outward disorder and claustrophobia that plague him, seems to leave him destined to perpetual homelessness. Through his tragic execution, Giovanni escapes the frightening spaces of Paris, but David is doomed to return to the city of his greatest loss and his greatest pain. Repatriating to the mythical wide-open spaces of America never can be a real alternative, for David's *paysage intérieur* leads him inevitably to the small airless places that reflect his inner suffocation. Further, repatriating would mean returning, at least metaphorically, to his father's house—a place David never will inhabit again. In spite of the final image of David walking outside, toward Paris, feeling upon him "the dreadful weight of hope" (224), it is hard to read this as a novel with a hopeful ending. Giovanni's death does not redeem David's life. The notion that "home is not a place but simply an irrevocable condition" (121) remains as painfully true as ever, and David's reactions to the places that surround him indicate, perhaps more vividly than any other details, the tortuous geography of his inner landscape.

NOTES

1. Many of these financial, personal, and social difficulties are discussed in Baldwin's essays of the 1950s and later. "Equal in Paris" (1955), in particular, relates Baldwin's wrongful arrest and traumatic detention in jail for the alleged theft of a bedsheet.

2. Two useful studies that examine in detail American writers and their encounters with expatriatism in Paris are Donald Pizer's *American Expatriate Writing and the Paris Movement* and Jean Méral's *Paris in American Literature*. Other interesting studies that explore the ways that writers invest cities with meaning are Melvin Dixon's *Ride Out the Wilderness: Geography and Identity in Afro-American Literature*, Richard Lehan's *The City in Literature: An Intellectual and Cultural History*, Hana Wirth-Nesher's *City Codes: Reading the Modern Urban Novel*, Burton Pike's *The Image of the City in Modern Literature*, and Blanche Housman Gelfant's classic *The American City Novel*. An interesting study of exile in Baldwin's work is Bryan R. Washington's *The Politics of Exile: Ideology in Henry James, F. Scott Fitzgerald, and James Baldwin*.

3. Emmanuel Nelson discusses several homophobic critical examinations of *Giovanni's Room* and other Baldwin novels in his 1991 article "Critical Deviance: Homophobia and the Reception of James Baldwin's Fiction."

WORKS CITED

Adams, Stephen. *The Homosexual as Hero in Contemporary Fiction.* New York: Barnes & Noble, 1980.

Baldwin, James. "Equal in Paris." *Commentary,* March 1955, 251–59.

———. *The Fire Next Time.* 1963. Reprint, New York: Vintage, 1993.

———. *Giovanni's Room.* 1956. Reprint, New York: Dell, 1988.

———. "The Male Prison." In *The Price of the Ticket: Collected Nonfiction, 1948–1985.* New York: St. Martin's, 1985, 101–06.

———. "Many Thousands Gone." In *Notes of a Native Son.* 1955. Reprint, Boston: Beacon Press, 1984, 24–45.

———. "Stranger in the Village." In *The Price of the Ticket: Collected Nonfiction, 1948–1985.* New York: St. Martin's, 1985, 79–90.

Dixon, Melvin. *Ride Out the Wilderness: Geography and Identity in Afro-American Literature.* Urbana: University of Illinois Press, 1987.

Fabre, Michael. *From Harlem to Paris: Black American Writers in France, 1840–1980.* Urbana: University of Illinois Press, 1991.

Gelfant, Blanche Housman. *The American City Novel.* Norman: University of Oklahoma Press, 1954.

Kennedy, J. Gerald. *Imagining Paris: Exile, Writing, and American Identity.* New Haven, Conn.: Yale University Press, 1993.

Leeming, David A. *James Baldwin: A Biography.* New York: Knopf, 1994.

Lehan, Richard. *The City in Literature: An Intellectual and Cultural History.* Berkeley: University of California Press, 1998.

Lutwack, Leonard. *The Role of Place in Literature.* Syracuse, N.Y.: Syracuse University Press, 1984.

Méral, Jean. *Paris in American Literature.* Chapel Hill: University of North Carolina Press, 1989.

Nelson, Emmanuel. "Critical Deviance: Homophobia and the Reception of James Baldwin's Fiction." *Journal of American Culture* 14, no. 3 (Fall 1991): 91–96.

Pike, Burton. *The Image of the City in Modern Literature.* Princeton, N.J.: Princeton University Press, 1981.

Pizer, Donald. *American Expatriate Writing and the Paris Movement.* Baton Rouge: Louisiana State University Press, 1993.

Wirth-Nesher, Hana. *City Codes: Reading the Modern Urban Novel.* Cambridge: Cambridge University Press, 1996.

Washington, Bryan R. *The Politics of Exile: Ideology in Henry James, F. Scott Fitzgerald, and James Baldwin.* Boston: Northeastern University Press, 1995.

another look at
Another Country

reconciling Baldwin's racial
and sexual politics

SUSAN FELDMAN

It is more than slightly ironic that James Baldwin's representations of homosexuality, of the possibility for an intense and redemptive love between men, often have been interpreted within a critical framework in which explorations of sexual identity and racial identity are viewed as mutually exclusive, as if Baldwin's representations of sexual relationships between men have little if anything to say about American race relations, past and present. That Baldwin's treatment of homosexuality often has led critics to question his allegiance to and concern for his own race is witnessed not only in Eldridge Cleaver's strongly homophobic attack on Baldwin and his novel *Another Country* in *Soul on Ice*—in which Cleaver accuses Baldwin of hating black men and having a "racial death wish" (101)—but also in the more subtle comments of literary critics who have criticized *Another Country* for its focus on sexuality and the novel's ostensible failure to explore the racist dynamics of American society.[1]

Where critics[2] have avoided such reductive readings of *Another Country*, offering insight instead into the novel's interrogation of how racial and sexual difference in the United States are constructed and articulated through interwoven discourses, new binary oppositions unfortunately emerge to displace the previously existing antagonism between race and sexuality. William Cohen's perceptive analysis, for example, successfully traces "the complex relations among the antinomies male/female, white/black, and heterosexual/homosexual through the novel," showing "the ways in which vectors of power relations themselves interact . . . in constituting the relationships among individual characters" (1). But while Cohen succeeds in reading the novel's interactive play among gender, race, and sexuality, he ultimately repeats the gesture of earlier critics by choosing to interpret Baldwin's treatment of sexuality through the logic of liberal humanism, so that in the final analysis sex is recognized "as an act that is always personal, never political" (9). "For Baldwin," Cohen maintains, "sexuality occupied the realm of the indisputably private, allowing a voice for individual desires to transcend social barriers" (16). By displacing the earlier opposition between race and sexuality into a new opposition between private and public, personal and political, Cohen essentially reaffirms previous conclusions that *Another Country,* which centers around a group of mostly white bohemian artists living in Greenwich Village during the 1950s, "appears more interested in the salvation of individual characters than radical social change" (1).[3]

It appears that Baldwin's belief in the redemptive quality of love and sexuality, though by now a critical commonplace, is itself in need of redemption, if only because the paradigms through which this belief has been interpreted seem to strip his novels of so much of their political content. The very fact that *Another Country* focuses more on love's inability to transcend social barriers for the only black male character suggests that Baldwin in no way regarded love, and its expression through sexuality, to be seen as a magical elixir capable of overcoming the psychological and social damage from oppressive social structures. On the contrary, in the case of *Another Country,* Baldwin depicts how love too often is seized as a means of self-avoidance, as a means of distancing oneself from one's past and one's responsibility to others.[4]

My reading aims not to challenge Baldwin's belief in the redemptive power of love, however, but to examine how his representation of love and sexuality in *Another Country* seeks to overcome the false opposition between private and social realms, between individual and collective change, by linking the repression of same-sex desire to America's past and present oppression of African Americans. To view Baldwin's representations of homosexuality strictly in "private" terms is to ignore how U.S. racial hierarchies traditionally have depended upon a homophobic discourse, how white patriarchal power has maintained its supremacy by locating in the bodies of those it sought to oppress the differences and excesses needed to justify oppression.[5] Because, as Paul Hoch has argued, the black male body historically has served as a site onto which white males have projected "those aspects of their own sexuality which society has made taboo" (54), Baldwin recognizes that any attempt to transform racist social structures must begin with the impulse of libidinal transfiguration. In this respect, Baldwin's social analysis can be likened to that of Freudo-Marxists Wilhelm Reich and Herbert Marcuse, whose work dismantles the simple opposition between the sexual and the political by exposing the connection between sexual repression and social oppression, and the manner in which structures of domination are maintained through repressed desire.[6] In *Another Country,* Baldwin demonstrates that overcoming the categorical barriers that prevent individuals from accepting others' differences only can be achieved by confronting our own buried pasts, our own repressed desires. Recognizing that these desires are constantly in flux is crucial to Baldwin's call for change, on an individual as well as a collective level. It is for this reason that his representations of homosexuality always are framed within a context of bisexuality, an important aspect of Baldwin's writing that continually has been overlooked.

Part of the critical difficulty in approaching *Another Country* involves coming to terms with the character of Rufus Scott, a young black jazz musician who, as the novel begins, is destitute, homeless, and struggling to survive yet another night on the streets of New York City. The opening section juxtaposes Rufus's attempts to satisfy his most immediate, present needs—to eat, to find a place to urinate, and to rest for a few hours—against his efforts to account for his past, especially his relationship with his last lover, Leona, a poor southern white whom he physically and mentally abused until she eventually was institutionalized. After briefly meeting a group of white artist friends in Greenwich Village, Rufus leaves with a few dollars to finally return to his family home in Harlem. In the course of the subway ride, however, Rufus suddenly "knew that he was never going home any more" (86). After passing his own station, Rufus gets off and commits suicide, eighty pages into the novel, by jumping off the George Washington Bridge.

Why Baldwin should so quickly and deliberately choose to write out the only black male character, the figure for his own self-representation, in a novel he insisted "he had to write"[7] has proven quite troubling to critics. Terry Rowden, for example, even has gone so far as to read Rufus's exclusion from the novel as a sign of Baldwin's own ambivalent relationship "not only to the sexuality of the black man, but to the simple fact of the existence of black men in society" (41). But rather than reading Rufus's absence as an indication that Baldwin was, on the one hand, either uninterested in addressing racism or, on the other, that "the critique Baldwin wanted to make about race he could only express fully in terms of sexuality" (Cohen 15), it might prove more constructive to examine why *Another Country* is a work Baldwin insisted he "had to write" and why Rufus ultimately is unable to return home. For the need to return home, to face the past, lies at the heart of this novel that Baldwin labored over for close to fourteen years as he struggled to come to terms with the nature of his own past, to accept both the suicide of a close friend upon whom the character of Rufus was based and his own retreat from responsibilities to his family and country. Commenting on his slow progress, Baldwin told a close friend that the characters were just "hanging around doing nothing . . . they seemed to be insisting on holding back the truth" (Leeming 133). In his characters, Baldwin recognized his own reluctance to face himself and his responsibilities to others, and from this he acknowledged that "it really was time to go home," to end his exile in Paris (Leeming 133).

This reluctance to uncover and accept the past is reflected in the struggles encountered by each of the novel's characters, who to varying degrees are all running away from a past they are unwilling to face, from the desire that threatens the security and safety of their own race or gender identities. Their unwillingness to explore the buried truths behind their experiences—the absence and loss which, left unexamined, renders them destined to repeat the past—makes them strangers to themselves and consequently to each other. Their retreat into art and love, as Baldwin makes clear, serves primarily as a means of escaping and not confronting the contradictions underlying their past. Through Rufus, Baldwin demonstrates the terrible cost of such escape, the dangerous and deadly consequences that result from self and social avoidance. By showing how Rufus's demise and the other characters' failure to acknowledge their complicity in the causes behind it threatens the other relationships in the novel, Baldwin seeks to illustrate to white America that "what is happening to every Negro at any time is also happening to you" (Leeming 204). If Baldwin has left critics questioning Rufus's role in the novel, perhaps it is because, as he writes in "Nobody Knows My Name" (1959), "The nation, the entire nation, has spent a hundred years avoiding the question of the place of the black man in it" (114). In *Another Country*, Rufus's absence is used to signify this failure to provide a place for the black male in the United States. Rufus, Baldwin claims, is the "black corpse floating in the national psyche— he and what he represents must be squarely faced if we are to find peace in our society" (Leeming 201).

The dangers of an unexamined past and the destructive possibilities that are borne from it are captured in the image of the runaway
subway car that Rufus envisions just before his death:

> He saw the train in the tunnel, rushing under water, the motorman gone
> mad, gone blind, unable to decipher the lights, and the tracks gleam-
> ing and snarling senselessly upward forever, the train never stopping
> and the people screaming at windows and doors and turning on each
> other with all the accumulated fury of their blasphemied lives. (85)

While the runaway train symbolizes the dangers of approaching the
future blindly, the "great scar of the tracks" (85) signifies the buried past
upon which the future inscribes itself. The train is "choked with people" who all stand or sit in the "isolation cell into which they transformed every inch of space they held" (85); "Many white people and
many black people, chained together in time and in space, and by history, and all of them in a hurry. In a hurry to get away from each other"
(86). But Baldwin demonstrates that the ability to run away and escape
history is a costly luxury that only those characters with class, race, or
gender privilege can afford: the white male characters all possess the
means to escape their pasts, while the black characters and Leona cannot escape theirs. As LeRoy tells Eric, "I can't be thinking about leaving. I got my Ma and all them kids to worry about . . . Ain't everybody's
old man runs a bank, you know" (203). In *A Rap on Race* (1971), Baldwin states that "no people nor individual can really escape, if that person is honest, history and the effects of history" (Standley 191).

It is precisely his honesty and his inability to avoid repeating and
passing on the effects of his own history that leads Rufus to suicide in
the opening chapter. While Baldwin has been criticized for not exploring in greater detail the historical forces accounting for Rufus's suicide,[8]
this refusal must be understood as deliberate, for to place Rufus's history strictly within a cause-and-effect narrative of racism would be to
deny him any responsibility in Leona's destruction; it would be to
depict individual subjectivity as entirely socially determined, and history as a narrative of easily represented causes and effects. Baldwin,
however, clearly is more interested in exploring the dialectical relationship between subjective and social forces, and the way in which
unconscious desires and fears can lead to individually and socially
destructive behavior. He invites us to read Rufus's death not merely as
an effect of racism, but as an effect of a repressed history, an unconscious cause of which racism is itself an effect. If Baldwin chooses to

focus most specifically on Rufus's relationship with Leona, it is because, as Fredric Jameson explains, "History can be apprehended only through its effects, and never directly as some reified force" (102).[9] And as Rufus's relationship with Leona makes quite clear, the historical causes and effects of racism are interwoven intricately with the history of sexuality, since the effects of racism on Rufus are expressed most visibly in the realm of sexuality.

Rufus's desire for Leona is tied inextricably to his memories of racial violence, for immediately upon hearing her Southern accent he recalls "his days in boot camp in the South and felt again the shoe of a white officer against his mouth" (12). Though the soldier "had vanished, had gone forever beyond the reach of vengeance" (13), Rufus found that he still could take vengeance through Leona, that racially motivated anger could be displaced in a gendered arena:

> He wanted her to remember him the longest day she lived. And shortly, nothing could have stopped him, not the white God himself nor the lynch mob arriving on wings. Under his breath he cursed the milk-white bitch and groaned and rode his weapon between her thighs. . . . A moan and a curse tore through him while he beat her with all the strength he had and felt the venom shoot out of him, enough for a hundred black-white babies. (22)

Through this relationship, Baldwin illustrates how misogynistic violence ultimately stems from male castration anxiety, from Rufus's own anxiety over his social disempowerment and the threat this disempowerment presents to his masculine identity. His paranoia that Leona is sleeping with other men reflects his own fears of emasculation and feminization. Rather than confronting these fears, however, Rufus uses sex as a weapon to avenge racism and to reaffirm his masculinity, ultimately delivering himself more fully into the power of the forces that sought to control him. In showing how racial rage can be transposed into sexual rage, how the violent denial of racial equality can result in the violent denial of sexual equality between man and woman, Baldwin locates the repressed history of racism in a fear of sexual equality (or sexual sameness), in the threatened collapse of the symbolic structure of sexual difference. The way white racist practices function to symbolically castrate the black male, to deny him access to power, yet simultaneously produce a hyper-sexualized image of black masculinity, illustrates how, within a white supremacist patriarchal culture, the black male becomes a site for the rearticulation of sexual difference. This structure of difference is reproduced within the black male, and figures prominently into the constitution of black male subjectivity.

Able to recognize, but not to fully understand and accept his role in Leona's destruction, Rufus eventually turns to his best friend, Vivaldo for comfort and support after a month of living on the streets. But when Vivaldo—the novel's staunchest representative of white liberalism—merely counsels Rufus to try to forget Leona, Rufus thinks to himself, "You can't forget anything that hurt so badly, went so deep and changed the world forever. It's not possible to forget anybody you've destroyed" (51). Vivaldo's failure to provide the understanding and compassion Rufus needs ultimately stems from an inability to acknowledge his own past, to acknowledge that "he had left something of himself back there on the streets of Brooklyn which he was afraid to look at again" (111). Just as the limitations of Richard, a successful but mediocre novelist, are apparent in his fear to confront "things dark, strange, dangerous, difficult, and deep" (112), it is Vivaldo's failure to reach beyond the "high, hard wall which stood between himself and his past" that keeps him from understanding the nature of Rufus's suffering and from reaching beyond the quarter-inch void that separates the two to comfort Rufus. Rather than trying to help his friend, Vivaldo wants to "go home and lock his door and sleep. He was tired of the troubles of real people. He wanted to get back to the people he was inventing, whose troubles he could bear" (71).

After Rufus's death, Vivaldo hopes to escape his own guilt and loneliness by entering into a relationship with Rufus's sister, Ida, a promising young jazz singer. "I think she has something to forget," he said. "I think I can help her forget it" (125). But passing one's life in "a kind of limbo of denied and unexamined pain" (128) is not the answer, as Baldwin makes clear, for it is merely a form "of taking refuge in the outward adventure in order to avoid the clash and tension of the adventure proceeding inexorably within" (133). The love Vivaldo so desperately desires remains impossible as long as he chooses to shut his eyes to both his own and Ida's past, as Ida tries to explain:

> "What I don't understand," she said, slowly, "is how you can talk about love when you don't want to know what's happening. And *that's* not *my* fault. How can you say you loved Rufus when there was so much about him you didn't want to know? How can I believe you love me? . . . How can you love somebody you don't know anything about? You don't know where I've been. You don't know what life is like for me." (324–25)

Like Leona, who insists that "people are just people as far as [she's] concerned" (13), Vivaldo refuses to explore and accept the differences between his own experience and that of Rufus, and it is precisely that refusal that blinds him to his own complicity in Rufus's death. "I know I failed him, but I loved him, too. . . . They're colored and I'm white but the same things have happened, really the same things" (113). Vivaldo's insistence that he and Rufus "were equals," his unwillingness to acknowledge that what happened to Rufus happened because he was black, ultimately stems from Vivaldo's fears of his own sexual desire for men, which seem to be so much a part of his repressed past. "You had to be a man where I come from, and you had to prove it, prove it all the time" (111), Vivaldo tells Cass after Rufus's funeral, as he describes an episode when he was younger and he and a bunch of friends "picked up this queer," then raped, beat, and left him for dead. It is this need to prove it all the time, to show that he and Rufus were sexual equals— "They had balled chicks together, once or twice the same chick—why?" (134)—that makes Vivaldo's relationship with Rufus "a game, a game in which Rufus had lost his life" (133).

As Vivaldo reflects back on this "game," he recalls the time in the army when he and a black buddy set their "minds at ease" by comparing the size of their genitals. Though he insists "there was nothing frightening about it," he simultaneously

> remembered occasional nightmares in which this same vanished buddy pursued him through impenetrable forests, came at him with a knife on the edge of precipices, threatened to hurl him down steep stairs to the sea. In each of the nightmares he wanted revenge. Revenge for what? (134)

Through this dream, Baldwin illustrates how, in the white male unconscious, the black male's threatening presence is tied to castration anxiety, to the threat of emasculation the black male presents on two distinct levels. The myth of a hyperbolic black male sexuality, as it has been constructed in the white imagination, not only is perceived as threatening in its own right, but this myth is itself a sign of the white male's libidinal investment in the black male body, a sign that white males have projected their own repressed or frustrated desires onto the black male body. When reflected back to the white male, the black male thus becomes the specter of the white male's repressed sexual desire for men, and the threat of emasculation that accompanies the expression of such desire in a society based on patriarchal heterosexuality. Because

Vivaldo's refusal to acknowledge the significance of racial difference clearly stems from his inability to explore his own desire for men, overcoming his fear of homosexuality becomes a necessary first step toward understanding and accepting his own complicity in Rufus's death.

In drawing the connection between the repression of same-sex desire and racism (which in the novel is equated with racial indifference), Baldwin reiterates both Reich's and Marcuse's argument that structures of domination are maintained through the cultural regulation and manipulation of sexual desire.[10] Freud himself never denied that "cultural frustration" of libidinal impulses "dominates the large field of social relationships between human beings" (97), for he argues in *Civilization and its Discontents* that "it is impossible to overlook the extent to which civilization is built up upon a renunciation of instinct, how much it presupposes precisely the non-satisfaction (by suppression, repression or some other means?) of powerful instincts" (97). But while Freud acknowledges that libidinal renunciation "dominates" human social relations, he fails to distinguish, as Marcuse points out, between the repression necessary for the perpetuation of civilization and the "surplus repression" specifically required to maintain relationships of domination (Marcuse 36). According to Marcuse, surplus repression is the primary means by which particular groups sustain their privileged positions at the expense of the advancement of the society as a whole. Although Marcuse does not address specifically Freud's claim that all social formations are derived from a sublimation of homosexual desire, we need not assume that *all* social formations depend upon the sublimation of same-sex desire. In cultures based on patriarchal heterosexuality, however, the surplus repression of same-sex desire clearly serves—as Baldwin shows in *Another Country*—as a foundational support for class, racial, and sexual hierarchies.

Marcuse's concept of surplus repression is helpful in explaining how unconscious and subjective structures are shaped by cultural forces—why sexual desire is never strictly a "private" affair. In order to establish heterosexual desire as the cultural norm, same-sex desire must continually be debased, and its expression accompanied by the threat of social abjection. Furthermore, individuals must internalize this threat, for as Marcuse explains, "The struggle against freedom reproduces itself in the psyche of man, as the self-repression of the repressed individual, and his self-repression in turn sustains his masters and their institutions" (16). Ultimately it becomes irrelevant whether same-sex desire actually exists within the psyche of man; what matters is that the *possibility* of its existence be the source of doubt and fear. So long as men associate the possibility of same-sex desire with the threatened loss of masculine privilege and feminization, they become subject to manipulation by social forces that are able to "stage and instrumentalize" unconscious fears and desires. As Baldwin illustrates through Vivaldo and Rufus, both of whom have internalized their culture's homophobia, the unconscious fear of emasculation can lead to both violent sexism and racism. What must be underscored, however, is how homophobia functions largely to maintain rigid gender roles and patriarchal power, since homophobia can maintain its force over the male psyche only so long as men recognize and accept the existing inequality between the sexes. Were men and women to be recognized as truly equal, the threat of loss attached to the expression of same-sex desire would disappear; there would be less danger in a man's assuming (or recognizing himself in) a passive or subordinate position.

Although Cohen argues that Baldwin "diverges little from the mainstream of traditional humanism" (Cohen 2) in his treatment of gender in *Another Country,* Baldwin's challenge to conventional gender roles is evident in the overdetermination of Rufus's and Vivaldo's masculine identity. Baldwin's rejection of collective inscriptions of homosexuality in the novel—often read by critics as a sign of his ambivalence toward his own homosexuality or as an indication that sex for Baldwin is never political—becomes more understandable perhaps if considered in relation to the barrier a rigid gender identity presents to the novel's interracial and romantic relationships. If Baldwin ultimately frames all of the novel's homosexual relationships between men within a context of bisexuality, he does so precisely in order to unsettle the privileged role gender plays in conceptualizations of sexuality.[11] Bisexuality challenges the assumption that an individual's gender identifications are necessarily stable or singular, and provides an understanding of desire freed from the specificity of the sexed and gendered body. As Juliet Mitchell notes, bisexuality reveals "the fictional nature of the sexual category to which every human subject belongs" (29).

More importantly perhaps, bisexuality provides Baldwin with a means of conceptualizing identity that unsettles an objectifying logic in which self-identity emerges through the appropriation of a distinct other, an identity that only can be maintained by disavowing the difference/other within the self. In *Another Country,* this disavowal of self-difference proves to be the greatest obstacle to both an understanding of racial difference as well as the possibility for love, which is why, for Baldwin, love and a rigid identity are ultimately incompatible. In saying this I realize I am collapsing the distinctions among racial, sexual, and gender identity, as well as seemingly contradicting a large body of criticism that attests to the importance of the theme of identity in Baldwin's work. What must be stressed, however, is that Baldwin does not conceive of identity in terms of essence: Identity for Baldwin is neither a static fixture that is constructed in opposition to external difference, nor is it that which transcends time, that which remains identical over time. Instead, identity is produced through temporal difference—it is the point at which the past, the present, and the possibilities for the future converge in the individual subject and assume meaning. This meaning is constantly in flux, as the past—"which preserves promises and potentialities which are betrayed and even outlawed" by society (Marcuse 19)—is never entirely complete and is constantly being rewritten as it is made available to the individual in the present. Bisexuality serves as a figure for Baldwin's concept of identity because it registers the contingency at the heart of identity, and demands that we note the disjunctions among past, present, and future possibilities.

The redemptive power of love in *Another Country* is recognized in the ability of desire to reveal and recover the past's lost promise and potential, yielding a new orientation on both the present and the future. For Baldwin, love is simultaneously "a miracle of release and coherence," but for love to prove redemptive, individuals first must be willing to risk losing their identity, if only to discover it again from a new position outside their previous frame of reference. Eric serves as Baldwin's representative for love's redemptive possibilities in the novel because unlike the other characters, who blindly pursue their future as a means of escaping the past, Eric willingly confronts his repressed past and brings it into the open. Eric stops and reflects upon the "backward light" of his life and comes to understand that the "aims of life are antithetical to those of the dreamer" (199), and that the encounters that took place between dreamers only served to drive truth out of this world. He faces the chaos and fear of life openly, recognizing

> that there were no standards for him except those he could make for himself. There were no standards for him because he could not accept the definitions, the hideously mechanical jargon of the age. . . . He did not believe in the vast, gray sleep which was called security, did not believe in the cures, panaceas and slogans which afflicted the world he knew; and this meant that he had to create his standards and make up his definitions as he went along. (212–13)

Most importantly, Eric realizes that "In order not to lose all that he had gained, he had to move forward and risk it all" (229–30). His willingness to leave France and the comfort of an Edenic relationship with his lover, Yves, to return home to America signifies a willingness to drag his secrets "into the light of the world, impose them on the world, and [make] them a part of the world's experience" (112).

While Eric clearly assumes a privileged position in the novel, it would be a mistake to regard Eric as a sexual saviour, as many critics have, or to read the sexual encounter between Vivaldo and Eric as Baldwin's imaginary solution to the racial and sexual tensions that *Another Country* explores. Rather, by providing Vivaldo with an opportunity to confront his repressed past, this encounter merely serves as a necessary first step toward breaking down the barriers that inhibit the recognition of other's differences. Through his relationship with Eric, Vivaldo for the first time is able to express his guilt over having failed Rufus, as he confesses

> I still wonder, what would have happened if I'd take him in my arms, if I'd held him, if I hadn't been—afraid. I was afraid that he wouldn't understand that it was—only love. Only love. But, oh, Lord, when he died, I thought that maybe I could have saved him if I'd just reached out that quarter of an inch between us on that bed, and held him. (342–43)

The scene that could not take place between Rufus and Vivaldo occurs between Vivaldo and Eric: "Here Vivaldo sat on Eric's bed. Not a quarter of an inch divided them" (344). Their sexual encounter, something Vivaldo "had long desired," becomes a means of reenacting the banished possibilities of the past, as Vivaldo fantasizes that he is making love to Rufus and then that he is Rufus, being made love to by Eric. As Cohen notes, "This sexual connection generates an orgasmic concatenation of identities, whereby Vivaldo conceives of himself as simultaneously gay and straight, male and female, white and black" (11), unsettling the series of binary oppositions that previously structured the novel's relationships.

Vivaldo's experience with Eric provides "a great revelation," liberating Vivaldo from his fears and leading to a heightened sense of consciousness. In learning to accept his repressed past, Vivaldo is able to open himself up to an understanding not only of Ida's and Rufus's past, but also to the repressed history of African Americans in a country that has lacked the courage to deal honestly and openly with the truth of its collective past. Only after his experience with Eric is Vivaldo finally willing to listen to the whole of Ida's story, to recognize in the woman he loves the effects of a history that "he had always known, but never dared believe" (412). As Ida admits to Vivaldo that she is having an affair with a white producer, her explanation circles back to Rufus and her child-hood. "Why must we always end up talking about Rufus?" Vivaldo questions, but as Ida tells her story, "now very quiet and weary, as though she were telling someone else's story" (413), Vivaldo comes to recognize that Rufus's story is Ida's story, and Ida's story remains inseparable from his own. No longer willing to be "protected," Vivaldo is left to wonder "what Rufus must have looked like in those days, with all his bright, untried brashness, and all his hopes intact" (416), just as he is left to wonder what Rufus's body must have looked like "so broken and lumpy" after it had been pulled out of the river. Against the promise and destruction of Rufus and the incoherent sobs of Ida, Vivaldo is forced to recognize the incoherence of his own life, of the truth "he did not know how he was going to live with" (431). His previous desire to "step out of this [racial] nightmare" (417) ultimately is replaced by the realization that he can't, that Ida's betrayal of his love is undeniably connected to his betrayal of Rufus, to America's betrayal of its black population.

"The problem of the American identity," Baldwin has repeatedly stated, "has everything to do with all the things that happened in this country but never have been admitted or dealt with" (Standley 26). Nor can they be dealt with, Baldwin suggests in *Another Country*, until we acknowledge that this history "is somewhere contained in all of us, in something we have not accepted about ourselves that is of utmost importance" (Standley 26–27). History, as Baldwin makes clear, is never merely to be confined to the past: it must constantly be read in that which is missing from the present, in that which limits the free expression of desire. That Baldwin's representations of sexuality for so long have been identified as apolitical, as irrelevant to questions of race, only points to the inadequacy of our conceptions of what counts as "political," to our critical failure to recognize that the boundary separating the personal and the political, the individual and the collective, is merely an illusion. Yet the history of this illusion, as Baldwin illustrates, is nothing less than deadly. To see beyond it is to imagine another country.

NOTES

1. According to Eldridge Cleaver in *Soul on Ice,* "There is in James Bald-win's work the most grueling, agonizing, total hatred of the blacks, particularly

of himself, and the most shameful, fanatical, fawning, sycophantic love of the whites that one can find in the writings of any black American write of note in our time" (99). For Cleaver, as for most black nationalists of the 1960s, homosexuality was perceived as the "white man's disease," and consequently black homosexuality was viewed as a form of racial self-hatred, as the ultimate sign of the black male's exploitation by and submission to white society. (See Cleaver's "Notes on a Native Son," 97–111.) The belief that black homosexuality is an adaptive reaction to white oppression has not entirely disappeared. In the 1990 book *The Isis Papers: The Keys to the Colors,* Dr. Frances Cress Welsing writes: "Black psychiatrists must understand that whites may condone homosexuality for themselves, but we as Blacks must see it as a strategy for destroying Black people that must be countered. . . . The racist system should be held responsible. Our task is to treat and prevent its continuing and increasing occurrence" (91).

David Bergman traces the effects attacks by Cleaver and other black critics had on Baldwin's career in "The African and the Pagan in Gay Black Literature." Bergman claims this criticism "helped to shape [Baldwin's] racial attitudes in middle age," and led Baldwin to abandon his focus on sexuality and devote himself more fervently to racial issues in his later work (148).

For a further example of the critical tendency to view Baldwin's treatment of race and sexuality as contradictory, see Terry Rowden's article "A Play of Abstractions: Race, Sexuality, and Community in James Baldwin's *Another Country.*" For a study of *Another Country*'s critical reception, see Mike Thelwell's chapter "*Another Country:* Baldwin's New York Novel" and Emmanuel Nelson's article "Critical Deviance: Homophobia and the Reception of James Baldwin's Fiction."

2. William Cohen's article "Liberalism, Libido, Liberation: Baldwin's *Another Country*" is the best study to date on the interrelationship among sex, gender, and race in that work. For a study of the connection between sexuality and race in *Giovanni's Room,* see Donald Mengay's article "The Failed Copy: *Giovanni's Room* and the (Re)Contextualization of Difference."

3. The conventional approach among scholars has been to read Baldwin's treatment of love and sexuality as evidence of the novelist's faith in the promise of liberal individualism, and to thus maintain that in Baldwin's fiction the sexual and the political, the private and public, are bipolar opposites. See, for example, Donald Gibson, "James Baldwin: The Political Anatomy of Space."

4. Baldwin addresses similar themes in his earlier novel *Giovanni's Room* (1956). David's (the white American narrator) attempts to escape himself and his past ultimately lead to his lover's, Giovanni's, death.

5. While antebellum biblical arguments attempted to prove from scripture that "the descendants of Ham had overdeveloped sexual organs and were the original Sodomites of the Old Testament," defending slavery on the grounds that blacks were now converted Christians, after Emancipation science was called upon to validate a white supremacy no longer fully guaranteed by law. Racial and sexual discourses converged in anatomical studies which located

perversion in black females and lesbians in their "abnormal" genitalia, while black males and homosexuals "became linked in sexological and psychological discourse through the model of 'abnormal' sexual object choice" (260). The racist fear of miscegenation and the myth of the black male rapist were naturalized and legitimated in a medical discourse of perversion. See Siobhan Somerville, "Scientific Racism and the Emergence of the Homosexual Body," 243–66.

It becomes even more problematic to read Baldwin's representations of homosexuality as apolitical if we remember that the novel is set in the 1950s, a time when the U.S. government was busy hunting down and persecuting homosexuals, who, by the nature of their "subversive" sexuality, were considered "perhaps as dangerous as the actual Communists" (95). According to Elaine Tyler May in *Homeward Bound,* "Gay-baiting rivaled red-baiting in its ferocity, destroying careers, encouraging harassment, creating stigmas" (94), for it was the government's belief that Communists could blackmail homosexuals into becoming spies owing to the homosexual's fear of exposure.

6. While the work of the Frankfurt School focuses almost exclusively on the relationship between sexual repression and economic oppression, my reading of Baldwin will concentrate on showing how sexual repression, and more specifically the repression of same-sex desire, contributes to racial and gender hierarchies. While racial oppression undeniably is connected to capitalism and class inequality in the United States, my focus will be limited to the relationship between race and sexuality in order to argue against the prevailing tendency to regard Baldwin as a liberal humanist who views sexuality strictly in terms of the "private" individual. For an important qualification on the Frankfurt School's approach to sexual repression see Note 10.

7. For background on the writing of *Another Country* see Mike Thelwell's article and David Leeming, *James Baldwin: A Biography.*

8. See Rowden for a particularly strong critique of Baldwin's ostensible failure to account for Rufus's history.

9. Fredric Jameson shares Althusser's conception of history as an "absent cause": "History is not a text, not a narrative, master or otherwise, but that, as an absent cause, it is inaccessible to us except in textual form, and that our approach to it and to the Real itself necessarily passes through its prior textualization, its narrativization in the political unconscious" (*The Political Unconscious: Narrative as a Socially Symbolic Act,* 35). My reading of *Another Country* aims to illustrate that it is this repressed history of racism that Baldwin is attempting to explore through his representations of homosexuality.

10. Although members of the Frankfurt School are noted for drawing attention to the ways in which repressed sexual desire functions to maintain oppressive social structures, most of the members' conclusions about homosexuality remain quite problematic. Erich Fromm, Wilhelm Reich, Max Horkheimer, and Theodor Adorno all tended to view the diversity of human desire as a result of inequality and the constraints placed on the free expression of a "naturally" heterosexual desire. Homosexuality was regarded as an

expression of social deformation, and the homosexual came to be regarded as the embodiment of authoritarian submissiveness. Herbert Marcuse, in contrast, seeks to "liberate sexual pleasure from the reproductive imperative" (*Eros and Civilization: A Philosophical Inquiry into Freud,* 313), and does not appear to view desire as "naturally" heterosexual. Yet like other members of the Frankfurt School, Marcuse tends to focus exclusively on the role sexual repression plays in maintaining economic inequality, ignoring in the process the role homosexual repression plays in gender and racial inequality.

11. A rigid homosexual identity merely obfuscates the relationship between sex and gender, since existing sexual categories are a constitutive feature of that same identity: To say that gay men are men who desire men, or lesbians are women who desire women, does little to challenge conventional understandings of what it means to be a man or a woman. Monique Wittig's assertion that "a lesbian is not a woman" can be understood precisely as an attempt to define homosexuality in a way that does not depend upon preexisting sexual categories.

WORKS CITED

Baldwin, James. *Another Country.* New York: Dial, 1962.

———. *Nobody Knows My Name.* New York: Dial, 1961.

Bergman, David. "The African and the Pagan in Gay Black Literature." In *Sexual Sameness: Textual Difference,* ed. Joseph Bristow, 148–69. London: Routledge, 1992.

Cleaver, Eldridge. *Soul on Ice.* New York: Dell, 1968.

Cohen, William A. "Liberalism, Libido, Liberation: Baldwin's *Another Country.*" *Genders* 12 (Winter 1991): 1–21.

Freud, Sigmund. "Civilization and its Discontents." *The Standard Edition of the Complete Works of Sigmund Freud.* Vol. 21. Trans. and ed. James Strachey. London: Hogarth, 1961.

Gibson, Donald B. "James Baldwin: The Political Anatomy of Space." In *James Baldwin: A Critical Evaluation,* ed. Therman B. O'Daniel, 3–18. Washington, D.C.: Howard University Press, 1977.

Halle, Randall. "Between Marxism and Psychoanalysis: Antifascism and Antihomosexuality in the Frankfurt School." *Journal of Homosexuality* 29, no. 4 (1995): 295–317.

Hoch, Paul. *White Hero, Black Beast: Racism, Sexism and the Mask of Masculinity.* London: Pluto Press, 1979.

Jameson, Fredric. *The Political Unconscious: Narrative as a Socially Symbolic Act.* Ithaca, N.Y.: Cornell University Press, 1981.

Leeming, David A. *James Baldwin: A Biography.* New York: Knopf, 1994.

Marcuse, Herbert. *Eros and Civilization: A Philosophical Inquiry into Freud.* Boston: Beacon Press, 1966.

May, Elaine Tyler. *Homeward Bound.* New York: Basic Books, 1988.

Mengay, Donald H. "The Failed Copy: *Giovanni's Room* and the (Re)Contextualization of Difference." *Genders* 17 (Fall 1993): 59–71.

Mitchell, Juliet. Introduction to *Feminine Sexuality: Jacques Lacan and the école freudienne,* ed. Juliet Mitchell and Jacqueline Rose. Trans. Jacqueline Rose. London: Macmillan, 1982.

Nelson, Emmanuel. "Critical Deviance: Homophobia and the Reception of James Baldwin's Fiction." *Journal of American Culture* 14, no. 3 (1991): 91–96.

Rowden, Terry. "A Play of Abstractions: Race, Sexuality, and Community in James Baldwin's *Another Country.*" *Southern Review* 29, no. 1 (Winter 1993): 41–50.

Somerville, Siobhan. "Scientific Racism and the Emergence of the Homosexual Body." *Journal of the History of Sexuality* 5, no. 2 (1994): 243–66.

Standley, Fred L., and Louis H. Pratt, eds. *Conversations with James Baldwin.* Jackson: University Press of Mississippi, 1989.

Thelwell, Mike. "*Another Country:* Baldwin's New York Novel." In *The Black American Writer.* Vol. 1. Ed. C.W.E. Bigsby, 181–98. Florida: Everett/Edwards, 1969.

Welsing, Frances Cress. *The Isis Papers: The Keys to the Colors.* Chicago: Third World Press, 1990.

Wittig, Monique. "One Is Not Born a Woman." In *The Straight Mind and Other Essays.* London: Harvester Wheatsheaf, 1992.

black-gay-man chaos in *Another Country*

CHARLES P. TOOMBS

James Baldwin's third novel, *Another Country* (1962),[1] explores the cultural madness and confusion that confronted black-gay-men[2] in their attempts to forge any kind of authentic existence in the United States of the 1950s and early 1960s. Race, racial matters, interracial pairings, sex, sexual identity confusion, sexual abuse and exploitation, notions of manhood, homophobia, and self-hatred are some of the issues this important novel engages, as Baldwin interrogates the cultural landscape that defames, debases, and, as in the case of Rufus Scott, destroys black-gay-man life, productivity, and genius in America at mid-century. Baldwin conceives all of the important characters to be nothing more than whores, and the women characters—Leona, Ida, and Cass—are not only actual whores in the fabric of the novel, but Baldwin "whores" and exploits them to help present his vision of black-gay-man life. Devoid, usually, of complex motivations for their actions, these women often are stripped to stereotypical meanderings that serve Baldwin's gay-informed aesthetic and criticism of America.

Baldwin's gay-informed aesthetic privileges the relationship between black characters who are gay (or bisexual) and their black communities. In this relationship, characters struggle to define and maintain their black identity, often confronting America's alienating and enstrangling cultural landscapes of racism and discrimination in the process. At the same time, these characters must create strategies for survival and viability in their black communities, where rampant homophobia lurks that threatens destroy whatever healthy sense of themselves they might develop. In unfolding this complicated relationship, Baldwin usually insists that these characters are well connected to their communities at some point in their personal and cultural development. Baldwin's black gay characters are, more than anything else, representative black people, who have been shaped by their cultural traditions and heritage yet must interact with the larger white American world that cares little for them.

Baldwin's gay aesthetic, moreover, does not separate the black gay character from a black ethos, and it is in keeping this connection that Baldwin shares an aesthetic with other black gay writers, such as Wallace Thurman, Essex Hemphill, and, more recently, James Earl Hardy and E. Lynn Harris. It is no easy task to create texts that refuse to sever black characters from their communities, when it is their communities—with their attitudes of hate, prejudice, intolerance, and love—that mean so much to black gay characters. One of Baldwin's techniques is to explore first the implications of his character being black in the United States, establishing a black identity battling with America's injustices (whether those injustices are clearly within the "white world" or within the "white world's" encroachment on the black community and black family). Then, as the character continues to define himself, grow, and fight with America, layers of complexity are added to his presence in the work and to his outer and inner motivations, such as homosexuality. Baldwin's texts insist that characters be unarguably black before their homosexuality takes up narrative space.

Black man homosexuality is at the core (indeed, is the core) of the often improbable and loosely plotted *Another Country*. Crucial to Baldwin's elucidation of this silent, ignored, and "counter-revolutionary" part of African American experience is his creation of women characters to brace, hide, confuse, and advance the chaos that is homosexuality in America during the 1950s, especially its black-gay-man version. The women characters, used as pawns by men and by Baldwin, lack depth, self-perception, and self-purpose. Instead, they function to reveal the deeply complex nature of being gay in America at mid-twentieth century. Moreover, while Eric and Yves are overtly homosexual, and Rufus and Vivaldo are, at best, gay men passing as disturbed bisexuals, the central story unfolds the chaos the black-gay-man, Rufus Scott, confronts in his failed struggle to live an authentic life. Before and after his death, Rufus is the catalyst—through his extraordinary impact on the lives of the other major characters—that moves the novel forward and the glue that holds it together. Several critics have noted this crucial role, though far too many of these discussions have emphasized Rufus's race rather than his sexual orientation to explain why he permeates the novel's structure and the characters' lives. While the importance of race cannot be ignored, its connection to sexual orientation, gender, and class must be engaged. To do so unleashes Baldwin's more dangerous and daring commentary on sexual and racial discourse. Nevertheless, when critics comment on homosexuality in the novel it is usually connected to Eric. The majority of critical responses have emphasized the novel's rendering of the confluence of a number of sexual, racial, and gender matters at mid-century, but few of these studies offer extended discussions of the key role Rufus's homosexuality plays. Roger Rosenblatt, for example, writes, "Homosexuality, in the person of Eric, becomes the main liberating force of the story" and thinks the novel is essentially about "sins of omission" and a "modern inferno" that contains them (91–92). James Campbell, while noting that Rufus is "probably Baldwin's most fully realized black character," thinks the major theme of *Another Country* is "the healing force of love and the difficulty of accepting it" (155, 154). Campbell says almost nothing about homosexuality in the novel. Trudier Harris's *Black Women in the Fiction of James Baldwin* is the most extensive study of his women characters, and while she acknowledges homosexuality as important in the novel, her major thesis centers on Ida Scott's improbability as a black woman character.

At the time it was published and today, *Another Country* is a problematic novel for African Americans. Its gay subject matter embarks on territory in the black experience that many African Americans refuse to acknowledge. Baldwin certainly was aware of the dilemma he faced as an artist[3] seeking to be true to his material and as a "race man" and civil rights activist who did not want to be divisive at a time when black unity was often the only hope for African Americans. In *Talking at the Gates: A Life of James Baldwin,* James Campbell writes that Baldwin wrote his friend Bill Cole to say that *Another Country* "was turning him into a mental and physical wreck. He was beginning to feel . . . that this was the novel he was destined not to survive" and that this "novel is based on his assumption that the two 'most profound realities' that the American citizen has to deal with are 'colour and sex'" (128, 134). Further evidence of the difficulties Baldwin knew he was taking on is the fact that he began *Another Country* shortly after *Giovanni's Room,* a gay novel with white characters. Adding race to this subject matter required innovative strategies, and in the years after the publication of *Another Country,* Baldwin often was ridiculed by other black leaders of the civil rights and later black power movements for his homosexuality. Eldridge Cleaver delivered the most famous of these attacks in his 1968 book *Soul on Ice,* declaring that Baldwin was unsuitable as a spokesperson for black issues. Cleaver, who repeatedly calls homosexuality a sickness and misreads Baldwin's writings, argues that Baldwin is not masculine enough, and states that "he [Baldwin] cannot confront the *stud* in others—except that he must either submit to it or destroy it" (106, italics added).

The strategy Baldwin uses to explore what it might mean to be a black-gay-man in 1950s America is to estrange Rufus and his sister, Ida, from the black community. Rufus is black, but he is not connected to the black community, even on those rare occasions when he is playing as a jazz drummer in Harlem nightspots. Most of the time he performs in clubs in Greenwich Village. The novel also expertly details Rufus's flight from his community to the larger, nonblack, world. Once Rufus serves in the Navy and travels in the United States and abroad, he never actually returns to Harlem, other than short visits to give his sister gifts and to see his mother. He apparently has no vital and meaningful relationship with his father, and we even learn that when Rufus was a late teen he no longer found black women desirable. Other than professional (the various black jazz musicians) and social (the alcohol-drug-sex parties) contacts of the most superficial kind, he does not have sustained relationships with any blacks including his sister, who seems to idolize him *because* he has escaped from the black community.

In short, Rufus is not presented as a black man. He is, if anything, an anomaly. This depiction is important, for to create Rufus as a black man deeply connected to his community and to make him gay would force Baldwin to explain the source of Rufus's attraction to men. One easily might argue that Rufus's attraction to his same sex began with black boys and men. Certainly Baldwin raised this possibility in *Go Tell It on the Mountain* (1953), where the fourteen-year-old John Grimes is sexually attracted to the seventeen-year-old Elisha. But while this gay subtext is barely explored in his first novel, Baldwin takes it up directly three years later in *Giovanni's Room.* Baldwin then diffuses the implications of examining homosexuality in the black community by casting Rufus out of that sphere and positioning him in the bohemian Village scene of the 1950s, where the subject might be more "safely" approached. Baldwin's awareness of homophobia in the black community[4] is evident in the novel when Ida tells Vivaldo that if Rufus and Eric had sex it is only because Eric "wanted to make him as sick as he is" (323). Ida apparently cannot even conceive of the idea that her brother might have sexual feelings for men.

Not only are Rufus and Ida estranged from the black community—its people, traditions, and rituals—the black community largely is absent from *Another Country*. Other than jazz, Ida's singing, the few times the Scott family is evoked, a few mentions of friends that Rufus or Ida had growing up in Harlem, and the black church (given largely from the perspective of white characters, Vivaldo and Cass, who attend Rufus's funeral), the black community is hardly to be found. This is a significant observation when Baldwin's entire canon is considered, given the prominent role of blacks and their heritage in those novels, essays, plays, and short stories. In his second and third novels, which explore gay subject matter, African American experience largely is invisible.[5] Ironically, the commentary on what it means to be black in a country that does not value this group is given by the two blacks, Rufus and Ida, who have left, spatially and culturally, their community.

In charting the path that leads to Rufus's failure to live an authentic life as a black-gay-man, Baldwin takes time to pause at one big stumbling block for all black men: manhood and masculinity. Because of the slave experience, many African American men have developed strange notions of what it means to be a man. For much of their history in America, black men have had to prove that they were human, that they were not "boys" and "uncles," and, after the Civil War, that they were entitled to full citizenship rights.

All of this "having to prove" has been exhausting and damaging for black men and others in their paths. For many black men, it often has meant accepting the weakly informed definitions of manhood and masculinity by those who oppressed them. Heterosexual black women and black gays and lesbians have suffered because far too many black men believed that their definitions of themselves were to be found in white patriarchy and its warped and convoluted hierarchies. For black heterosexual women, after emancipation and into the late nineteenth century, this meant black men tried to subdue, subjugate, placate, and otherwise keep them in their place. Although these efforts failed for a variety of reasons—especially the primary economic role black women played in the black family and community[6]—black women were still verbally, emotionally, and physically abused as black men attempted to live up to the white man's fantastical definitions of manhood and masculinity. Black men, because of the constant threats they faced—they could be lynched or beaten at any time in the post-Civil War South as well as much of the North and West by any white man or even white boy—assumed exaggerated notions of manhood in their own communities. They became, or tried to become, "super-masculine, super-men." For such individuals a white woman on their arm, if they were lucky (considering the dangers that such a display would provoke), or in their bed was the sign that they had arrived. One consequence for black men of this "super-masculinity" was a lack of tolerance, respect, or acceptance of difference, whether that difference was because of one's gender or sexual orientation. In addition to the tremendous suffering of black women because of this exaggerated masculinity, something black feminist discourse has articulated so succinctly in the last twenty-five years, black-gay-men also were silenced and disregarded. And just as black women have done, they discovered ways to tell their stories, to combat oppressive environments within their own communities, and to create places where there were no spaces.[7]

Rufus has accepted the dominant culture's superficial and inauthentic definitions of manhood and masculinity. In his fear of his homosexuality, he exhibits "super-masculinity," and in his encounters with women and gays, he berates, abuses, and tries to exert some nonexistent power over them. Consider for a moment what Baldwin reveals of Rufus's relationship with Eric, the white southern man who "loves" Rufus (but who actually suffers from "jungle fever" or a severe case of "dinge queenism").[8] The only time that Baldwin presents Rufus in an actual sexual encounter with a man—although the narrator does inform the reader that during the last four months of his life, when Rufus was desperate and homeless, he sold his body to white men—is given in this way:

> "You act like a girl—or something." . . . "I'm not the boy for you. I don't go that way." . . . But with his hands on Eric's shoulders, affection, power, and curiosity all knotted together in him—with a hidden, unforeseen violence which frightened him a little; the hands that were meant to hold Eric at arm's length seemed to draw Eric to him; the current that had begun flowing he did not know how to stop. . . . [and later when Rufus remembers this first sexual experience with Eric] He had despised Eric's manhood by treating him as a woman, by telling him how inferior he was to a woman, by treating him as nothing more than a hideous sexual deformity. (45–46)

Rufus's involvement with women also is noteworthy, as it reveals how well "super-masculinity" serves the black man who has homosexual desires but cannot face them honestly. Rufus's first meeting with Leona and the night of partying and sex that follows captures the essence of straight and gay black men who acquiesce to "super-masculinity." In addition, Baldwin's portrayal of Leona—the poor white from Georgia who has escaped a number of restrictions and injustices the South imposes on women—reveals his lack of concern for the motivations, complexities, and psychological states of his female characters. They function largely as cardboard characters who serve the text by helping to hide its most cogent and searing story: black male homosexuality at mid-century. Leona, in particular, is whored by Baldwin and Rufus, as both manipulate and use her. Baldwin uses Leona to complicate and mask Rufus's sexuality under a veil of bisexuality and confusion. As long as Rufus is having sex with Leona, beating her, and otherwise dominating her, his sexuality is beyond suspicion. And, since Rufus is estranged from the black community (he is just a black man gone crazy in the bohemian jungle of Greenwich Village) and yet still accepts one of its values, "super-masculinity," what he does to Leona is completely acceptable to black male readers. He is just being a "man." Certainly analyses of Rufus's character have not considered the crucial role his homosexuality plays in his demise, as most criticism has little to say about this aspect of the novel. Instead, critics emphasize the role race plays in destroying Rufus's life. And even more important than Baldwin's treatment of Leona is how Rufus uses her to attenuate his self-hatred because he is both black and gay. His ruthless behavior toward Leona, both as a sexual object and as a subject (he does recognize "that Leona was a person and had her story"), are his attempts to keep at bay homosexual feelings that are becoming impossible for him to control or deny (13). The authority and license he exercises over Leona, a part of his "super-masculinity," allow him to function during the last seven months of his life.

When he first meets Leona, this power immediately is revealed. At a Harlem jazz club, significantly, one of the rare ones actually "owned and operated by a Negro," he notices the blonde Leona after having played drums. It is telling that he also observes that she is "over thirty probably, and her body was too thin. Just the same, it abruptly became the most exciting body he had gazed on in a long time" (9). It does not matter what she looks like, as long as she is white, preferably blonde. She becomes, then, a white woman for him to possess and to have displayed on his arm as a cultural trophy. When he tells her, after only mentioning his name, to get in a cab and go with him to an after-set party, his power is revealed. When she hesitates just a bit, asking him if it is okay if she comes along, Rufus states in his display of masculinity and power, "If it wasn't all right, I wouldn't ask you. If I say it's all right, it's all *right*" (emphasis in text 10). As they enter the building of the party on Riverside Drive in Harlem and wait for the elevator, amid small talk, the narrator records a few of Rufus's thoughts. "Suddenly, his days in boot camp in the South and [he] felt again the shoe of a white officer against his mouth. He was in his white uniform, on the ground, against the red, dusty clay. Some of his colored buddies were holding him, were shouting in his ear, helping him to rise. The white officer, with a curse, had vanished, had gone forever beyond the reach of vengeance" (13). This quotation is central to an understanding of how "super-masculinity" serves the black man, whether straight or gay. Rufus will mention a long list of injustices that whites, particularly "the man," have inflicted upon him and other blacks. The juxtaposition of "white," "red," and "colored" is telling. White men have made colored "buddies" bleed for centuries, and continue to do so in 1950s America.[9] The white officer was "beyond the reach of vengeance," but the white woman is not; she is right next to Rufus.

Vengeance can, in fact, be enacted upon the white thing that has caused black men to bleed, and it apparently does not matter to Rufus, or to other black men, that the gender has changed. Part of this vengeance is the mere fact that the black man can sexually possess the white man's woman. This is especially important since so many black men have lost their lives or their sexual organs because white men assumed they desired their women, whether they did or not. Something else also happens when black men challenge white male authority by assuming authority over white women in sexual encounters: the rage, that so many black men spend countless hours creating numerous tactics to suppress, erupts. Unfortunately for women like Leona, who have their own reasons for becoming involved with black men, this anger often means that white females become the victims of violence, verbal, physical, and emotional. Black women know all too well the consequences of black men's rage against white injustice.[10]

Significantly, before Rufus gets too far along in his night of partying and sex, he takes the time to call Vivaldo. The short conversation the two friends have presents the reader with something else to consider that relates to Rufus's use of "super-masculinity" to assuage his homosexual feelings. Leona, or any white woman (or gay man in the example of Rufus and Eric), helps Rufus to be the big man. His conversation with Vivaldo first suggests that the men have sexual feelings for one another, an idea indicated when Vivaldo asks Rufus if "it's worthwhile making it up there [to the party]." In response, Rufus says, "Well, hell, I don't know. If you got something *better* to do—" (emphasis in text). Vivaldo immediately says "Jane's here" (15). Rufus and then the narrator discuss and describe Jane as gray and unattractive. The "something *better* to do" is the first indication that mutual sexual attraction and its resulting tension are a part of Rufus's and Vivaldo's friendship. If Vivaldo were not with Jane, and if Rufus were to abandon Leona, perhaps this would be the night for them to express sexually their feelings for one another. After some jousting about their heterosexual virility, Rufus tells Vivaldo "You better *quit* trying to compete with me. *You* ain't never going to make it" (15). The door to Rufus's closet barely was cracked open, and a quick return to "super-masculinity" closes it tightly again.

It is not surprising that for Rufus, the party's host is both a model of the "super-black man" and someone to fear. Black men like the host make it even more difficult for black-gay-men to emerge from the closet, for these men ridicule, humiliate, and figuratively and literally kill black-gay-men. The host is described as

> a big, handsome, expansive man, older and more ruthless than he looked, who had fought his way to the top in show business via several of the rougher professions, including boxing and pimping. He owed his present eminence more to his vitality and his looks than he did to his voice, and he knew it . . . and Rufus liked him because he was rough and good-natured and generous. But Rufus was also a little afraid of him; there was that about him . . . which did not encourage intimacy. He was a great success with women, whom he treated with a large, affectionate contempt. (16)

This description is an apt one that encompasses many of the values that Rufus has assumed. The host is noted for his roughness, ruthlessness, physical prowess, sexual vitality, and contempt for women, traits accompanied by anger and rage against white men. He tells Rufus that "It's these *respectable* [white] motherfuckers been doing all the dirt. They been stealing the colored folks blind, man. And niggers helping them do it" (16, emphasis in text).

Rufus's initial sex act with Leona—and it is a sex act, not love-making—shows how he has internalized the values associated with the host and exposes the delusional power and authority associated with "super-masculinity." Their coming together on the balcony of the Harlem flat is violent, rough, even ruthless. The narrator records that Rufus

> pulled her to him as roughly as he could. . . . He knocked the glass out of her hand. . . . Go ahead, he thought humorously; if I was to let you

go now you'd be so hung up you'd go flying over this balcony, most likely. . . . "Go ahead, fight. I like it. Is this the way they do down home?" (20)

He is motivated and excited by the power that he wields over this white woman, and he thinks his sexual prowess is so great that if he were to stop his seduction, Leona would be so out of sorts that she would jump off the balcony, so turned on is she by Rufus. And he likes the slight resistance she initially offers. He likes it when his women resist or fight. Why? Such fighting makes his power seem even greater, for, of course, he, the robust black man in his sexual and physical prime, will triumph over the slight, even frail, Leona.

That she is white is crucial to the vengeance that he believes he is taking on the white man who has victimized and brutalized him and a long history of "colored buddies" and who continues to deny black men social, civil, economic, and political opportunities. After penetrating her, his innermost thoughts reveal the direct relationship of how his taking of Leona represents his own impotence against the white men who actually control power and authority in America. Immediately before he climaxes, he thinks "nothing could have stopped him, not the white God himself nor a lynch mob arriving on wings. Under his breath he cursed the milk-white bitch and groaned and rode his weapon between her thighs. . . . A moan and a curse tore through him while he beat her with all the strength he had and felt the venom shoot out of him, enough for a hundred black-white babies" (22). The narrator's language makes it explicit that Rufus's sexual conquest of Leona is motivated by his desire for vengeance against the white man. A "white God" and a "lynch mob" are evoked at exactly the time he reaches his climax, the physical and emotional sign of his sexual prowess. The "white God" is telling, for many versions of the Judeo-Christian tradition in America have conspired with the white man to keep the black man in his subordinate place, and "lynch mobs" have killed or castrated black men to destroy the very "weapon" that he now uses against Leona. And for Rufus, it is important that his "weapon" shoots "venom" and that it is productive, capable of creating a "hundred black-white babies," real or physical evidence of the black man's vengeance and conquest of the white man's worst fears. Rufus's thinking seems to run this way: You will not allow me access to real sources of power in this country, so I will use my weapon to create havoc on your most precious object, the one you have put on any number of pedestals—the white woman. I will despoil her and present you with evidence of your soiled property, "black-white babies." After the sex act, Baldwin shows the inadequacy of Rufus's thinking, of "super-masculinity," by having Leona declare, "I ain't going to be having no more babies. . . . He [her white husband] beat that out of me, too" (22). Ironically, Leona's statement reveals the triumph of the white man once again.

Although the text does not make it explicitly clear, this indication of the white man's triumph might account partially for Rufus's continued victimization of Leona after they begin a relationship. Rufus is still fighting for victory over the white man. Once Leona moves in with Rufus, their sex acts continue to be violent, and the conversations they have in a number of contexts—their sordid apartment, bars, walks in the park—are dominated by Rufus's rage against the white power establishment. One key scene underscores the connection in Rufus's mind between sexual prowess over Leona and its relationship to white power, or the white man. After Leona moves in, she tries to appease Rufus and his rage, tries to make peace, looking to him to be her Black Knight in Shining Armor, someone who will mend the years of abuse she suffered from her husband and the southern milieu, where white women have little authority in their relationships with white men. If they have power at all, it is over black women and black men, and perhaps over their own children. In Leona's case, she does not have authority even over her child, who was taken from her by her husband supposedly because of her drinking. Although the narrator presents few details of her relationship with her husband, her drinking and sexual liaisons with black men suggest the extent of her unhappiness and her feeble attempts to seek refuge elsewhere.[11]

The text further suggests that her relationships with black men account for how readily she takes up with Rufus on the night they meet, as well as her later comments in which she declares there is nothing wrong with being black. She so often tries to convince Rufus that she is not like other southern whites. Her sexual relations with black men in the South (if they happened) do explain some of her actions, for she defies her culture's values (which brutalize white women and restrict their possibilities) by challenging the unreasonable fear of white men—black men having sex with their women. Her attempts to show Rufus that she is, somehow, on his side fail miserably, however. The text demonstrates how Leona's simple and innocent gestures toward racial healing and reconciliation become the fuel that unleashes Rufus's rage toward white power, and this rage almost always has a sexual connotation.

"Rufus," Leona had said—time and time again—"ain't nothing wrong in being colored."

Sometimes, when she said this, he simply looked at her coldly, from a great distance, as though he wondered what on earth she was trying to say. His look seemed to accuse her of ignorance and indifference. Sometimes, when she said that there was nothing wrong in being colored, he answered, "Not if you a hard-up white lady."

The first time he said this, she winced and said nothing. The second time she slapped him. And he slapped her. They fought all the time. They fought each other with their hands and their voices and then with their bodies: and the one storm was like the other. Many times . . . he had, suddenly, without knowing that he was going to, thrown the whimpering, terrified Leona onto the bed, the floor, pinned her against a table or a wall; she beat at him, weakly, moaning, unutterably abject; he twisted his fingers in her long pale hair and used her in whatever way he felt would humiliate her most. It was not love he felt during these acts of love: drained and shaking, utterly unsatisfied, he fled from the raped woman into bars. In these bars no one applauded his triumph or condemned his guilt. He began *to pick fights with white men.* (52–53, italics added)

Here Baldwin specifies in an exacting prose[12] how Rufus's entire ill-advised relationship with Leona is tied to his vengeance and battle with white men. No, she cannot understand his life in America as a black man. No matter how intimate she thinks she has been with black men in the South, she does not understand them, and she should not be around them, for in the 1950s in African American experience, black men use white women in their fight with white men. Even Baldwin uses them, and when he is through with Leona, she is promptly excised from the text. She said something Rufus did not like, "that there was nothing wrong with being colored," and he exploded. He believes and knows there is something wrong with being "colored." Everything we know of his experience informs us of this belief. Rufus has not reached the stage in his development where he can be happy with his black self.[13] Too many of his belief systems are derived from Eurocentric views of the world and human life. He hates himself, and he really wants to be the very white man that he tries so futilely to destroy. His dilemma is certainly that which the W.E.B. Du Bois articulated in his 1903 *The Souls of Black Folk.* Rufus's "double-consciousness" is at least tripled, likely quadrupled or more. He is living what it means to exist in a country that does not value him. He knows of the extra strength it takes to keep himself from falling asunder. His strength has made it possible for him to exist as long as he has (keep in mind that he commits suicide in his late twenties) and in his sexually confused state of mind.

Throughout his brief appearance in the novel, Rufus is psychologically and culturally crazy; the cultural schizophrenia has caught up with him and is kicking his ass. He has overpowering homosexual feelings and desires, he is poor, he is an artist, he is a proud race man. He refuses to say that injustices are not happening to him. He copes, although, unfortunately for him, too much of Rufus has been obliterated by white, male, heterosexual, cultural hegemony. He questions, he fights, he challenges, he rages against Eurocentric cultural values, interpretations, but he finally and tragically accepts these limited views of the world and universe. As a black-gay-man, with no space to operate, so to speak, he takes on a number of guises in his struggle to create a space where he can live.

Some of these he should have put in the nearest dump, however. Instead of trying to be the big, bad, black, virile, promiscuous, vicious, cool (or down with it), I can do it all alone, "super-masculine" brother, Rufus should have taken the path followed by his forefathers, who did not acquiesce or succumb to white people's definitions of the world, who took what was here and made it their own, who said, "Oh, this is your religion, your philosophical ethos, your look at the world. Well, this is mine. You present some of us in bondage with this Christian religion. Well, I will read and interpret your Bible for you to you. You do not want me to read and write because being illiterate will help you to continue your limited world view. Well, I will learn, and every other slave that I can teach to read and write, I will do so proudly."[14] With no black cultural values or black people to assist him, Rufus is doomed to being alone, as he is shortly before he dies on the George Washington Bridge, and none of his white "friends" tried to save him. Keep in mind that Rufus's most intense relationships are with white people; even his relationship with his sister, Ida, is suspect, for in that relationship he largely represents himself as the strong, "super-masculine" black man. Admittedly, black cultural values of the mid-1950s privilege homophobia (as do the white cultural values that he embraces); nevertheless, Rufus might have been able to find enough cultural resources to help him love most of himself. If he had remained connected to blacks and black culture, it even is possible that he might have met a black-gay-man, like himself (they did exist).[15] Instead, as the narrator's description of Rufus's relationship with Leona so vividly shows, he is reduced to beating and belittling a crazy, frail, and powerless white woman as a vent for his sense of his own worthlessness in the white man's world.

Rufus's relationship with Vivaldo—his so-called best friend, who had to be white—should have provided him with some insight into the uselessness of privileging white men's values. In estranging Rufus from the black community, to avoid facing head on the implications of black male homosexuality in the African American experience, Baldwin provides no opportunities for him to have meaningful experiences with blacks. As a best friend, however, Vivaldo failed Rufus miserably—in large part because of two key aspects of their relationship that make it impossible for them to have a healthy friendship. The first is that Rufus knows of Vivaldo's jaunts to Harlem to buy black woman for sex, while the second is that Vivaldo knows he has homosexual feelings for Rufus and realizes that Rufus has similar feelings for him.

The part of Rufus's being that is black and proud, or at least shouts the slogan anytime he can, should have something to say about Vivaldo's treatment of black women as bitches to be used at his discretion. In this, Vivaldo uses women the way Baldwin uses them in this novel: as whores to service the needs of men. The text only mentions these sexual escapades as a part of the two men's bragging of their virility and "studness."[16] As a black man and a white man, the two are in competition, and their sexual boasting conceals the real competition between black and white men in the United States, something that Baldwin makes explicit in his analysis of Rufus's relationship with Leona. That relationship, as previously discussed, is not about Rufus and Leona; it is about Rufus and white men. Yet Rufus has nothing to say against Vivaldo's actions, which mirror, in miniature, the white man's privilege, license, and authority over black women during slavery and after. What happened to Rufus's rage and vengeance? What accounts for Rufus's ability to accept or tolerate Vivaldo? It cannot be because Rufus thinks Vivaldo is a good and decent person. The text does not support such a reading. For months Rufus has been desperate, broke, homeless, but he does not go to Vivaldo until the night he has decided to kill himself. Rufus has a great deal of mistrust of Vivaldo, but he still does not put Vivaldo in the same category of white men that fuels his rage.

The answer is that although neither man is honest enough with himself to admit it, the two commune despite their differences because of something they have in common: their homosexuality. On the night of his death, after four months of living on the streets and prostituting himself to *white* men, Rufus comes to see Vivaldo, immediately after he has turned down a white man's offer, and he and Vivaldo have the following conversation:

> "Have you ever wished you were queer?" Rufus asked suddenly.
>
> Vivaldo smiled, looking into his glass. "I used to think maybe I was. Hell, I think I even *wished* I was." He laughed. "But I'm not. So I'm stuck."
>
> Rufus walked to Vivaldo's window. "So you been all up and down that street, too," he said.
>
> "We've all been up the same streets. There aren't a hell of a lot of streets. Only, we've been taught to lie so much, about so many things, that we hardly ever know *where* we are."
>
> Rufus said nothing. He walked up and down. (51–52, italics in text)

The above passage is remarkable. These men have known each other for years, but only on the night of his death does Rufus broach the subject of homosexuality openly. The most telling observation, however, is the dishonesty that permeates Vivaldo's words. He keeps his head down, looking into his glass; he laughs; he admits to wishing he were gay, but concludes he is not, and then he has the nerve to go on and to talk about lies. Because he is lying when Rufus needs him to tell the truth, it is not surprising that the response by Rufus—who knows Vivaldo has flirted with him before—is to say nothing. Even when Rufus was with Leona, Vivaldo comments one day, as Rufus pulls the covers off, stands and stretches while naked, "You're giving quite a show this afternoon" (25). There must have been many times when Vivaldo has admired and desired Rufus's penis. Vivaldo's dishonesty at this crucial moment in Rufus's life becomes a final blow for Rufus, who really does not have anyone. And yet the reader knows that Vivaldo has had an active homosexual life. When he was in his own community in Brooklyn, working at the warehouses, he was proud to be around all of the "manly" men, "Only—it was they who saw something in him which they could not accept, which made them uneasy" (61). As a teen, he and his friends had often had group sex with gay boys, usually taunting and humiliating them in the process, but when Vivaldo tells Rufus that he is not gay it is the biggest lie. Several months after Rufus's death, after Vivaldo and Ida have begun a relationship from hell, he cheats on her with Eric and easily assumes the "passive role": "Now, Vivaldo, who was accustomed himself to labor, to be the giver of the gift, and enter into his satisfaction by means of the satisfaction of a woman, surrendered to the luxury, the flaming torpor of passivity, and whispered in Eric's ear a muffled, urgent plea" (385).[17] The narrator does not record this plea, but surely it is "Fuck me." He has no regrets. He tells Eric it probably will not happen again, but he leaves that option open. And in his sleep before he and Eric have sex, Vivaldo dreams of Rufus. In the dream he tells Rufus not to kill him and that he loves him. That he dreams Rufus would want to kill him is an indication, on a subconscious level, that Vivaldo knows he is partially responsible for Rufus's death for not owning up to the homosexual desires that might have saved them both. On a conscious level, or at least a verbally artic-ulated one, before Vivaldo and Eric go to sleep, before they have sex, Vivaldo tells Eric that, on the night when he had taken Leona from Rufus's apartment, after Rufus had beat her, and returned to find Rufus in bed, "I had the weirdest feeling that he wanted me to take him in my arms. And not for sex, *though maybe sex would have happened.* I had the feeling that he wanted someone to hold him, to hold him, and that, that night, it had to be a man" (342, italics added). But Vivaldo does not hold him. Vivaldo has never given Rufus what he needed, and will not or cannot give Ida what she needs either.

It is Vivaldo's dishonesty with himself that makes the already prob-lematic relationship with Ida even more so, at novel's end. First, how-ever, it is necessary to consider how useful Ida has been to Baldwin as a device to elevate racial matters over sexual ones. In this considera-tion, Ida becomes the novel's biggest whore and a largely implausible one at that, given how her entire presence is forced and out of place. That she initially would have some contact with Rufus's white friends makes sense, as it is his disappearance that prompts her to seek them out for possible information on his whereabouts. But her continued involvement with them lacks credibility given her portrayal as being every bit as race conscious and militant as Rufus. Baldwin establishes her as a viable black entity first, one fueled by a barely controllable rage against whites who make it so difficult for black people to live in Amer-ica. When she first meets Cass, Richard, and Vivaldo (who she has not seen since she was a teen-ager) and gives all of them a bit of "black atti-tude," it is consistent with how Baldwin creates her as an authentic black character who really does not like white people. Her later, more intimate involvement with these characters makes little sense, how-ever. Readers might understand her involvement as a part of an attempt to punish them for what she believes they have done to destroy Rufus, but her sleeping with the enemy requires a higher level of character motivation—one that Baldwin never reveals.[18] That Ida might want to use white people to seek revenge against them for their failure to be real friends to Rufus works in terms of how Baldwin manipulates his black characters to carry his vision of racial matters in America at midcentury. It is understandable that Ida initially might perceive a closer relationship with Vivaldo as a way to get back at him for failing to assist Rufus, since Vivaldo has been presented to her by Rufus as his best friend. To use this white man the way she has used so many others is plausible. She will do her best to make him suffer. But when she develops feelings for him, the novel has done little to prepare the reader to understand her motivation. Their relationship is one in which they fight most of the time, with most of their arguments centering on Vivaldo's lack of understanding of Ida as a black woman. In allowing Ida to develop feelings of love for Vivaldo despite his lack of respect and understanding of her as a black woman, Baldwin signals his own disregard for her status in America as a black woman, at least in this novel. That is, though Baldwin spends some narrative space detailing how white men think of black women as little more than whores, even his characterization of Vivaldo fits this assessment, and Ida knows white men think of her in this way and she uses them accordingly, Baldwin nevertheless disregards both Ida's knowledge of white men's attitudes of her and other black women when he allows her to love and sleep with the enemy. The interesting matter is why Ida would allow herself to be taken in by a white man, such as Vivaldo, who continually has shown that black women do not count in his vision of the world, other than for momentary sexual gratification. It may be possible that Ida has motivation for loving Vivaldo, but readers are never privy to it. Ida sought out to pay Vivaldo back for his neglect of her brother, but when she falls in love with him, it is possible to see how women characters, once again, are sacrificed by Baldwin in his telling of homosexual desire and confusion of his male characters. Vivaldo and Ida's relationship shifts the focus away from the homosexual stories that provide most of the novel's meaning.

When Baldwin reveals that Ida loves Vivaldo, he does so *after* Vivaldo and Eric's homosexual affair, a liaison that apparently was quite gratifying to both. By introducing Ida's love for Vivaldo and his statement of love to her, Baldwin is able to close on a heterosexual note—even if their final relationship makes little sense given their earlier portrayal. One supposes that on the surface Baldwin assumes his readers will buy the idea that people are capable of forgiving, and that love conquers all, apparently even the white man's thinking of black women as immoral, instinctual whores. But the ending suggests something else as well. Ida's love for Vivaldo might temporarily keep him in the heterosexual world, but his homosexual desires and his attitudes toward race and gender matters are powerful undercurrents that he and the novel have not resolved. Baldwin's final comments on the relationship of Vivaldo and Ida suggest its future.

Ida has confessed her initial design to use him and then Ellis to further herself and her singing career. But, she says, along the way she actually fell in love with him. Vivaldo has little response, although in her confession she becomes the very kind of black "whore" that he consistently has abused. She also is just like her brother, in that attached to her personal confession is the rage she has toward the white world. Vivaldo failed Rufus, and every indication is that he will fail Ida, too. He does not have the capacity to understand black people's dilemmas in America, even though he can be sexually intimate with them; in this he is similar to Leona. After Ida's confession, "She looked directly at him, and an unnamable heat and tension flashed violently alive between them, as close to hatred as it was to love" (431). And Vivaldo tells her "'You seem to forget that I love you'" (431). What will Ida do with the rage and hatred that are a part of her being as a black woman in America? When she has had a bad day, one replete with all kinds of physical and psychological assaults, how will she respond to the white man in her bed? Will she understand that she is in fact sleeping with the enemy? What will she do with this understanding if it comes? She inherently knows, and told this to Vivaldo, that Vivaldo had something to do with her brother's death. If he talks to her the way he did with Eric about Rufus, she will have evidence of his guilt. And Vivaldo, as dishonest as they come, what will he really do with his homosexual desires now that they were so beautifully expressed with Eric? Will they disappear or haunt him? Nothing indicates that Vivaldo values monogamy; he already has cheated on Ida with Eric. And what about this love Ida and Vivaldo supposedly feel for each other? One might consider Toni Morrison's statement on love when she states that Cholly Breedlove, who raped his daughter Pecola, did love her: "Love is never any better than the lover. Wicked people love wickedly, violent people love violently, weak people love weakly, stupid people love stupidly" (*The Bluest Eye* 159).

Rufus (and Ida) put too much faith in Vivaldo. When Vivaldo tells him that he is not gay, Rufus takes his plan to kill himself to its final stage. On the George Washington Bridge, before Rufus takes his plunge, he thought of Eric, Ida, and Leona, but not Vivaldo. Perhaps he finally realized that what Vivaldo represented—white, dishonest, and "supermasculine"—were the very things he should have avoided, but of course it is now too late.

That Rufus was not successful in negotiating new—although still quite restricted and oppressive—cultural landscapes, and the novel does not make certain Ida's fate in the chaos of the American nightmare of the 1950s, *Another Country* moves the African American novel to a place where it can see new vistas. It skillfully and subtly looks at submerged subject matter in the African American experience. Some black men are gay, and though Rufus could not accept this part of his being, Baldwin prepares his own stage and the stage for other black writers, to create black gay characters who are integrated into their communities and who do "survive whole."[19]

NOTES

1. All citations are from James Baldwin, *Another Country,* 1962, Reprint, *Griot Editions: Voices of the African Diaspora,* 1994, Quality Paperback Book Club by arrangement with Alfred A. Knopf.

2. I use the term "black-gay-man" to suggest that the gay man who is black is always black first. He cannot, like many gay white men, just be gay. Racial matters in America prevent him from doing so.

3. What Baldwin faced as a black writer is quite similar to what many black writers have faced, as they must deal with their allegiance to race and to art. The classic example of this dilemma is Langston Hughes's "The Negro Artist and the Racial Mountain," 1926.

4. An important discussion of homophobia in the black community is found in Barbara Smith's "Homophobia: Why Bring It Up?" in *The Lesbian and Gay Studies Reader,* edited by Henry Abelove, Michele Aina Barale, and David M. Halperin. One of Smith's statements that relates so directly to Rufus's fate in *Another Country* is "Homophobia is usually the last oppression to be mentioned, the last to be taken seriously, the last to go. But it is extremely serious, sometimes to the point of being fatal" (99). Other works addressing this issue include: Sheldon Waldrep's "'Being Bridges': Cleaver/Baldwin/Lorde and African-American Sexism and Sexuality" in *Critical Essays: Gay and Lesbian Writers of Color* edited by Emmanuel S. Nelson; *In the Life: A Black Gay Anthology* edited by Joseph Beam; and *Brother to Brother: New Writings by Black Gay Men* edited by Essex Hemphill and conceived by Joseph Beam.

5. In later works, namely the 1979 novel *Just Above My Head,* Baldwin positions black-gay-men rooted in and integral members of the black community.

6. Many examples from black feminist discourse can support the above claim. Paula Giddings's *When and Where I Enter: the Impact of Race and Sex in America* was an influential text on my thinking in the mid-1980s.

7. The works of Joseph Beam, Samuel Delany, Melvin Dixon, E. Lynn Harris, Essex Hemphill, Marlon Riggs, and others are continuing a black-gay-man literary tradition that writers such as Baldwin, Countee Cullen, Langston Hughes, Claude McKay, Richard Bruce Nugent, Wallace Thurman, and others created.

8. In gay culture, a "dinge queen" is a white man who is obsessed with the black male, his skin, his hair, and especially his penis. The black man is an object of the white man's desire; rarely is the black man considered a subject. And in these pairings, the white man usually has little interest in the black man's culture and history, and the race-specific oppressions he must combat. The opposite of the dinge queen is the "snow queen." The "snow queen," and Rufus qualifies as one, loves everything about the white body and hates his own black skin. There are also heterosexual versions of each of the above.

9. Whenever Rufus and Leona are out in public, white men stare at them with eyes that could kill. Once when Rufus, Vivaldo, and Jane were at a club and Jane was drunk and loud, white men in the bar came to her defense, thinking that Rufus must have done something to her, and they beat Rufus to the point where he requires medical attention (Baldwin, *Another Country*, 31–35).

10. This is a major theme in the writings of black women (for example, Zora Neale Hurston, Gayl Jones, Terry McMillan, Toni Morrison, Gloria Naylor, Ann Petry, Joyce Carol Thomas, and Alice Walker, among others).

11. At several moments in Baldwin's brief and surface account of Leona's life we are led to believe or consider that Leona has had sex with black men before Rufus. She never says directly, but Rufus assumes she has, and Baldwin suggests on more than one occasion he has said to her "'Your husband and all those funky niggers screwed you in the Georgia bushes'" (Baldwin, *Another Country*, 56). Furthermore, on the few times that Baldwin represents Leona's and Vivaldo's interactions, she tells Vivaldo that "'He [Rufus] says I'm sleeping with other colored boys behind his back and it's not true, God knows it's not true'" (55).

12. This prose style is associated with Henry James, who was a major influence on Baldwin's creation of prose fiction. Baldwin particularly appreciated James's contribution to American realism of the importance of psychological precision in delineating character. The way that language, if used expertly, is capable of reproducing the human mind. For an excellent discussion of James's connection to Baldwin's fiction, see Charles Newman's "The Lesson of the Master: Henry James and James Baldwin," in *Modern Critical Views: James Baldwin* edited by Harold Bloom.

13. See the William Cross model of the stages many black people go through on their road to a healthy black self. Rufus does not reach the stage of immersion, where the black person deliberately seeks to learn all that he can about his race and culture, which can then lead to internalization, where the black person essentially loves himself. The Cross model is contained in *Black Psychology*, ed. Reginald Jones, 81–98.

14. I will never forget a winter seminar in which I participated at San Diego State University several years ago. Frances Smith Foster was the discus-

sion leader, and she introduced new ideas and new areas of investigation for scholars of black literature. The most relevant for the present discussion is her statement that black writers wrote to black readers or hearers. From the beginning of Africans' encounters with whites in what is now the United States and elsewhere in the Americas and the Caribbean, they privileged reading and writing, and the sophisticated level of thinking that is required for both. The majority, the masses, although from separate ethnic groups in Africa, once they arrived in the new world, conspired together to do real battle with white people. Forefathers and foremothers, bringing to America the best of African traditions, such as the communal self or kinship, and not the worse, such as female circumcision and the lifelong horrors associated with it as Alice Walker so tragically renders in *Possessing the Secret of Joy,* immediately planted their culture and their traditions into the American soil. They communicated to one another through song and word; they braved all kinds of risks against their bodies and minds to articulate their beings. They resisted in whatever way they could, as David Walker, in his *Appeal,* and Henry Highland Garnet, in "An Address to the Slaves of the United States of America," announced the call. These are two of many black writers and other activists who created black definitions of the world. Both Walker's and Garnet's writings are directed to black people. Their ideas insist that black people can resist white cultural hegemony and manufacture their own values.

15. See Eric Garber's "A Spectacle in Color: The Lesbian and Gay Subculture of Jazz Age Harlem" in *Hidden from History: Reclaiming the Gay & Lesbian Past* edited by Martin Duberman, Martha Vicinus, and George Chauncey, Jr. Garber provides a detailed examination of black gay life in Harlem of the 1920s and 1930s, and, although a good deal of it was underground, his most significant point is that it was present. It also certainly is present in the Harlem of the 1950s.

16. There is one exception to this. Vivaldo recalls one night when he went uptown to Harlem in search of a black "whore." On that night the woman set him up, and her pimp, or just her friend, the text is not clear on this, gives Vivaldo the kind of response that Rufus should have: "'You goddamn lucky you *didn't* get it in' [the black man said]. 'You'd be a mighty sorry white boy if you had. You wouldn't be putting that white prick in no more black pussy, I can guarantee you that'" (Baldwin, *Another Country,* 63).

17. The night before Vivaldo and Eric have sex, he lies to Harold, a gay white artist. Harold wants to have sex with him, and Vivaldo says he does not go that way; yet he does sleep in Harold's arms.

18. Trudier Harris in *Black Women in the Fiction of James Baldwin* concludes that although Ida serves many purposes in the novel "she is still an elusive entity" and "Baldwin never really explains how a black woman . . . could so thoroughly sever connections with all bases of support contained [in her black community]" (126).

19. Grange Copeland in Alice Walker's first novel, *The Third Life of Grange Copeland* (1970), concludes that his granddaughter Ruth must do more than survive, she must survive whole.

Works Cited

Baldwin, James. *Another Country.* 1962. Reprint, New York: Quality Paperback Book Club, 1994.

———. *Giovanni's Room.* New York: Dial, 1956.

———. *Go Tell It on the Mountain.* 1953. Reprint, New York: Dell, 1974.

———. *Just Above My Head.* New York: Dial, 1979.

Beam, Joseph, ed. *In the Life: A Black Gay Anthology.* New York: Alyson, 1986.

Campbell, James. *Talking at the Gates: A Life of James Baldwin.* New York: Viking, 1991.

Cleaver, Eldridge. *Soul on Ice.* New York: Dell, 1968.

Delaney, Samuel. *The Motion of Light in Water: Sex and Science Fiction in the East Village, 1957–1965.* New York: Arbor House/Morrow, 1988.

Dixon, Melvin. *Vanishing Rooms.* New York: Dutton, 1991.

———. *Love's Instruments.* Chicago: Tia Chuca Press, 1995.

Du Bois, W.E.B. *The Souls of Black Folk.* 1903. Reprint, ed. David W. Blight and Robert Gooding-Williams, 38–40. Boston: Bedford, 1997.

Garber, Eric. "A Spectacle in Color: The Lesbian and Gay Subculture of Jazz Age Harlem." In *Hidden from History: Reclaiming the Gay & Lesbian Past,* ed. Martin Duberman, Martha Vicinus, and George Chauncey, Jr., 318–31. New York: New American Library, 1989.

Garnet, Henry Highland. "An Address to the Slaves of the United States of America." 1843 (when speech was first presented); 1848 (when speech was first printed). In *The Norton Anthology of African American Literature,* ed. Henry Louis Gates, Jr. and Nellie Y. McKay, 280–85. New York: Norton, 1997.

Giddings, Paula. *When and Where I Enter: the Impact of Race and Sex in America.* New York: Morrow, 1984.

Harris, E. Lynn. *Invisible Life: A Novel.* New York: Anchor, 1994.

———. *Just As I Am: A Novel.* New York: Anchor, 1995.

———. *And This Too Shall Pass: A Novel.* New York: Doubleday, 1996.

Harris, Trudier. *Black Women in the Fiction of James Baldwin.* Knoxville: University of Tennessee Press, 1985.

Hemphill, Essex, ed. *Conditions.* 1986.

———. *Brother to Brother: New Writings by Black Gay Men.* Conceived by Joseph Beam. New York: Alyson, 1991.

———. *Ceremonies: Prose and Poetry.* New York: Plume, 1992.

Hughes, Langston. "The Negro Artist and the Racial Mountain," *The Nation,* 23 June 1926.

Hurston, Zora Neale. *Their Eyes Were Watching God.* 1937. Reprint, Urbana: University of Illinois Press, 1978.

Jones, Gayl. *Eva's Man.* New York: Random House, 1976.

———. *White Rat: Short Stories.* New York: Random House, 1977.

Jones, Reginald L., ed. *Black Psychology.* 2d ed. New York, Harper and Row, 1980.

McMillan, Terry. *Mama.* Boston: Houghton Mifflin, 1987.

Morrison, Toni. *The Bluest Eye.* 1970. Reprint, New York: Pocket Books, 1972.

Naylor, Gloria. *The Women of Brewster Place.* New York: Viking Press, 1982.

———. *Linden Hills.* New York: Ticknor & Fields, 1985.

———. *Bailey's Café.* New York: Harcourt Brace Jovanovich, 1992.

Newman, Charles. "The Lesson of the Master: Henry James and James Baldwin." In *Modern Critical Views: James Baldwin,* ed. Harold Bloom, 45–57. New York: Chelsea House, 1986.

Petry, Ann. *The Street.* Boston: Houghton Mifflin, 1946.

Riggs, Marlon. *Tongues Untied* (documentary). 1992.

Rosenblatt, Roger. "Out of Control: *Go Tell It on the Mountain* and *Another Country.*" In *Modern Critical Views: James Baldwin,* ed. Harold Bloom, 77–96. New York: Chelsea House, 1986.

Smith, Barbara. "Homophobia: Why Bring It Up?" In *The Lesbian and Gay Studies Reader,* ed. Henry Abelove, Michele Aina Barale, and David M. Halperin, 99–102. New York: Routledge, 1993.

Thomas, Joyce Carol. *Marked by Fire.* New York: Avon, 1982.

Waldrep, Sheldon. "'Being Bridges': Cleaver/Baldwin/Lourde and African-American Sexism and Sexuality." In *Critical Essays: Gay and Lesbian Writers of Color,* ed. Emmanuel S. Nelson, 167–80. New York: Harrington Park, 1993.

Walker, Alice. *The Third Life of Grange Copeland.* New York: Harcourt Brace Jovanovich, 1970.

———. *In Love and Trouble.* New York: Harcourt Brace Jovanovich, 1985.

———. *The Color Purple: A Novel.* New York: Harcourt Brace Jovanovich, 1982.

———. *Possessing the Secret of Joy.* New York: Harcourt Brace Jovanovich, 1992.

Walker, David. "Appeal, in Four Articles Together with a Preamble, to the Coloured Citizens of the World, but in Particular, and Very Expressly, to Those of the United States of America." 1829. In *David Walker's Appeal,* ed. Charles M. Wiltse. New York: Hill and Wang, 1964.

"masculinity" and (im)maturity

"The Man Child" and other stories in Baldwin's gender studies enterprise

YASMIN Y. DEGOUT

BALDWIN AS GENDER STUDIES THEORIST

There were no standards for him because he could not accept the definitions, the hideously mechanical jargon of the age. . . . And this meant that he had to create his standards and make up his definitions as he went along.   *—James Baldwin*

"Race and sex have always been overlapping discourses in the United States. That discourse began in slavery," says bell hooks, who stresses "the ways racism and sexism are interlocking systems of domination which uphold and sustain one another" (*Yearning* 57, 59). Baldwin adds to and complicates this undertaking by exploring a broader set of interconnected ideologies:

> Well, now we've really, you know, we've walked into very marshy ground because those terms, homosexual, bisexual, heterosexual are 20th-century terms which, for me, really have very little meaning. I've never, myself, in watching myself and watching other people, watching life, been able to discern exactly where the barriers were. ("Race, Hate" 54)

Baldwin's fiction not only plays upon the instability of these terms and the false boundaries between them but also draws this discussion into the related deconstruction of gender itself—specifically, notions of manhood—as that discourse underlies both sex-gender prejudices and racism, revealing, in fact, how these related constructs underpin the entire hegemonic hierarchy.

In "Here Be Dragons," published in *Playboy* in 1985 as "Freaks and the American Ideal of Manhood," Baldwin simultaneously reconstructs and destroys the host of primary labels that constitute the mythology of American identity politics, disputing American/Western notions of dualism that conflate, link, and bifurcate notions of male/heterosexual/white/monied with notions of female/gay/Black/poor (Fig. 1). Figure 1 attempts to represent the myriad interacting strands of bifurcating identity construction represented and debunked by Baldwin throughout his canon, keeping in mind the injunctions made by Judith Butler:

> And clearly, listing the varieties of oppression, as I begin to do, assumes their discrete, sequential coexistence along a horizontal axis that does not describe their convergences within the social field. A vertical model is similarly insufficient; oppressions cannot be summarily ranked, causally related, distributed among planes of "originality" and "derivativeness." (*Trouble* 13)

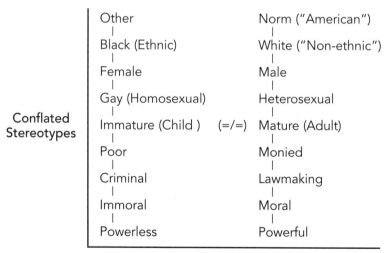

Supposed Oppositional Constructs

Figure 1. Myths of identity constructs and binary oppositions demystified by Baldwin in "Here Be Dragons."

This figure does not present a hierarchy but rather a series of linked constructions and their purported oppositions, though, as Butler's own language implies, written language forces the *appearance* of such a vertical and horizontal imaging. Importantly, though this chapter reads Baldwin's revision of sexual and gendered identity, Butler's analysis reveals the need to recognize the interrelations among "oppressions"—which is, indeed, comparable to Baldwin's own enterprise—and she theoretically validates the manner in which this study deliberately reads the interconnection of sex-gender, racial, and other identity constructs.

The conflations and binary oppositions (of stereotypes) debunked by Baldwin in "Here Be Dragons" (Fig. 1) need little explanation. Conflations of women with children, African Americans with poverty, gay men with "femininity," and so on are prevalent in sexist, racist, and homophobic discourses (such as phrenology), as well as in popular media. Ruth Bleier, in "Science and Belief," uncovers such ideology throughout preemancipation print, mapping the discourse of 'scientists' who "used craniometry to 'confirm all the common prejudices of comfortable white males—that blacks, women, and poor people occupy their subordinate roles by the harsh dictates of nature'" (114). Similarly, in tracing the historical genesis of the concept of heterosexuality, Jonathan Katz asserts: "Each of heterosexuality's founding fathers was also 'white,' and ... the residue of a white perspective may also be found within theories of heterosexuality. Freud's association of 'civilization' and heterosexuality, the 'primitive' and homosexuality, comes to mind" (18). Likewise, links between "the medicine of perversion and the programs of eugenics" (118) and the advent of "racism in its modern 'biologizing,' statist form" (149) are found throughout *The History of Sexuality* (e.g., 26, 54), and though Michel Foucault does not draw these out, neither does he pretend to.

This is done most fully by current authors—those following Foucault and, notably, following Baldwin—such as Elisabeth Young-Bruehl, whose 1993 article "Discriminations: Kinds and Types of Prejudices" stresses that "the topic of how racism and sexism are both distinct and related has been especially slow to surface" and that African Americans who "called for attention to the sexual dimensions of racism were not listened to" (61–62). Young-Bruehl notes the contribution of authors such as Frantz Fanon and Baldwin in this context. In fact, Lee Edelman's chapter "The Part for the (W)hole: Baldwin, Homophobia, and the Fantasmatics of 'Race'" includes a brief reading of *Just Above My Head* but also discusses Baldwin and his work more generally, using it to examine how racism is "suffused with homophobia" (48). Of real interest is that each aspect of demystification is referenced and treated by Baldwin in the short space of his last autobiographical treatise, "Here Be Dragons," which reformulates and crystallizes an enterprise he has undertaken since the late 1940s.

This autobiographical narrative is couched, however, in a political text on androgyny and on the American idea(l) of masculinity as it affects the American idea(l) of manhood. This strategy both universalizes the autobiographical subject and implicates the reader in a system of American mythology and sexual denial that are disrupted, for Baldwin, by homoerotic love. Further, unlike Judith Butler, who views identity as constituted through repeated performance (e.g., "Imitation" 18), Baldwin posits a notion of identity as constituted through the "eye" of another (i.e., one's parents, one's lover), through which the sexual is linked to the Self and because of which one's sexuality is defined by the direction of one's own gaze.

That these mythologies are reinscribed in Baldwin's text only to be deconstructed is characteristic of a number of gay autobiographical texts, accounting for the manner in which Baldwin places identity contestation within the sexual arena.[1] The autobiographical root of this practice for Baldwin himself is identified in "Here Be Dragons" as his youthful relationship with a Spanish-Irish racketeer in Harlem: " All of the American categories of male and female, straight or not, black or white, were shattered, thank heaven, very early in my life" (681). Baldwin's goal in "Here Be Dragons," then, was to shatter these categories and mythologies for others so that they could define themselves as well. In doing so, his essay references many of the issues that characterize gay autobiographies in general, including 1) the idea of being (self-)identified as gay, 2) the impulse toward (gay) liberation, 3) the conscious struggle to define oneself against societal labeling, 4) the attention to the idea of a gay community, and 5) the attention to the development of a political sensibility, as well as the other distinct features and experiential moments that characterize much of gay men's self-writing but that also have parallels in the tenets of the black womanist theory, such as summarized by Jennifer Jordan (107–8).

In undertaking this project in "Here Be Dragons," Baldwin asserts both that "the American idea of sexuality appears to be rooted in the American idea of masculinity" and that "the idea of one's sexuality can only with great violence be divorced or distanced from the idea of the self" (678). He goes on:

> The American *ideal*, then, of sexuality appears to be rooted in the American ideal of masculinity. This ideal has created cowboys and Indians,

good guys and bad guys, punks and studs, tough guys and softies, butch and faggot, black and white. It is an ideal so paralytically infantile that it is virtually forbidden—as an unpatriotic act—that the American boy evolve into the complexity of manhood. (678)

It is through such statements that Baldwin presents and dismantles American myths and stereotypes, implying through rhetorical structure, through the use of the series, and through the overall trajectory of the larger discussion of homophobia and gender prejudice how these stereotypes are both alternately conflated with each other and partitioned into opposing camps (see Fig. 1).

Further, even in navigating the interaction of race and sex in a racist and homophobic society—one in which he is discriminated against as gay in the black community (681–82) and in which he is stereotyped as "black" in the gay (then "queer") and alternative communities of the Greenwich Village (685–86)—Baldwin refuses to be defined by limiting sex-gender stereotypes. Regarding the "queer" world, he asserts that "the mirrors threw back only brief and distorted fragments of myself" (685), and similarly, regarding effeminacy (or derogatory charges of it), he asserts "that many of the people I met were making fun of women, and I didn't see why. *I* certainly needed all of the friends I could get, male *or* female" (685). Here, Baldwin refuses to accept limiting notions of (sexual) identity or to enforce camps created by gender stereotypes, opting for and thereby creating a paradigm of "brother"hood (itself a gender-misnomer).

As the essay progresses, other camps are broken down; Baldwin, for example, through his own persistence, desegregates an Italian bar in the Village:

> it seemed to me that I was no longer black for them and they had ceased to be white for me . . . and exhibited not the remotest interest in whatever my sexual proclivities chanced to be.
>
> They had fought me very hard to prevent this moment, but perhaps we were all much relieved to have got beyond the obscenity of color. (687)

Hence, in the larger discussion of sex, gender, sexism, and homophobia, Baldwin does not lose sight of the impact of race and the manner in which stereotypes work with and against each other—as well as the need to break down all of these stereotypes and the camps created by them—nor does he fail to acknowledge the distinction between stereotype and cultural or individual reality. Like many of his essays, then, "Here Be Dragons" is the story of the racialization of individual consciousness in America and the subsequent need to disrupt this progression. Here, in addition to that story and inseparable from it, is the story of sexualization (and engendering) and the subsequent need to disrupt that progression. While the complexity of Baldwin's essay cannot be rendered here in its entirety, even this brief reading reveals how Baldwin's discourse on sexuality and gender in such pieces engages a myriad of theoretical and political issues at the core of current feminist, gay, and gender studies.

The discussion in "Here Be Dragons" is preceded by an ongoing discussion found in Baldwin's nonfiction that theorizes the sex-gender complex and related stereotypes. Beginning with "The Male Prison," published in 1954 as "Gide as Husband and Homosexual," Baldwin addresses homosexuality and related gender issues, and as early as "Carmen Jones: The Dark Is Light Enough" (1955), Baldwin points out how sexuality is linked to racialized bodies in stereotypical ways by popular American media. Though the complexity of such arguments cannot be rendered here, these articles clearly identify the persistence of this discourse in Baldwin's nonfiction canon. In fact, "The Discovery of What It Means to Be an American" contains what may be read as a statement of Baldwin's overarching sex-gender enterprise: "to free ourselves of the myth of America and try to find out what is really happening here" (175). Here and elsewhere, one finds Baldwin prefiguring discussions in the contemporary theoretical arena regarding the postmodern conceptions of identity and of the relationship between identity and the simulacra of mass-media images such as those discussed by Jean Baudrillard (166–72).

Such a reading of Baldwin's nonfiction reveals that he fills gaps in theoretical practice such as those noted by Joseph A. Boone and Michael Cadden, who "lament . . . the invisibility of heterosexual, bisexual, and gay male feminists both in contemporary literature and, despite their demonstrable feminist activity, in the culture at large" (6). Such an interpretation also reveals that Baldwin fills gaps found in feminist and black feminist criticisms—the latter focussing upon the double- or triple-marginality of black and radical black women as these groups constitute exclusive, counter-mythologizing bodies—repeating the paucity of male voices noted by Boone and Cadden.

Despite Marcus Klein's suggestion that Baldwin substitutes sexuality for identity (29), Baldwin's attention to the constructed nature of both sexuality and identity does not sustain this reading. The task undertaken here is the excavation of how this theoretical undertaking—demystification of American mythology through the rubric of gender—is rendered with complexity in Baldwin's short fiction, specifically through his critique of "masculinity."

In fact, any reading of Baldwin's fiction reveals him to be progenitor of many of the theoretical formulations currently associated with feminist, gay, and gender studies, making it possible to raise questions central to current critical practice within these fields in the context of his works. How are representations of masculinity and of the homoerotic placed in the context of national identity politics, social hierarchy, and personal psychology, and how is patriarchy seen to function in the texts of black (gay) male authors? To what degree does self-conscious gay fiction reify or resist the social construction of the gay subject as Other, and how does Baldwin's narrative and rhetorical strategy function across this continuum?

In suggesting that gendered discourse within Baldwin's *fiction* is both representational and theoretical, this chapter focuses on the politics of gender representation in this work and on the links Baldwin identifies between sex-gender ideology and other facets of identity construction. The way Baldwin re-visions notions of gender and sexuality and debunks conflations of this ideology with other identity signifiers ultimately deconstructs the (American) idea(l) of masculinity (or manhood) as it affects and is critiqued through characters presenting a range of genders and sexualities. Baldwin ultimately reveals in his fiction how sexism and heterosexism affect women and men in a gendered society and how gender constructs are inseparably linked to race, class, and other identity categories.

"MASCULINITY" AND AMERICAN MYTHOLOGY: "THE MAN CHILD" AND OTHER STORIES

Baldwin sees violence against African-American males (and unlike Cleaver, gay men and women) in psychoanalytical terms. For him violence against male homosexuals is society's acting out of a collective mirror stage of infantilism. It is fear of confrontation with oneself and fear of touch from others. (Waldrep 174)

Gender constructs and sex-gender prejudices most often are critiqued by Baldwin through depictions that reveal how social constructs function negatively in society and produce harmful behavior that resonates within and across the spectrum of American identity politics. Notions of masculinity (or manhood)—creating gendered violence, homophobia, and sexism—are shown to place limitations on lived experience, individual potential, and interpersonal relationships, and are shown to interact with other prejudices and ideologies, here examined primarily in terms of race.

Examples from *Going to Meet the Man* reveal that Baldwin's critique of the notion of masculinity—a notion inherently heterosexual and intrinsically related to other discourses—began in his early short stories as revealed through heterosexual characters. And though his strongest critique of "masculinity" appears primarily in gay characters, this reading focuses on how Baldwin uses heterosexual male characters in selected short fiction in this enterprise. This critique cannot be separated from the general critique found in his larger canon but is undertaken here to preview that larger critique, to give attention to characters often overlooked in discussions of Baldwin and sex-gender constructs, and because Baldwin himself begins his critique through these characters.

When *Going to Meet the Man* was published by Dial Press in 1965 under the editorial supervision of E. L. Doctorow, the publishers asserted of the collection that "every situation is firmly rooted in the world as we know it today, and the characters are so accurately perceived and truthfully rendered that the overall effect is almost musical—in that we may still hear music long after it is played" (dust jacket). Although W. J. Weatherby suggests that critics were "generally respectful" and offers a typical example from *The Saturday Review* (268), biographer James Campbell writes that the collection "was not well received," with Campbell himself critiquing the title story for its "position of moral bias" and reading the collection itself in terms of "the possibility of an actual decline in the quality of his [Baldwin's] work" (203).

While no story in the collection has been anthologized more frequently or received more critical attention than "Sonny's Blues," which has garnered a plethora of scholarly articles and the most rigorous treatments, literary critics have given select attention to individual pieces, treating form, symbols and racial/national themes and treating the work in the context of Baldwin's larger canon.[2] Such critical attention has re-visioned initial critical reception of the work. In fact, increased attention to "Going to Meet the Man" (as well as *Giovanni's Room* and *Another Country*) with the advent of gay and gender studies has allowed a re-vision of the "narrative of decline" as Campbell and others have applied it to Baldwin's works—"Going to Meet the Man" itself already having been re-claimed from Campbell's later valuation through attention to its complex treatment of gender studies issues.

Many of the stories in *Going to Meet* (with the exceptions of "Sonny's Blues" and "Going to Meet the Man") have received sparse critical attention, but none has been more overlooked than "The Man Child." According to biographer David Leeming,

> An improbable tale of veiled homosexuality culminating in a child's murder at the hands of his father's best friend, it is of interest to the Baldwin scholar as the only fiction of his (besides *Giovanni's Room*) that contains no black characters. In fact, the first version of the piece had been written during the same period as *Giovanni*. (248)

Two bonds are emphasized in the work—that between Jamie and his dog, and that between Jamie and Eric's father, the former (Jamie) having driven his wife to run away and the latter (Eric's father) having helped to create the circumstances that caused his wife's temporary hospitalization. That Eric's father symbolizes the white, monied, ruling class is stressed repeatedly in the text. Jamie, for example, calls Eric's father "the giant-killer, the hunter, the lover—the real old Adam, that's you." He goes on: "I know you're going to cover the earth. I know the world depends on men like you" (55). This kind of language is repeated by Jamie in other parts of the text (e.g., 61) and is substantiated when Eric's father provides Eric with an extended narrative of patriarchal hegemony regarding his inheritance of the land (59–60).

If this facet of the text is heavy-handed, other important implications of the story are complex and subtle. That the hierarchical relationship between Eric's father and Jamie parallels the hierarchical and abusive relationship between Jamie and his dog is understated but repeated throughout the text, the dog alternately representing the friendship of the men (49) and serving as an alter ego for Jamie—conveying his uselessness (51) and his displaced anger (57)—that symbolically and vicariously reveals Jamie's debasement at the hands of Eric's father (53).

Though the homosocial facet of their relationship is repeatedly stressed (50, 54, 62), Baldwin also reveals the functioning class distinction between them; Jamie works on Eric's father's land (49) and resents his friend's prosperity: "You got it all—the wife, the kid, the house, and all the land" (54). More subtle is how the text implies a homoerotic subtext to the homosocial bond between the two men, who "had grown up together, gone to war together, . . . never . . . to be divided" (49):

"Hell, no," said Jamie, "I'm not old. I can still do all the things we used to do." He put his elbows on the table, grinning. "I haven't ever told you, have I, about the things we used to do?"

"No, you haven't, . . . and I certainly don't want to hear about them now."

"He wouldn't tell you anyway," said Eric's father, "he knows what I'd do to him if he did." (52)

That this passage refers to a homoerotic bond is further implied by another exchange between Jamie and Eric's father (55), and is subtly suggested in the moments of affection and tenderness between them (55, 57). Hence, the implication is that the homoerotic urge—or rather, the inability to either affirm or acknowledge it—is, at least in part, what undermines the white male hegemony.

This type of interaction between the homosocial and the homo-erotic is central to Eve Kosofsky Sedgwick's analysis in *Between Men: English Literature and Male Homosocial Desire*:

To draw the "homosocial" back into the orbit of "desire," of the poten-tially erotic, then, is to hypothesize the potential unbrokenness of a continuum between homosocial and homosexual—a continuum whose visibility, for men, in our society, is radically disrupted. (1–2)

In suggesting that this continuum is operant in Baldwin's characteri-zation of the relationship between Jamie and Eric's father—that their inability to participate in or recognize the need for the continuum destroys them—I am arguing that Baldwin participates in both femi-nist and gay liberation imperatives, making obvious the area in which these constitute the same discourse and the same practice.

Even more subtle, however, are the implications that Jamie claims some right of ownership over Eric and that Eric's parents, as well as Jamie, have some foreknowledge of their son's murder. This is evident in an exchange between Jamie and Eric's father:

"Little Eric's getting big," he heard his father say.

"Yes," said Jamie, "they grow fast. It won't be long now."

"Won't be long *what*?" he heard his father ask.

"Why, before he starts skirt-chasing like his Daddy used to do," said Jamie. (53)

The concern of Eric's father is telling, as is the description of events following Eric's mother's miscarriage. Eric's mother "shrunk within herself, away from them all, . . . but, oddly, and most particularly, away from Jamie. . . . [It was] as though she had been startled by some new aspect of something she had always known" (62–63). Similarly, Jamie's assertion that "a man's got a right to do as he likes with whatever's his" (51) and his overtly symbolic act of giving Eric the first piece of his birthday cake "on the silver blade" of a cutting knife (61) foreshadow his murder of Eric at the end of the story, both having implications for the reading of that later scene.

The effect that this construct of manhood in the white male hegemony has upon white women is evident in the history of Eric's mother and the noted absence of Jamie's runaway wife, placing this story in the canon detailed by Sandra M. Gilbert and Susan Gubar in *The Madwoman in the Attic* of studies on and literary manifestations of "the ways in which patriarchal socialization literally makes women sick, both physically and mentally" (53). That Jamie's wife has escaped this fate by running away is used by Eric's father as evidence of Jamie's lack of "masculinity" (e.g., 54, 56) and to negatively characterize gay (and/or homosocial) desire (54). Jamie is thus an obvious example of the dying hegemony, having lost his land and his wife, living a life of isolation and alcoholism, and having no heirs in a patriarchal system where these are prized. Both men, however, catalyze their own fates, symbolically spending their evenings getting drunk at The Rafters.

Eric's father, through his own greed, also creates his own demise, for Jamie—whose land Eric's father has bought cheaply—is prompted to kill Eric, an only heir. Symbolically (if heavy-handedly), Eric is killed by Jamie the day after his father takes him to survey their land (Eric having imitated his father, "looking over [the land] calmly, pleased, knowing that everything he saw belonged to him" [64]). Jamie's decision to carry out this murder becomes evident after Jamie is embarrassed by Eric's father at his own birthday party—after which he becomes "more silent than ever" (62)—and appears to be cemented by the pronouncement that Eric's mother can no longer have children (62). "'This land,' said Jamie, 'will belong to no one'" (66), even though he had just asserted his love for Eric's father. It is because this love is not returned adequately (e.g., at the birthday party) that Jamie is compelled to act, an implication evident in the narrative structure, which largely recounts the events of the birthday party in the past tense, pointing to this event as a causal turning point. Eric's plea—that if Jamie spares his life and kills his father instead, he (Eric) will be Jamie's little boy forever and give Jamie all of the land—clearly establishes the work's pathos as the demise of the monied class.

This is also the pathos of "Going to Meet the Man," which is perhaps Baldwin's most obvious, focused, and pointed treatment of the links between racial and sexual constructs. The lynching in this story is both the site of Jesse's racialization and Baldwin's metaphor for this process: Jesse's memory moves from Otis, "a black friend" of his childhood (208), to "the bad nigger" (212), "the man" who is being punished (215), and then to "the black body" "on the ground," "spread-eagled with what had been a wound between what had been legs" (217). That is, racialization proceeds from the idea of an African American as an individual to the idea of the African American as an indistinguishable racialized and sexualized (de-sexed) black body—a body identified not as an individual but as a racial and sexual category, a body made sexual not only in its nudity but also through the very act of castration that also signals (e.g., for Jesse) the threat of this race-sex category. Roger Whitlow, in fact, describes lynching itself as a sexual experience, "a white southern folk ritual, a primitive sex rite in which the society experiences, through the mutilation of the 'outcast' figure, a communal orgasm" (196). According to Peter Freese, the "socialization" afforded by Jesse's experience of the lynching inextricably links Jesse's racial and sexual attitudes (177). "For Jesse, the sadist," he says, "sexual excitement is linked with the notion of black skin, accompanied by fear, released by violence" because his "sexual awakening is connected with the violent emasculation of a black man" (178).

For Jesse, sexual (ab)use of black women, rape of black women, and unjust arrest of black women "come to the same thing" (199). This information—Jesse's desire for sexual encounter with a black woman in order to overcome his impotence—is conveyed at the story's beginning, perhaps implying that his arousal in the company of black men is a form of substitution, with black men "feminized" in his sexual yearning. Rather, it seems clear that blackness itself is eroticized by Jesse, both alluring and threatening. Blackness itself (black culture, black color) is thus "feminized" as the object of Jesse's self-perceived heterosexual desire and thereby relegated to a lower position in the hegemonic hierarchy in terms of both race and gender. In this story, Baldwin both recreates and debunks these conflations within American mythology.

Those who socially defy Jesse's perception of their identity are then social and literal outlaws, and Baldwin both metaphorically and literally draws upon Jesse's representation as a police officer. The similar characterization made policemen (including officer Bell in *If Beale Street Could Talk* [133, 212]) reinforce the sociopolitical links being made between racism and sexualization of the black body (especially on the sadomasochistic level), as well as morality and law (see Fig. 1). As police officers, these men reflect the moral and legal order of the community at large: In his youth, they were "models" for Jesse, for "what it meant to be a man" (205). "Manhood" is here equated with racism, (false) moral authority and (immoral) legality, all of which are demystified in the representation of Jesse. Thus, "The Man Child" and "Going to Meet the Man" both dramatize Baldwin's assertion that "when a structure . . . becomes too expensive for the world to afford, when it is no longer responsive to the needs of the world, that structure is doomed" ("White Racism" 442).

Baldwin's critique of the American notion of masculinity is found in other stories in *Going to Meet the Man*. In "The Rockpile" and "The Outing," it is seen via the characterization of Gabriel Grimes; in "Sonny's Blues" and "This Morning, This Evening, So Soon," such normative American identity constructs are linked, respectively, to class and race. Turning to "Previous Condition," however, one may note the exchange between Peter and his landlady:

> "This is a white neighborhood. I don't rent to colored people. Why don't you go on uptown, like you belong?"
> "I can't stand niggers," I told her. . . . I wanted to kill her. . . . I was aware of my body under the bathrobe; and it was as though I had done something wrong, something monstrous, years ago, which no one had forgotten and for which I would be killed. (76–77)

Passages such as this reveal both the source and effect of Peter's bitterness. Further, this scene contains an associative link between Peter's racialized body (as it is racialized by the presence and attitudes of his landlady) and a body thereby sexualized, both in imagined nudity (nudity at once revealing blackness and sexuality) and in the sexual tension within the scene, both covertly conveyed by the landlady's forceful intrusion into Peter's private (domestic) space (the symbolic penetration of cultural rape) and explicitly conveyed by the their verbal exchange: "Get out of the door. . . . I want to get dressed. . . . You wanna come in and watch me?" (76). Interestingly, this parallels how Ruth is typed by her family in "Come Out the Wilderness," in which her assumed sexual activity leads her brother to call her "black and dirty" (181), an association that leads her to Paul, whom she wants to "release her from the prison" of the color of her skin (195). These conflations also function in her own pathway of desire and relational choices. In Baldwin's representation, then, African American men are sexualized because of racism, which also applies to African American women—who are racialized because of sexism as well, even within the African American community. In each of these cases, "blackness" is a negative qualifier, one linked to an assumption about sexual desire or sexual activity.

Here, in refusing to be limited by stereotypes, Peter almost unquestioningly *accepts* these very stereotypes, and these stereotypes resonate not only on the level of race but also on the level of gender, toward women of both races: "I know what I'm going to do. I'm gonna go back to my people where I belong and find me a nice, black nigger wench and raise a flock of babies" (81). One finds that Peter reflects upon the African American community in purely negative and stereotypical terms that combine racial and gendered attitudes; his reaction to prejudice and indoctrination rob him of the ability to recognize his racial heritage outside of this warped perspective so that he can neither use his past nor feel at home in his own community: he has "got no story" (84–85). "Previous Condition," "Come Out the Wilderness," and "Going to Meet the Man," like "The Man Child," detail the indoctrination of central characters into the limiting racial or sex-gender constructs operant in American mythology, linking these identity qualifiers and calling for revision of them.

Within this critique, one also may note the prevalence of children as centers of consciousness and as minor characters, as well as the inclusion of childhood episodes for adult protagonists. These include (in addition to Eric, Jesse, Peter and Ruth) John Grimes, who is coming of age in the atmosphere of terror wrought by his father ("Rockpile" and "Outing"); Sonny and his brother, living in the wake of family and social destruction wrought by the perpetual car (of racism) that claims their uncle and so many of the children around them ("Sonny's Blues"); and little Paul, who is about to encounter American racism for the first time as his father returns home ("This Morning"). Baldwin thus constructs a variety of narratives that chronicle the process of maturation and highlight ideological irruptions in it created by societal ideologies, this narrative recurrence itself drawing the reader's attention to Baldwin's critique of indoctrination into American mythology. In titling the collection *Going to Meet the Man*, Baldwin renders coming of age in the wake of hegemonic ideology as an encounter with normative assumptions symbolically specified as institutionally white and male in origin—i.e., as "the man." In using "the man" to specify this discourse, Baldwin, as did the popular colloquialism of his time, underscores the gendered denominator of this discourse, rendering "masculinity" as a model of identity resulting in a larger behavioral complex that is linked to broader societal ideologies.

"MASCULINITY" AND NARRATIVE STRATEGY: CRITICAL AND THEORETICAL IMPLICATIONS

In ironic contrast to his reception in the early 1960s and his own preference to take more of a public stand on racial rather than sexual issues, Baldwin's literary stature has a strong presence in the growing field of lesbian and gay studies. (Spurlin 179)

Any reading of the critical reception of Baldwin as a gay writer reveals a historical imperative to make audible gay voices within the African American (literary, critical, and socio-political) arena, and more comprehensive assessments of such reception are just beginning to be made. Lorelei Cederstrom's 1984 article "Love, Race and Sex in the Novels of James Baldwin" is joined by Emmanuel Nelson's more comprehensive 1991 treatment in "Critical Deviance: Homophobia and the Reception of James Baldwin's Fiction" and by William J. Spurlin's "Rhetorical Hermeneutics and Gay Identity Politics: Rethinking American Cultural Studies." According to Nelson, silence on the part of "at least some of the critics" "is a deliberate ploy," "a carefully defined political posture," "a strategy of enforcing invisibility" (95). In excavating the notion of masculinity as it appears in Baldwin's short fiction, this chapter pinpointed moments in which this oeuvre speaks against a variety of exclusions by linking feminist, gay, and gender studies issues. Moreover, though its exclusion of the homoerotic is only part of Baldwin's critique of American "masculinity," such a reading is incomplete without consideration of the manner in which narrative and rhetorical strategy function within his revisionary gender enterprise and specifically within gay studies theory. The strategies used in the short fiction characterize Baldwin's literary approach and find consistent parallels in his longer fiction, some of which will also be referenced here.

Among the narrative devices employed by Baldwin to control the readers' perception of homoerotic material include the use of Eric's father ("Man Child") as an interpretative commentator on the construct of "manhood" (e.g., as lacking in Jamie), and the use of Jesse ("Going to Meet") as a figure through whom to construct the ideological link between racialized and sexualized desire (eroticizing blackness, male and female, through the heterosexual gaze). A parallel in the long fiction is found in the character Hall Montana's rendering of Arthur's history in *Just Above My Head* (as seen in his commentary on Arthur's experience with Guy). However, Baldwin's use of heterosexual (or heterosexually identified) characters as surrogates through which to explore and voices through which to comment upon gay/homoerotic experience may be seen to also serve a silencing function, "naturalizing" gay experience at the same time that the subject is "denied the authority of cultural voice" (DuCille 105). Such narration allows one to level against this strategy Arthur Flannigan-Saint-Aubin's primary contention with the writing collected in *Brother to Brother: New Writings by Black Gay Men* (1991):

> the black heterosexual father, uncle, brother . . . provides the tone and determines the ultimate meaning encoded in the text. . . . The reader, in other words, must play the role of a black heterosexual reader because he is the one who is encoded and dramatized within the text and he is the one, therefore, who gives the text coherence. (386)

Flannigan-Saint-Aubin finds this forced affinity part of the text's failure to create "a real space," "a safe place," "for the black gay male reader" (383), a replication of exclusion and one that dates Baldwin's fiction within the evolving canon of gay fiction. The reader, however, must determine how successful this structural technique is and whether (or when) the use of the heterosexual "surrogate" to "authenticate" gay experience in fact reifies the very societal paradigm it purports to write against.

Reading Eric's father within the homoerotic subtext of "The Man Child" affords another analysis of Baldwin's narrative technique and other parallels with his longer fiction. It allows one to apply questions regarding narrative strategy to the "super" "masculinity" of gay (or bisexual) male characters in Baldwin's longer fiction—such as Eric Jones in *Another Country* and David (e.g., his reaction to the "fairies") in *Giovanni's Room*—whose stereotypical "masculine" characterization allows John Lash to hypothesize the "cult of phallicism, the fear and admiration and worship of the male sex organ" (133). While David's behavior may be seen as debunked via his characterization—as is the abuse of Jamie by Eric's father in "The Man Child"—as the manifestation of his own self-hatred, Eric Jones's characterization is not dismissed so easily. One may consider George Chauncey, Jr.'s discussion in "Christian Brotherhood or Sexual Perversion? Homosexual Identi-ties and the Construction of Sexual Boundaries in the World War I Era." Chauncey describes how gay military men in Newport formed a known community and how they defined gay identity—the term "queer," for example, being reserved for "passive" sexual partners only, while the "trade" who interacted with them were considered heterosexual by both themselves and military officials (296–97). Interpreted within the terms of Chauncey's analysis and within the homosocial/homoerotic fabric of the story, the characterization of Eric's father—despite his symbolic representation as the dying white hegemony—also may be described as fulfilling the same textual and political role as the surro-gate heterosexual narrative voice, dangerously reifying the notion of the heterosexual "norm" and implicitly suggesting that stereotypical (i.e., sexist and bifurcating) gender roles determine (acceptable) gay identity, replicating the dualism found in American mythology.

Alternately, one may consider Eric's father, as well as Eric Jones *(Another Country)* and others, in light of Richard Dyer's discussion of gay stereotypes. Of the "Macho," Dyer asserts:

> It is an exaggerated masculinity, and indeed its very exaggeratedness marks it off from the conventional masculine look on which it is based. . . . Camp, drag and macho self-consciously play the signs of gen-der, and it is in the play and exaggeration that an alternative sexuality is implied—sexuality, that is, that recognizes itself as in a problematic relationship to the conventional conflation of sexuality and gender. (40, 42)

Dyer's reading, like that of Butler, allows one to consider the subver-sive potential of the "Macho," as it problematizes "masculinity" by revealing its constructed nature, posing an alternative in "super" "mas-culine" "drag." As theorists suggest of drag, such "masculinity" may be seen as "role-playing" that "de-natures identity and sexuality, con-fronting heterosexist essentialism with the artifices of gender and the errant play of desire" (Tyler 32). Allen Ellenzweig makes a similar argu-ment in his seminal text *The Homoerotic Photograph: Male Images from Durieu/Delacroix to Mapplethorpe,* discussing, for example, the sanction-ing of male nudes through classical imagery and male bonding rites (i.e., wrestling), techniques "used to reinforce the very eroticism they are meant to sanitize" (34). Considered through this framework, the use of surrogate voices and the characterization of figures such as Eric's father, Eric Jones, and Jesse may be seen as acts of resistance in which Baldwin forces reader repositioning, as also seen in his rhetorical use of the third person and of the discourse of androgyny in "Here Be Dragons."

This strategy is seen to have even greater revolutionary potential when one considers arguments such as those by Eve Sedgwick and Lee Edelman. Edelman's *Homographesis: Essays in Gay Literature and Cultural Theory* suggests that the need to identify "homosexual difference" (3), either in literature or in bodies, serves both the political right and the political left (as alternative readings made here of Baldwin's strategy would verify). Pointing to the manner in which society has attempted to morphologize gay communities, Edelman uses the term "homograph" to refer to the hidden difference that threatens to disrupt the basis of heterosexual identity. Characterization of Eric Jones and of Eric's father in "The Man Child" and the use of surrogates plays upon the idea of the "homograph," the invisible difference, by disrupting gender categories as they function within the gay community—forgoing the "feminization" of the gay character or of homoerotic desire (as is the case, for example, in the characterization of Jamie).

As Nelson asserts, "Baldwin's heightened maturity is also evident in his refusal to categorize men into the conventional and rigidly distinct camps of homosexuals and heterosexuals. He views human sexuality in terms of a homosexual-heterosexual continuum" ("Novels" 14). In fact, heterosexually identified characters like Eric's father (paralleled by Rufus and Vivaldo in *Another Country*) allow Baldwin to separate sex from self-perceived sexual identity altogether, the homoerotic being available to all men. Baldwin's narrative strategy may even heighten what Edelman describes as an actual "assault." In reading Baldwin in the context of Fanon, he suggests that the homoerotic "signifies for the dominant order as an act of aggression," representation of gay male sexuality, like "blackness," being

> an assault that sodomitically unmans the very body through which that dominant order represents itself; for the eye compelled to 'take in' such a vision paradigmatically experiences the involuntary penetration that the subject fears to suffer elsewhere. (65)

Use of heterosexual and "male" engendered characters works to preclude the heterosexist reader's desired distance from this "assault."

Through narrative strategy and characterization, then, Baldwin obliterates the traditional categories of sexual preference and gender as they are typed onto heterosexual and gay male characters, re-visioning the sexual Self and the gendered Self by calling for the revision of "masculinity" and the redefinition of "manhood," even if gender divisions often remain intact as they are applied to women characters or male-female relationships. According to Kendall Thomas, "Moreover, Baldwin's own experience persuaded him that 'homosexual' was not a 'noun' but a 'verb,'" Baldwin speaking in terms of those whom he loved and those who loved him (60). Eric's father, unlike David and Giovanni, also is characterized in terms much broader than sexual preference (e.g., class, profession, and symbolic function) resisting the notion that sexual identity is all-encompassing. Here and elsewhere, Baldwin simultaneously reveals the complicity of African American communities in ideological constructions and indicates how sex-gender and racial images are separate from and observed by the so "marked" subject. By existing within and thereby disrupting such boundaries (on the printed page), Baldwin emphasizes the constructedness of these categories as well as the relationships between them. The implications are both overtly political and theoretical, directly engaging the projects of gay and lesbian studies.

According to Adrienne Rich, one must view "the institution of heterosexuality itself as a beachhead of male dominance" (64):

> I mean the term *lesbian continuum* to include a range . . . of woman-identified experience. . . . embrac[ing] many forms of primary intensity between and among women, including the sharing of a rich inner life, the bonding against male tyranny, the giving and receiving of practical and political support. (79–80)

By revealing a political agenda that acts across the boundaries of sexual preferences, Rich's continuum also seems to point toward a sex-gender continuum, forcing one to question the placement of men—gay, heterosexual, or bisexual—who also share "a rich inner life, the bonding against male tyranny," etc., and who also are affected negatively by the myth of compulsory heterosexuality and by male hegemony. Baldwin allows one to suggest a revision of Rich's paradigm, particularly as its position needlessly replicates a form of exclusionism. Rich's assertion that "part of lesbian experience is, obviously, to be found where lesbians, lacking a coherent female community, have shared a kind of social life and common cause with homosexual men" (80) denies that such cross-gendered political bonding may have any richness of its own; it is described in terms of "lack."

Though Rich argues against the inclusion of men in her continuum, her issues suggest another point of view:

> The lesbian trapped in the closet, the woman imprisoned in prescriptive ideas of the "normal," share the pain of blocked options, broken connections, lost access to self-definition freely and powerfully assumed. . . . We have been stalled in a maze of false dichotomies[,] . . . but the absence of choice remains the great unacknowledged reality. (88)

The applicability of such statements to male gay experience can easily be gleaned. What may be more difficult to ascertain is how the heterosexual male—even the heterosexist male—also is "imprisoned in prescriptive ideas" that thwart "access to self-definition," that is, the manner in which men are engendered. What may be equally difficult to ascertain is how men, like women, have also sought to undermine the oppression of male hegemony. By revealing patriarchy's impact on heterosexual and gay male characters (such as Eric's father and Jamie), by showing the oppressive nature of negative gendered discourse and its oppressive functioning within male homosocial/homosexual communities (also as seen via Eric's father and Jamie), and by depicting women both as they are negatively affected by sexism (such as Eric's waning and barren mother and Jamie's runaway wife) and as they provide verbal critiques of behavior enacted as "masculinity," Baldwin himself re-visions Rich's lesbian continuum to include those male voices able to question such prescriptions, constituting what can be called a cross-gendered "feminist" continuum—here specified as feminist because its political aims originate in that ideological complex. Though women's verbal critique is gleaned more readily in Baldwin's longer fiction (e.g., via Florence in *Go Tell*), as is the effect of (hetero)sexism on the gay community (e.g., *Giovanni's Room* and *Just Above*), it also is clear that all of these critiques began in his short fiction, here noted particularly in "The Man Child," but also visible in characters including Ruth ("Come Out"), Jesse (*Going to Meet the Man*) and Peter ("Previous").

One cannot assert the need for such a re-vision without questioning the political implications of such a recommendation. Rich makes clear (1) that women in general and lesbian women in particular are affected specifically by particular brands of sexualization (81), (2) that "woman-identification is a source of energy, a potential springhead of female power" (88), (3) that lesbian experience must be seen as more than "female versions of male homosexuality" (80), and (4) that there is a particular need to recover women's/lesbians' historiography. What is at stake, then, is the possibility that the inclusion of male voices—the expansion of this rubric through the inclusion of authors such as Baldwin—may subvert the unique actualities of women's oppression, may subvert the real need to recover women's voices and authority, may subvert the power of the women-bonding-against-male-oppression imperative. Nevertheless, Baldwin and Rich share the need to deconstruct the sex-gendered codes that maintain patriarchy.

TOWARD A CONCLUSION: GENDER REINITIATION

Baldwin dares to speak out against racism and to write poignantly of homosexuality while not conforming to black or white social expectations about masculinity himself. This cultural resistance . . . was regarded, in the context of the early sixties and the rhetorical strategies used to represent him as a homosexual, as an assault on dominant cultural practices. (Spurlin 178)

The reading of "Here Be Dragons" undertaken above uncovers it as a political treatise demanding the disruption of the (African) American subject's indoctrination into the racialized, engendered, and sexualized discourse of the American milieu. Similarly, readings of Baldwin's short stories have revealed that "the coming of age story" is rewritten pervasively as "the narrative of indoctrination" in Baldwin's canon through child protagonists and childhood episodes in the short stories. Moving beyond the scope of this chapter, such episodes are revisited in the longer narratives through all of the major protagonists—little Eric revisited in David *(Giovanni's Room)* and Eric Jones *(Another Country)*, Jesse and Otis revisited through Eric and LeRoy *(Another Country)*, Peter revisited through Leo Proudhammer *(Tell Me How Long the Train's Been Gone)*, Ruth revisited through Tish *(If Beale Street Could Talk)* and Julia *(Just Above)*, Elizabeth and Richard *(Go Tell It)* revisited through Tish and Fonny *(Beale Street)*, Johnnie and David ("The Outing") revisited through Arthur and Jimmy *(Just Above)*, Crunch revisited through Jimmy Miller *(Just Above)*, and so on.

These narratives afford reconsideration of Marcus Klein's assertion that "Baldwin's chief occupation is actually his own childhood. 'Identity' is something that one once had, or at least almost had, in the past, in childhood. And indeed, the child who has not yet quite defined himself but who has not yet either been lost is, an inventory would prove, Baldwin's favorite subject" (20). What one finds is that Baldwin's occupation with childhood and its link to identity formation undertakes a rewriting of the American coming of age narrative at the same time that it re-visions a variety of the interrelated identity constructs into which the subject is thereby initiated—gender, specifically "masculinity," functioning centrally among these. On this level, genre—that of the *bildungsroman*—becomes the site of a larger rhetorical strategy used by Baldwin to comment upon American mythology—revisiting and revising the notion of maturity, the effects of indoctrination, the quest for self-definition, the prescribed "ideals" of such a quest, the (relational) landscape in which the quest takes place, the site of Otherness in which the "hero" is tested, and actuality of "danger" (the touch of another) encountered on such a journey.

In comparing southern coming of age narratives by William Faulkner and Padgett Powell, for example, Marcel Arbeit finds the construction of ideal sociological landscapes with "rigid moral codes" where "boys, coming of age, can easily come to terms with the omnipresent issues of race, identity and morals, and learn to face immorality and evil in the surrounding world more efficiently" (282). In Reinhard Kuhn's wider ranging analysis of the archetype of "the enigmatic child"—characterized as "a stranger to this world, sufficient unto himself, incapable of communication and yet the bearer of important tidings" (262)—he suggests that this trope signals "a combination of nostalgia for the past and a longing for a new and transcendental future" but is also "a profound tragedy, for on the one hand he [the child] is eternal and on the other hand constantly menaced by extinction. . . . [H]e must die, for if he did not he would grow up to be an ordinary mortal" (263).

While this is true for little Eric, his slaughter at the hands of Jamie itself signals a "transcendental future"—the demise of the system of patriarchal indoctrination symbolized by the narrative of inheritance that he accepts but which dies with him. More importantly, it signals an interruption in the ideology that disrupts transcendental maturity, seen on the level at which the narrative itself identifies homophobia, classism, sexism, and other ("masculine") ideologies as what (through Jamie) ends Eric's maturation process (i.e., by causing his death). In the transition from the short story to the longer narrative, Baldwin complicates the process of indoctrination (continuing his critiques of engendered camps) and offers resistance in the form of pedagogical alternatives. Both Eric Jones *(Another Country)* and Arthur Montana *(Just Above)* are seen to create (socio-ideological) spaces in which the ideological and behavioral qualifiers of "masculinity" are challenged, creating "other countries."

Baldwin's rewriting of the American coming-of-age narrative, then, critiques the moral codes that Arbeit finds to be idealized in Faulkner and Powell and challenges the equation of "grow[ing] up to be an ordinary mortal" with "maturity." Baldwin, in fact, is specifically concerned that the child *does* grow up and also that the child grows out of the simplistic binary oppositions (Fig. 1) sustained by the "paralytically infantile" American ideal of masculinity ("Here Be" 678). In the process, Baldwin re-visions feminist and gay studies theories and enters the emerging field of gender studies by placing these theories in the context of one another and within broader identity politics—a process through which he broadens the scope of critical fields and creates new linkages over old boundaries.

NOTES

Epigraph: James Baldwin, *Another Country* (New York: Vintage International), 1962, 212–13.

1. Representative works include Paul Monette's National Book Award winning autobiography *Becoming a Man,* historian Martin Duberman's *Cures: A Gay Man's Odyssey,* and Simon Watney's critical article "Ordinary Boys."

2. This scholarship on "Sonny's Blues" includes articles by Keith E. Byerman, "Words and Music: Narrative Ambiguity in 'Sonny's Blues,'" John M. Reilly, "'Sonny's Blues': James Baldwin's Image of Black Community," and articles collected by Therman B. O'Daniel in *James Baldwin: A Critical Evaluation.* In the context of Baldwin's other works, see articles by Edward Margolies, who treats Baldwin's rendering of the black church in "The Negro Church: James Baldwin and the Christian Vision," and C.W.E. Bigsby, who focuses largely on racial issues in "The Divided Mind of James Baldwin."

WORKS CITED

Arbeit, Marcel. "Coming of Age in Faulkner's *The Reivers* and Padgett Powell's *Edisto.*" In *Faulkner, His Contemporaries, and His Posterity,* ed. Waldemar Zacharasiewicz, 276–83. Transatlantic Perspectives 2. Tübingen, Germany: A. Francke Verlag, 1993.

Baldwin, James. *Another Country.* New York: Dial, 1962.

———. "Carmen Jones: The Dark Is Light Enough." In *The Price of the Ticket: Collected Nonfiction, 1948–1985.* New York: St. Martin's, 107–12. Originally published as "Life Straight in De Eye," *Commentary,* January 1955.

———. "The Discovery of What It Means to Be an American." In *The Price of the Ticket: Collected Nonfiction, 1948–1985.* New York: St. Martin's, 171–76. Originally published in *The New York Times Book Review,* 25 January 1959.

———. "Here Be Dragons." In *The Price of the Ticket: Collected Nonfiction, 1948–1985.* New York: St. Martin's, 677–90. Originally published as "Freaks and the American Ideal of Manhood," *Playboy,* January 1985.

———. "The Male Prison." In *The Price of the Ticket: Collected Nonfiction, 1948–1985.* New York: St. Martin's, 101–5. Originally published as "Gide as Husband and Homosexual," *The New Leader,* 13 December 1954.

———. *Giovanni's Room.* New York: Dial, 1956.

———. *Go Tell It on the Mountain.* New York: Dell, 1953.

———. *Going to Meet the Man.* New York: Dial, 1965.

———. *If Beale Street Could Talk.* New York: Signet, 1974.

———. *Just Above My Head.* New York: Dial, 1979; New York: Laurel, 1978/79.

———. "Race, Hate, Sex, and Colour: A Conversation with James Baldwin and Colin MacInnes." Interview by James Mossman. In *Conversations with James Baldwin,* ed. Louis H. Pratt and Fred L. Standley, 46–58. Jackson: University of Mississippi Press, 1989. Originally published in *Encounter,* 25 July 1965.

———. *Tell Me How Long the Train's Been Gone.* New York: Laurel, 1968.

———. "White Racism or World Community?" In *The Price of the Ticket: Collected Nonfiction, 1948–1985.* New York: St. Martin's, 435–42. Originally published in *Ecumenical Review,* October 1968.

Baudrillard, Jean. *Selected Writings.* Ed. Mark Poster. Stanford, Calif.: Stanford University Press, 1988.

Bigsby, C.W.E. "The Divided Mind of James Baldwin." In *Modern Critical Views: James Baldwin,* ed. Harold Bloom, 113–29. New York: Chelsea House, 1986. Originally published in *Journal of American Studies* 13, no. 3 (December 1979).

Bleier, Ruth. "Science and Belief: A Polemic on Sex Differences Research." In *The Impact of Feminist Research in the Academy,* ed. Christie Farnham, 111–30. Bloomington: Indiana University Press, 1987.

Boone, Joseph A., and Michael Cadden. Introduction to *Engendering Men: The Question of Male Feminist Criticism,* ed. Joseph A. Boone and Michael Cadden, 1–7. New York: Routledge, 1990.

Butler, Judith. *Gender Trouble: Feminism and the Subversion of Identity.* New York: Routledge, 1990.

———. "Imitation and Gender Insubordination." In *inside/out: Lesbian Theories, Gay Theories,* ed. Diana Fuss, 13–31. New York: Routledge, 1991.

Byerman, Keith E. "Words and Music: Narrative Ambiguity in 'Sonny's Blues.'" In *Critical Essays on James Baldwin,* ed. Fred L. Standley and Nancy V. Burt, 198–204. Boston: G. K. Hall, 1988. Originally published in *Studies in Short Fiction* 19 (1982): 367–72.

Campbell, James. *Talking at the Gates: A Life of James Baldwin.* New York: Viking, 1991.

Cederstrom, Lorelei. "Love, Race and Sex in the Novels of James Baldwin." *Mosaic* 17, no. 2 (Spring 1984): 175–88.

Chauncey, George, Jr. "Christian Brotherhood or Sexual Perversion? Homosexual Identities and the Construction of Sexual Boundaries in the World War I Era." In *Hidden from History: Reclaiming the Gay & Lesbian Past,* ed. Martin Bauml Duberman et al., 294–317. New York: New American Library, 1989.

Duberman, Martin. *Cures: A Gay Man's Odyssey.* New York: Dutton, 1991.

DuCille, Ann. "'Othered' Matters: Reconceptualizing Dominance and Difference in the History of Sexuality in America." *Journal of the History of Sexuality* 1, no. 1 (July 1990): 102–30.

Dyer, Richard. *The Matter of Images: Essays on Representations.* New York: Routledge, 1993.

Edelman, Lee. *Homographesis: Essays in Gay Literary and Cultural Theory.* New York: Routledge, 1994.

Ellenzweig, Allen. *The Homoerotic Photograph: Male Images from Durieu/Delacroix to Mapplethorpe.* New York: Columbia University Press, 1992.

Flannigan-Saint-Aubin, Arthur. "'Black Gay Male' Discourse: Reading Race and Sexuality between the Lines." In *American Sexual Politics: Sex, Gender, and Race since the Civil War,* ed. John C. Fout and Maura Shaw Tantillo, 381–403. Chicago: University of Chicago Press, 1993.

Foucault, Michel. *The History of Sexuality: An Introduction.* Vol. 1. Trans. Robert Hurley. New York: Vintage, 1990.

Freese, Peter. "James Baldwin: 'Going to Meet the Man' (1965)." In *The Black American Short Story in the 20th Century: A Collection of Critical Essays,* ed. Peter Bruck, 171–85. Amsterdam: B. R. Gruner Publishing, 1977.

Gilbert, Sandra M., and Susan Gubar. *The Madwoman in the Attic: The Woman Writer and the Nineteenth-Century Literary Imagination.* New Haven, Conn.: Yale University Press, 1984.

hooks, bell. *Yearning.* Boston: South End Press, 1990.

Jordan, Jennifer. "Feminist Fantasies: Zora Neale Hurston's *Their Eyes Were Watching God." Tulsa Studies in Women's Literature* 7 (1988): 105–17.

Katz, Jonathan Ned. *The Invention of Heterosexuality.* New York: Dutton, 1995.

Klein, Marcus. "A Question of Identity." In *Modern Critical Views: James Baldwin,* ed. Harold Bloom, 17–36. New York: Chelsea House, 1986. Originally published in *After Alienation: American Novels in Mid-Century* (New York: World Publishing, 1970).

Kuhn, Reinhard. "The Enigmatic Child in Literature." In *The Philosophical Reflection of Man in Literature: Selected Papers from Several Conferences Held by the International Society for Phenomenology and Literature in Cambridge, Massachusetts,* ed. Anna-Teresa Tymieniecka, 245–64. Boston: D. Reidel, 1982.

Lash, John S. "Baldwin Beside Himself: A Study in Modern Phallicism." In *James Baldwin: A Critical Evaluation,* ed. Therman B. O'Daniel, 47–55. Washington, D.C.: Howard University Press, 1977. Originally published in *CLA Journal* 8, no. 2 (December 1964): 132–40.

Leeming, David A. *James Baldwin: A Biography.* New York: Knopf, 1994.

Margolies, Edward. "The Negro Church: James Baldwin and the Christian Vision." In *Modern Critical Views: James Baldwin,* ed. Harold Bloom, 59–76. New York: Chelsea House, 1986. Originally published in *Native Sons: A Critical Study of Twentieth-Century Black American Literature* (New York: J. B. Lippincott, 1968).

Monette, Paul. *Becoming a Man.* San Francisco: Harper Collins, 1992.

Nelson, Emmanuel S. "Critical Deviance: Homophobia and the Reception of James Baldwin's Fiction." *Journal of American Culture* 14, no. 3 (Fall 1991): 91–96.

———. "The Novels of James Baldwin: Struggles of Self-Acceptance." *Journal of American Culture* 8 (1985): 11–16.

O'Daniel, Therman B., ed. *James Baldwin: A Critical Evaluation.* Washington, D.C.: Howard University Press, 1977.

Reilly, John M. "'Sonny's Blues': James Baldwin's Image of Black Community." In *James Baldwin: A Critical Evaluation,* ed. Therman B. O'Daniel, 163–69. Washington, D.C.: Howard University Press, 1977. Originally published in *Negro American Literature Forum* 4, no. 2 (July 1970): 56–60.

Rich, Adrienne. "Compulsory Heterosexuality and Lesbian Existence." In *Women: Sex and Sexuality,* ed. Ethel Spector Person and Catharine R. Stimpson, 62–91. Chicago: University of Chicago Press, 1980.

Sedgwick, Eve Kosofsky. *Between Men: English Literature and Male Homosocial Desire.* New York: Columbia University Press, 1985.

Spurlin, William J. "Rhetorical Hermeneutics and Gay Identity Politics: Rethinking American Cultural Studies." In *Reconceptualizing American Literary/Cultural Studies: Rhetoric, History, and Politics in the Humanities,* ed. William E. Cain, 168–83. New York: Garland Publishing, 1996.

Thomas, Kendall. "'Ain't Nothin' Like the Real Thing': Black Masculinity, Gay Sexuality, and the Jargon of Authenticity." In *Representing Black Men,* ed. Marcellus Blount and George P. Cunningham, 55–69. New York: Routledge, 1996.

Tyler, Carole-Anne. "Boys Will Be Girls: The Politics of Gay Drag." In *inside/out: Lesbian Theories, Gay Theories,* ed. Diana Fuss, 32–70. New York: Routledge, 1991.

Waldrep, Shelton. "'Being Bridges': Cleaver/Baldwin/Lorde and African-American Sexism and Sexuality." In *Critical Essays: Gay and Lesbian Writers of Color,* ed. Emmanuel S. Nelson, 167–80. New York: Haworth Press, 1993.

Watney, Simon. "Ordinary Boys." In *Family Snaps: The Meaning of Domestic Photography,* ed. Patricia Holland and Jo Spence, 26–34. London: Virago, 1991.

Weatherby, W. J. *James Baldwin: Artist on Fire.* New York: Donald I. Fine, 1989.

Whitlow, Roger. "Baldwin's *Going to Meet the Man*: Racial Brutality and Sexual Gratification." In *Critical Essays on James Baldwin,* ed. Fred L. Standley and Nancy V. Burt 194–98. Boston: G. K. Hall, 1988. Originally published in *American Imago* 34, no. 4 (1977): 351–56.

Young-Bruehl, Elisabeth. "Discriminations: Kinds and Types of Prejudices." *Transition* 60 (1993): 53–69.

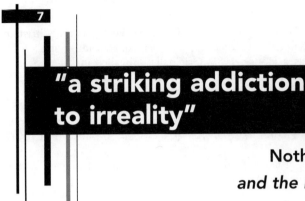

"a striking addiction to irreality"

Nothing Personal
and the legacy of the
photo-text genre

JOSHUA L. MILLER

New forms in art are created by the canonization of peripheral forms.
— *Viktor Shklovsky*

Photography is unclassifiable. . . . Whatever it grants to vision and whatever its manner, a photograph is always invisible: it is not it that we see.
— *Roland Barthes*

In the relation between a photograph and words, the photograph begs for an interpretation, and the words usually supply it. . . . Yet it might be that the photographic ambiguity, if recognized and accepted as such, could offer to photography a unique means of expression. Could this ambiguity suggest another way of telling?
— *John Berger*

The camera can be lenient; it is also expert at being cruel. But its cruelty only produces another kind of beauty . . . it is not surprising that some photographers who serve fashion are also drawn to the non-photogenic.
— *Susan Sontag*

I always prefer to work in the studio. It isolates people from their environment. They become in a sense . . . symbolic of themselves. . . . The photographs have a reality for me that the people don't.
— *Richard Avedon*

To an ever greater degree the work of art reproduced becomes the work of art designed for reproducibility.   —*Walter Benjamin*

"We are unbelievably ignorant concerning what goes on in our country," James Baldwin declares at the outset of *Nothing Personal*, "to say nothing of what goes on in the rest of the world—and appear to have become too timid to question what we are told" (Baldwin *Price* 387).[1] Intentional, self-directed ignorance is perhaps the most Baldwinian of topics. Ironically, one of his most inventive and compact articulations of both the manifestations and the consequences of such ignorance largely has been ignored by scholarly and critical establishments. *Nothing Personal*—a collaboration with his high school friend, the photographer Richard Avedon—examines both the seduction of illusions and the possibilities for subversion of the artist's position in regard to the ignorance of "our country" (as Baldwin archly puts it). Practicing what it preaches, *Nothing Personal* problematizes the "timid[ity]" of both literary and national forms of belonging through a visual and textual performance of mobility.

As powerfully as *Nothing Personal* resonates with the politics of the early 1960s that joined the two artists, the work is simultaneously in dialogue with a genre rarely considered in the history of U.S. cultural production. *Nothing Personal* emerges from a number of intersecting (and perhaps even contradictory) histories. Formally as well as substantively, it draws on and complicates at least two genres: documentary-based social activist literature as well as an emerging African American tradition of photo-text narratives. This chapter interprets Baldwin and Avedon's collaboration in the context of both documentary and African American photo/text works. As is evident from even a quick perusal, however, the lasting significance of *Nothing Personal* may lie in its rejection of the terms of its predecessors, opening the doors to daring experimentation that combines photographic iconography and text.

The form of *Nothing Personal* makes it difficult to categorize, largely because this genre's history has been so long ignored. By 1964, the year that Baldwin and Avedon published their book, the photo-text form already had a long and complex history. Baldwin and Avedon knew that they were inserting themselves into a debate that began in the nineteenth century over new technologies and the representation of classed, racialized, gendered, and sexualized bodies.[2] Melding photo images with texts is nearly as old as photography itself, but the photo-text genre runs parallel to and often calls into question other literary forms such as realism and reportage. The works of this form rarely depend on an uncritical mutuality between image and text. Unlike journalism, which strives to create out of photography the category of objective "evidence," the images and texts in this genre often exist in a productive form of dissonance, each calling the other into question. One of the earliest and most astute observers of the use of photography to provide material "evidence" is Walter Benjamin. In his famous essay "The Work of Art in the Age of Mechanical Reproduction," Benjamin argues that around 1900, Eugène Atget's photographs of Paris begin this process. "With Atget," he suggests, "photographs become standard evidence for historical occurrences, and acquire a hidden political significance. They demand a particular kind of approach" (226). Benjamin's point about the "hidden political significance" of photos as historical evidence will reemerge later in this chapter.[3]

Photo-text works utilize journalistic methods, but they also parody them, critique them, and scrutinize the notion of evidence itself—particularly visual evidence, which has taken on increasing importance in twentieth century U.S. culture.[4]

THE DOCUMENTARY ORIGINS OF PHOTO-TEXT COLLABORATIONS: "THE MOTIONLESS CAMERA AND THE PRINTED WORD"

Although it was not the first book to use photographs interspersed with textual elaboration, Jacob Riis's *How the Other Half Lives* (1890) remains one of the genre's most powerful and effective early works. A Dutch immigrant and a journalist, Riis took a camera into New York's poorest slums to literally make visible the dire state of the poverty-stricken. Using invasive and unsettling images of claustrophobic living conditions, Riis implicates the reader (viewer) of the text. His book is an exhortation for Christian charity, interpolating the guilty reader with the accusing question, "What are you going to do about it?" (Riis 2). Photographs, like statistics and anecdotes in this work, form the "bald facts" that Riis wants to hoist in front of citizens who have ignored the strangers in their midst for too long (223). An investigative journalist to the core, Riis does not want to attract readers' attention to himself at all. *How the Other Half Lives* is a spectacularly effective piece of reportage precisely because Riis effaces his own role as the mediator and the conveyor of images and information through the scientific tone of his text, and the stark, objectively offensive quality of his photographs.

One can easily view Riis's photography, at its most mundane as well as poetic, as an investigation of space, or the lack thereof. In screeching contrast to the lyrical "literature of place" that U.S. authors had been attempting to construct in the half-century up to that point, Riis's work can only be described as marking a literature of anti-place or nowhere. Juxtaposing Riis's work with that of Ralph Waldo Emerson, Henry Thoreau, and Walt Whitman makes this contrast over the meaning of space even more jarring.

Riis considered himself a chronicler of urban chaos and misery, in the Anglo-American reform tradition.[5] But what distinguishes him from previous journalists is his use of photography to elaborate the textual sociological points. In *How the Other Half Lives,* the photographs do not simply illustrate the points that Riis makes, they *overpower* the dry, factual, scientific tone of his words.[6] In some cases, the photographs portray exactly the person that Riis describes in his text (see, for example, the "particularly ragged and disreputable tramp," pp. 64–67). More often than not, however, the photographs portray the more abstract qualities of desperation and yearning that Riis clearly felt his words could not convey (see, for example, photograph 1).

In the implicit competition between image and text for the reader's attention, Riis privileges the voyeuristic impulse to which the emergent technology of photography gives rise. Riis's message renders the messenger unworthy of consideration. He refers to himself in the text only anecdotally and with hesitation; his photographs do not include his shadow or any evidence of his presence, except, of course, the fact of the picture itself (see photograph 2).

If Riis's work hints at a concern that the competition between image and text will valorize the former at the expense of the latter, James Agee's "Preface" to *Let Us Now Praise Famous Men* (1941) articulates a cautious, uneasy alliance between word and image, a writer and a photographer working jointly to depict the lives of southern tenant farmers. Agee and Walker Evans's goal is clearly documentary; they aim to (as Roy Striker put it later) "introduc[e] America to Americans" and produce a record of everyday U.S. lives (Levine 288). For this purpose, the photo-text combination forms an ideal mode of narration. Warren Susman argues that during the 1930s, "the sophisticated uses" to which photography and film were put "created a special community of all Americans (an international community previously unthinkable). The shift to a culture of sight and sound was of profound importance . . . it helped create a *unity of response and action*" (Levine 288, italics added). Although this assessment undoubtedly overstates the complex histor-

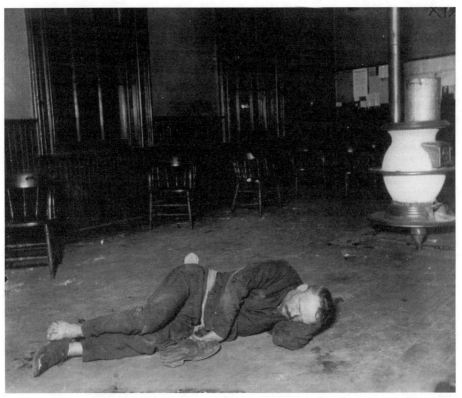

Photograph 1. Police Station: Lodging House, Quarters for the Night. **Museum of the City of New York, Jacob A. Riis Collection, #243.**

ical relationship between visual culture and polemical purposes, Susman's point that potent cultural shifts in the thirties created kinds of communities based on both visual iconography and documentary ideals is worth pursuing beyond the thirties.

The "immediate instruments" at their disposal, as Agee puts it, are "the motionless camera and the printed word" (Evans and Agee xiv). This surprising juxtaposition (what exactly *is* the relation between "motionless" and "printed"?) demonstrates nicely how the two artists and activists work together, yet use different tools and terms. Like the comparison between immobility and print, Agee and Evans refer to one another's work implicitly (obvious correlations exist, on both levels), but they certainly do not blend seamlessly into one another. Lest one mistake the relationship between Evans's photographs and Agee's

Photograph 2. Old Mrs. Benoit in her Hudson Street attic (Indian woman), Ca. 1898. **Museum of the City of New York, Jacob A. Riis Collection, #300.**

text, the writer informs readers that "the photographs are not illustrative. They, and the text, are coequal, mutually independent, and fully collaborative" (xv). To this end, Evans's photographs appear as the first pages of the work, untitled and unexplained, separated from the nearly 500-page text by the title page. In this case, unlike Riis's text, the photographs and text have different ambitions, however similar their subjects may be. In living with, talking to, and attempting to inhabit the lives of three southern tenant farming families, Evans's photographs tell a different story than Agee's challenging narrative. Where Agee's descriptive passages will enter into his subjects and claim a knowledge of their interior, hidden lives, Evans's photographs are unmistakably concerned with the external. By leaving his images utterly wordless (without captions or even identifications), Evans decontexualizes them. In contrast, Agee continually tries to penetrate the mysteries not only of his subjects, but also of Evans (and, by extension, of photography) as well. As Carol Shloss points out, "Agee's struggle to come to terms with the camera forms a coherent and powerful subtext, an underground commentary, making this book a central document—perhaps *the* central document—of art's struggle with social responsibility during the Depression" (Shloss 180, emphasis in original).

Evans's photographs, like those of Riis, encapsulate a complex dynamic of absences and presences. Evans's subjects often are posed awkwardly, playing to the camera's eye, yet unable (or unwilling) to hide the difficulties in their midst. Many of the people in Evans's portraits stare directly back at viewers. Their eyes have an intensity, particularly the piercing stares of the children (photograph 3). As Agee writes, "It is not going to be easy to look in their eyes" (189). In another photograph, Evans literalizes absence by portraying a man's dusty, worn boots standing empty and unlaced, a ghostly reminder that there is always more backbreaking work to be done the next day (photograph 4). This photo,

Photograph 3. **Library of Congress (LC-USZ62-13832). Photograph by Walker Evans.**

Photograph 4. **Library of Congress (LC-USZ62-17922). Photograph by Walker Evans.**

like his numerous shots of rickety, wooden houses, eschews exploration of the pain within by focusing on the symbolic aspects of the external (photograph 5).

Like Riis, Evans and Agee seek to document the lives that they encounter. But where one might classify Riis's text as based on the realism of reportage, Agee continually refers to the fact that he and Evans are themselves "quite monstrously alien human beings, in the employment of still others more alien" (13).[7] Agee's perspective on his subjects betrays a distinctly un-Riisian guilt as outside observers who

> pry intimately into the lives of an undefended and appallingly damaged group of human beings, an ignorant and helpless rural family, for the purpose of parading the nakedness, disadvantage and humiliation of these lives before another group of human beings, in the name of science, of "honest journalism" (whatever that paradox may mean). (7)

Paula Rabinowitz argues that Agee's "dilemma about his relationship to his subjects" spurs his anxiety about the form of the text (49). In other words, his concern with representation takes on formal dimensions in this strangely circular and shapeless narrative. As a reporter

Photograph 5. **Library of Congress (LC–USF342-RA8133A). Photograph by Walker Evans.**

and a documenter, Agee's job is to make sense of the tenant farmer families' lives for his readers, and we must be able to understand the farmers' lives through his account. Part of his method of doing this, as in the quoted section above, is to describe the families along familiar class and gender lines ("an undefended and appallingly damaged group"). By objectifying and classifying his subjects, Agee examines the narrative forms of both documentary and photo-text works.[8] Agee's fragmentary, elliptical narrative depends on the communication ruptures spurred by his dissatisfaction with his writerly possibilities: "If I could do it, I'd do no writing at all here. It would be photographs; the rest would be fragments of cloth, bits of cotton, lumps of earth, records of speech.... As it is, though, I'll do what little I can in writing" (13). Since documentary evidence, the physical shards of historical memory, requires narration, Agee resigns himself to imperfectly filling in the gaps with his prose.

"It Squeezes Out of Us What We Leave Unspoken": African American Innovations on the Photo-Text Genre

Still riding the crest of his best-selling 1940 novel *Native Son,* Richard Wright immediately turned his attention (and sudden fame) to a study of photographic representation of African Americans. As a writer deeply concerned with the searing impact of iconic stereotypes, Wright's purpose was to counter the conventional images of African Americans. In the aftermath of the phenomenal success of *Let Us Now Praise Famous Men* and the other products of photography during the 1930s, Wright saw that even the most well-intentioned reporters and ethnographers positioned themselves as outsiders who penetrate a subculture in order to expose its underlying poverty and decay. Alan Trachtenberg notes that, after the notable successes of *Let Us Now Praise Famous Men* and *You Have Seen Their Faces* by Margaret Bourke-White and Erskine Caldwell (1937), "a rash of picture-and-word books appeared between 1938 and 1941 on the themes of rural poverty, the small town, the Negro, the condition of agriculture—and in one case, Archibald MacLeish's *Land of the Free* (1938), accompanying a long poem" (Trachtenberg 252–53). In part, Wright's book is a response and a corrective to these other attempts to depict African American life. However, it is also a historical narrative in its own right.

In *12 Million Black Voices* (1941), Wright's narrator speaks in the first-person plural, articulating from within the African American story of twentieth-century migration. As he puts it in the "foreword," he constructs the work "to seize upon that which is qualitative and abiding in Negro experience, to place within full and constant view the collective humanity whose triumphs and defeats are shared by the majority" (Wright xx).

From the beginning, Wright addresses a collective narrative to the white reading public that claims to "know" African Americans, but in fact peers through lenses distorted by racist imagery:

> Each day when you see us black folk upon the dusty land of our farms or upon the hard pavement of the city streets, you usually take us for granted and think you know us, but our history is far stranger than you suspect, and we are not what we seem. (10)

Wright, in ways that resonate with his other writings of the period (such as *Native Son* and *Black Boy*), uses the photographic material to transform traditionally derogatory images of black Americans. Above all else, *12 Million Black Voices* constitutes a sophisticated effort to overturn the agency that produces racist stereotypes. Rather than relying on others to tell African American history through images, Wright inserts himself in the role of editor and mediator.

Unlike Riis, Evans and Agee, and most of the earlier photo-text collaborators, Wright neither took his own photographs, nor participated in their creation. In 1940, Viking Press asked him to compose a text to accompany photographs culled by Edwin Rosskam from the Works Progress Administration's Farm Security Administration. With the photographs in one hand and stacks of sociological and historical texts on African American life in the other, Wright took immense interest in the interplay between word and image. His initially brief text grew (through multiple revisions) into a manuscript of more than fifty pages.

The originality and power of *12 Million Black Voices* arises not from the historical drama that Wright lays out. The story of African American migration from Jim Crow segregation in the rural South to another form of segregation in the industrial and urban North already had been told in many forms by the early 1940s. In this work, however, Wright seizes upon ingrained images of racial stereotypes and challenges the modes of visuality that uphold them. "Our outward guise still carries the old familiar aspect which three hundred years of oppression in America have given us," he writes with an image of a bent worker below, "but beneath the garb of the black laborer, the black cook, and the black elevator operator lies an uneasily tied knot of pain and hope whose snarled strands converge from many points of time and space" (11). Throughout this work, Wright utilizes the language of visuality (particularly verbs such as see, seem, appear, gaze, show, etc.) in order to argue that what one sees—in photographs as in everyday life—is utterly constructed by preconceptions of racialized difference.

To counter these negative images of African Americans, Wright keeps the photographs themselves at the center of the work. It is Wright's presentation of them as both representative and misrepresentative of the ever-changing realities of African American lives that gives this book its power. Ingeniously, Wright uses the most conventional images of blacks in servile roles ("the black maid," "the black waiter," "the black stevedore") to prod readers into the realization that these are violently distorted stereotypes rather than accurate depictions of African American life (see photographs 6 and 7). Wright juxtaposes these first suspect images with those that fill the rest of the book, of violence and compassion, isolation and community, material poverty and spiritual wealth. Both individually and collectively, Wright emphasizes the sense of inner strength that the photographs imply. He draws the varied photographs together under the themes of persistence and growing self-definition. In fact, definitions—both textual and visual—help shape the work. Using words to scrutinize the power of racist language and photographs to do the same for racist imagery, Wright aims at a new definition for an entire people:

> The word "Negro," the term by which, orally or in print, we black folk in the United States are usually designated, is not really a name at all nor a description, but a psychological island whose objective . . . artificially and arbitrarily defines, regulates, and limits in scope of meaning the vital contours of our lives, and the lives of our children and our children's children. (30)

Throughout *12 Million Black Voices,* Wright deepens the central idea that both verbal and visual definitions restrict African American expression by relegating it to stereotypical forms of literature or labor. This "psychological island" that constrains the term "Negro" takes hold through iconography as pervasively as it does through language. Some of the photographs themselves (such as photograph 8) are complex and eloquent expressions of the loneliness of this psychological island.

If the third section of *12 Million Black Voices*—"Death on the City Pavement"—sounds a pessimistic note on the position of African Americans in the North, the concluding section challenges readers with a call to action.[9] Alongside images of political protest and personal fulfillment, Wright concludes:

> We black folk, our history and our present being, are a mirror of all the manifold experiences of America. What we want, what we represent,

Photograph 6. The black waiter. **Library of Congress (LC-USF33-20988-M5). Photograph by Jack Delano.**

what we endure is what America *is*. If we black folk perish, America will perish. If America has forgotten her past, then let her look into the mirror of our consciousness and she will see the *living* past living in the present . . . through the tales of slavery told by our black grandparents, to the time when none of us, black or white, lived in this fertile land. (146, emphasis in original)

Photograph 7. The black stevedore. **Library of Congress (LC-USF34-34558-D). Photograph by Russell Lee.**

When Wright commands, "Look at us and know us and you will know yourselves," he compels readers to continually reexamine the very images in this work. The photograph that faces this injunction depicts a young man standing in the doorway of a wooden shack, looking up into radiant sunlight with a look of promise and determination (pho-

Photograph 8. There are times. . . . **Library of Congress (LC–USF34–44563-D). Photograph by Jack Delano.**

tograph 9). The modesty of his surroundings is infused with the hope in the man's face. One cannot help but note the neatness of the house with bottles gathered in a barrel and the ground swept clean. In this final image, as in the rest of the book, Wright challenges readers/viewers to look beyond built-in, preprogrammed images of African Americans to the complicated realities within: "The differences between black folk and white folk are not blood or color, and the ties that bind us are deeper than those that separate us. The common road of hope which we all have traveled has brought us into a stronger kinship than any words, laws, or legal claims" (146).

In the history of the photo-text genre, Wright's method both builds on those of predecessors and represents a significant shift. His purpose in *12 Million Black Voices* is not to challenge the evidentiary or documentary mode of photography in general, but to *subvert* this power, the authority of images, in the service of a corrective antiracism.[10] Hous-

Photograph 9. Back yard of alley dwelling. **Library of Congress (LC-USF-34-239-D). Photograph by Carl Mydans.**

ton Baker sums up this subversion as "the voicing of a collective coun-termotion to Western material acquisitiveness and its desire for stable authority and domination" (Baker 111).[11] But it is not only the textual description of the folk that makes the collective story central, as the photo-images fill verbal absences. From this subversion—and from the aesthetic pleasure of the photographs themselves—emanates Wright's lyrical and passionate prose. Ralph Ellison, a photographer himself and author of the novel that virtually defines the literary relationship between race and visibility, finds reading *12 Million Black Voices* "a deeply emotional experience" (Ellison 11/3/41). In one of the longest and most intimate letters Ellison ever wrote to Wright, he suggests that the lyrical photo-text work ultimately may be an even more powerful statement than Wright's celebrated first novel:

> Be proud to place the book beside *Native Son*. For while in the novel you sliced deep and twisted the knife to open up the psychic wound, *12 Million Black Voices* seizes hold to epochs and a continent and clears them of fog, and it squeezes out of us what we leave unspoken. Some could deny N.S. but all but a few of us have come along the path set down here ... the book makes me feel a bitter pride.

Ellison immediately recognizes Wright's attempt to subvert the role of iconographic stereotypes and celebrates the fact that "we have begun to embrace the experience and master it, and we shall make of it a weapon more subtle than a machinegun ... I think it significant that I can feel pride of this kind in a Negro *book*" (Ellison, emphasis in original). And *12 Million Black Voices* was not Wright's only foray into the photo-text genre. In 1951, he published an article titled "The Shame of Chicago" in *Ebony* that was accompanied by photographs of Chicago's south side neighborhoods by Wayne Miller.[12] Michel Fabre also notes that Wright contacted photographer Helen Levitt with regard to a collaboration on Harlem (Fabre 267).

To the extent that *12 Million Black Voices* is a weapon against racism, Langston Hughes and Roy DeCarava compose their 1955 work *The Sweet Flypaper of Life* as a hymn to personal expression. In contrast to Wright's mobile "we" (which, at various points, denotes men, women, African Americans, Americans, etc.), Hughes's narrator is a particular fictional character, Sister Mary Bradley, who threads DeCarava's photographs together into a representative story that dramatizes the life of a community. The move, from *12 Million Black Voices* to *Sweet Flypaper,* is aesthetic as well as political. DeCarava's gorgeous photographs demonstrate a wide range of African American urban life in rich detail.

The tightly reflexive relationship between image and text constitutes another significant distinction between Wright's work and *Sweet Flypaper.* Hughes wrote the text directly from DeCarava's photographs and intensifies their interrelationship by repeatedly referring to them explicitly. Hughes ends most of the textual passages with colons, as if the photograph below continues the sentence or amplifies its meaning. This interplay throughout the work allows Hughes to name the figures who appear in the images and to characterize them as familiar friends. Hughes's narrator, Sister Mary, introduces characters through verbal stories that include the photographs within the plot. For example, she describes the warm relationships between her children and grandchildren ("Never saw a baby so crazy about its daddy") as she refers to DeCarava's photographs of a man cradling an infant while engaged in a discussion (62). Hughes also uses DeCarava's photos of Harlem streets, city laborers (and strikes), and churches to project the community's political, economic, and spiritual life. Sister Mary herself views Harlem through the lens of her own window: "Yes, you can set in your window anywhere in Harlem and see plenty. Of course, some windows is better to set in than others mainly because it's better inside, not that you can necessarily see any more" (98).

Hughes and DeCarava's work falls squarely in line with the history of photo-text collaborators who use both media in the attempt to represent a collective narrative. In this case, Hughes uses a fictionalized narrator (rather than Wright's more explicit move to speak for a community), to keep readers' attention focused on DeCarava's photographs. Sister Mary refers to the photographs with pride, as if they are snapshots from her personal album, or as if the reader is with her viewing the actual people on a walk through Harlem on a warm summer afternoon. In this way, Hughes's sense of the importance of DeCarava's photographs anchor *The Sweet Flypaper of Life* in the documentary tradition, even if they are among the most aesthetically concerned members of that tradition. Both the aesthetics and the politics of Harlem are at stake in this collaboration. DeCarava does not attempt to conceal the suffering of African Americans, but his photographs implicitly argue (as Hughes's text *explicitly* argues) for the richness of ordinary lives. This notion of recognizing the complexly quotidian elements of African American life fits *Sweet Flypaper* within the documentary tradition, even as Hughes and DeCarava avoid the ethnographic pitfalls of reportage that ensnare Agee and Evans and (to a perhaps lesser extent) Richard Wright.[13]

NOTHING PERSONAL: THE PHOTO-TEXT COLLABORATION IN THE AGE OF CIVIL RIGHTS

Roland Barthes suggests that powerful images, rather than being static, demand effort from their viewers: in "'good' photographs

... the object speaks, it induces us, vaguely, to think. . . . Ultimately, Photography is subversive not when it frightens, repels, or even stigmatizes, but when it is pensive, when it thinks" (Barthes 38). Barthes's notion of subversive images as those that impel thought links Agee and Evans with Baldwin and Avedon. Evans's portraits, like Avedon's, fall aesthetically somewhere between mug shots and fashion portfolios. Both photographers intentionally distort the boundaries between "high" art and popular culture. But, in the interconnection between image and text, Baldwin and Avedon seek to undermine radically the documentary relation between photo and word. Instead of *providing* context for the images (as Riis, Agee, Wright, and Hughes all do in varying ways), Baldwin and Avedon wrench figures from their contexts and re-present them against a harsh, uncompromising, unmistakably white background. Rather than relying upon the "evidential" status of illustration, Baldwin textually destabilizes, decontextualizes both the familiar (i.e., "public") and the unfamiliar personas that Avedon captures (Barthes 113). The genre of photo-text collaboration drew on documentary literatures of the late nineteenth and early twentieth centuries. As artists as well as documentary historians, Riis, Evans, and Agee are intimately concerned with concepts of evidence, moral authority, historical truth, and narrative. But Baldwin and Avedon mark a distinct shift away from evidence[14]; their collaboration questions the very idea of the historian's (or storyteller's) agency in giving definitive meaning to images. If the documentary's function is to stabilize the meaning of certain pictures and events in history, "freezing the images within their frames for later instructional use," Baldwin and Avedon turn this proposition on its head (Rabinowitz 17). Their joint effort uses both overdetermined images (i.e., Gov. George Wallace, poet Allen Ginsberg) as well as underdetermined ones (i.e., anonymous faces in a mental institution) to pry the pedagogical ("instructional") impulse away from the genre of the photo-text.

At the same time, Baldwin and Avedon also mark their distance from the emerging tradition of African American photo-text collaborations. Unlike Richard Wright's new grand narrative of African American history and DeCarava and Hughes's intimate view into Harlem life, Baldwin and Avedon's work is not intended as a seamless combination of images and words that refer to and reinforce one another. While the texts of both Wright and Hughes carefully contextualize the accompanying images, Baldwin only makes the most oblique references to the photographs in *Nothing Personal*.[15] By design, the language of the writing fits only loosely with the language of the photographs. *Nothing Per-*

sonal is far from a seamless narrative, and it seems to flaunt its very formlessness with rapid shifts of subject (in both image and text) and sudden juxtapositions. For much of the text, jarring shifts challenge readers to bridge the gaps without authorial aid or explanation. Baldwin and Avedon defer ultimate answers by constantly adjusting their line of inquiry, from the national to the personal, from the familiar to the unfamiliar, from the historical to the immediately contemporary. In direct contrast to Wright's commanding use of the first-person plural to speak *for* the "12 Million Black Voices," Baldwin's use of the subject "we" slides from one group to another. At various moments in the text, this pronoun refers to African Americans, Americans, Baldwin himself, artists, perceptive individuals, etc. In this way, the status of the speaking subject of *Nothing Personal* is changing continually.

These unsettling shifts illuminate the artists' objectives. By 1963, Avedon was a highly successful fashion photographer followed by a wide audience in magazines such as *Vogue* and *Harper's Bazaar*. Baldwin already had become a major writer whose essays and books had turned him into an international figure. Baldwin and Avedon, who had known each other for more than two decades, sought to combine their separate audiences with an unlikely coffee-table book.[16] This attempt to inform Avedon's fashion audience about the civil rights movement led to the unusual format: oversized pages and text, enormous photographs, and a strikingly white cover.

The response, from reviewers as well as consumers, was both immediate and unambiguous. *Time* magazine called Baldwin's "brief" text "oddly irrelevant, obviously hasty, [and] too often drawn on by his sheer flow of language into shrill overstatement" ("American Gothic" 110). This reviewer lamented the "slippery bias" of both Baldwin's text and Avedon's photos. In *The Nation*, Lincoln Kirstein chose to bestow "the prize for unworthiness," out of the entire year's publications, on "*Nothing Personal*, the coffee-table horror supreme" (Kirstein 471). But the most devastating review appeared in *The New York Review of Books*. In a tone of disbelief, Robert Brustein wrote that "*Nothing Personal* shows us an honorable tradition of revolt gone sour, given over to fame and ambition, discredited by shadowy motives, twisted by questionable ideals, turned into a theatrical gesture by café society performers" (Brustein 11). This "hypocritical charade" in which nearly "everyone present is seen with a hideously jaundiced eye" merely "falsifies rather than reveals reality" (10–11). Similarly, the London *Times Literary Supplement* concluded that "this remains a paradoxical and in some ways a dishonest work. The camera can lie in more ways than one" ("Dark

Exposure" 1122). This reviewer called the fusion of Baldwin's "brief prose sermon" with Avedon's "lenses of a darker hue" an "obscene" combination (1122).

Such violently unfavorable coverage ensured that *Nothing Personal* sold poorly, was remaindered at bookstores, and ended up reprinted in an unsolicited paperback edition. Baldwin's biographers generally have reinforced the harsh impressions of contemporary reviewers by barely mentioning the work in the context of his life (Leeming 226–27, Campbell 174). In historical retrospect, however, the enduring power of both the images and the language of this unique work become clear. In the context of both documentary and African American artistic photo-text works, the formal innovations and political commentaries seem even more prescient.

The form of *Nothing Personal* is like no other photo-text collection. Avedon's photographs are gathered in four thematically arranged sets, with Baldwin's text interspersed between them, while a short concluding section of text includes photos within it. The text also never refers explicitly to one photo or another, although the final section comes closest to commenting implicitly on the images.[17] While the two talked about the project during both the writing and the photographing, they chose not to give the text and the images obvious relations. Avedon relates that "Baldwin had a good idea what I was doing, and actually did see some of the photographs in the process of being organized. We deliberately talked about not illustrating one another, but obliquely worked out of the same sources, in different directions" (Avedon, letter to author). The overall structure is quilt-like: stories wrapped in arguments that fuse the metaphorical with the tangible (in particularly Baldwinesque fashion). *Nothing Personal* has a mobile form, and it is itself a meditation on framing: both Baldwin's textual framing of national and personal dilemmas, and Avedon's uncompromising portraits that veer nearer to and further from his subjects' faces.

Baldwin's overall argument largely depends on his mobile metaphor of the "witness," an observer whose perspective on the nation emerges from both within and without; as neither an outsider nor an insider, the witness is a dynamic participant who can take on the roles of either patriot or expatriate.[18] Just as Baldwin subverts presumed dichotomies (such as gay/straight, black/white, hope/fear, individual/collective) throughout his fiction and nonfiction (itself a dichotomy that has not served Baldwin criticism well), the narrator of *Nothing Personal* blurs the distinction between his words and Avedon's photos, sometimes ignoring the images, at other times, implicitly engaging them.[19]

In contrast to Riis's investigation of urban poverty and Evans and Agee's focus on rural class and gender, Baldwin makes contemporary mythologies of race and sexuality his central subject. He marks a definitive shift away from the poetics of documentary by refusing to state a single subject or target of his study. Unlike Agee, who repetitively bounds his comments with reservations about his own practice of ethnography, Baldwin wants to claim that he is a part of the phenomenon he examines. He emphasizes his own role as subject (and author) rather than anxious outsider by beginning the text of *Nothing Personal* with a textual picture of himself, lying immobile in bed, staring at the flickering images of commercials. Flipping channels randomly (long before the cynically appropriate term "channel-surfing" was coined) with his "remote control gadget," Baldwin notices that the form of sexuality that television constructs is a plastic, empty, "soulless" expression of commodified desire (381). The visually enhanced body parts actually take on the characteristics of the commodities that they are trying to sell, that they "represent," such as "teeth gleaming like the grillwork of automobiles," "eyes as sensuous and mysterious as jelly beans," and "hair sprayed to the consistency of aluminum" (381). However, these "uplifted" and "corrected" body parts represent something deeper than crass commercialism to Baldwin; they suggest a sexuality that has forsaken mutual communication. The characters on the screen "happily blow smoke in each other's face" (and, one might add, in that of the television audience), yet "perhaps—poor, betrayed exiles—they are trying to discover if, behind all that grillwork, either of them has a tongue" (382).

Taking the images that television commercials present as clues to the state of both contemporary sexuality and communication (because, for Baldwin, these are always synonymous terms), he concludes that consumerist, visual culture has castrated masculinity ("the male certainly doesn't have a tongue") and reduced communication to jingles (382–84). The (missing) tongue, a symbol of sexuality as well as an organ of communication, is symptomatic of what is absent from U.S. culture. The result of this cultural silencing is that the media (or "communications industries" as they are referred to today) such as film, print, and television are "communications whose role is not to communicate, but simply to reassure" (387). In response to the generic, oppressively uninspired images of telegenic sexuality, Baldwin suggests that personal, intimate communication has shriveled up. With Perle Mesta's craggy, pained face staring from the opposite page, Baldwin writes of the faces he observes during a typical walk in New York (pho-

Photograph 10. Perle Mesta, Hostess. **Photograph by Richard Avedon. March 11, 1963, New York, New York. © 1963 Richard Avedon.**

tograph 10). The faces he views, like many of the faces that Avedon captures, discount meaningful communication before it can even occur: "How did they become—these faces—so cruel and so sterile?" (384) Only on the rarest of occasions does he encounter faces that possess the emotional freedom to warm the chilly city; "a boy and a girl, or a boy and a boy" who express "something to which the soul responded. . . . One felt that one might approach them without freezing to death" (385).

Although he does not mention it explicitly, Baldwin implicitly contrasts his description of television's banal and "dispiriting" images of sexuality with Richard Avedon's unsettling first series of portraits. As the absolute antithesis of the gleaming, spotless, surgically improved bodies on TV, Avedon's portraits capture familiar faces from unexpected angles and distances. The result is a collection of photos that challenges viewers to reconsider their preconceptions of both public and private figures. Avedon's lens seems poised to record and magnify every wrinkle or flaw on his subjects' faces. Perle Mesta, for example, a Washing-

Photograph 11. The Generals of the Daughters of the American Revolution. **Photograph by Richard Avedon. October 15, 1963, Washington, D.C. © 1963 Richard Avedon.**

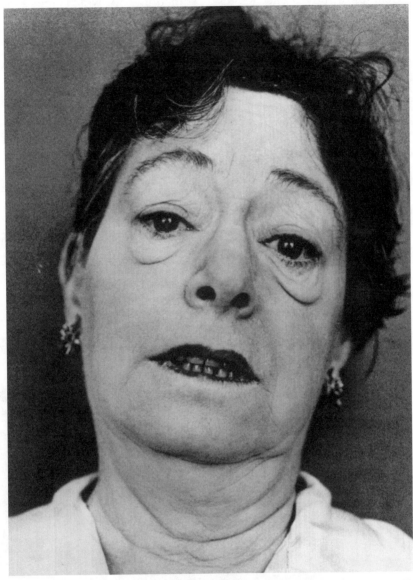

Photograph 12. Dorothy Parker, Writer. **Photograph by Richard Avedon. June 17, 1958, New York, New York. © 1958 Richard Avedon.**

ton "hostess," appears in an extreme close-up, the harsh lights illuminating rows of creases around her eyes and deep lines running from her chin to the bottom of her neck. In the next image, "the Generals of the Daughters of the American Revolution"—a group remembered for preventing Marian Anderson from singing in 1964 Washington, D.C.'s Constitution Hall (Washington, D.C.)—appear as a disorganized and distracted set of vain elderly women (photograph 11). At the center is a woman with her back turned, presumably trying to decide how they should arrange themselves. One easily can imagine Avedon eagerly snapping the picture as they are in the midst of preparations.

Another example of iconic femininity under Avedon's lens is his pairing of Marilyn Monroe with Dorothy Parker in the second series of portraits (photographs 12 and 13). The close-up of Parker's bloated, baggy face is magnified even further, blown up to cover the entire page. On the facing page, Monroe appears in miniature, less than a quarter

Photograph 13. Marilyn Monroe, Actress. **Photograph by Richard Avedon. May 6, 1957, New York, New York.** © 1957 Richard Avedon.

of the size of the Parker picture. The movie star seems unusually distracted and unfocused. Although she is as glamorous as always, all of her usual signs of beauty—lips, hair, birthmark, and partially exposed breasts—are scaled down and deprived of their usually seductive qualities. The result is that Monroe begins to appear as deflated as Parker. The juxtaposed images, wit drowned in alcohol and beauty calcified by Hollywood, present both of these endlessly reproduced women (in books, films, etc.) in strikingly unusual views. In the thirty portraits that make up the second and third photographic sets, not one depicts a conventional sexiness or even physical attractiveness. These images take public personae and re-present them in unfamiliar ways that compel us to reconsider the individual behind the persona. They subvert our received notions of personality and fame in exactly the manner that Barthes suggests in *Camera Lucida*. The disparity between generic images of sex, gender, and power and those in Avedon's photos is even greater as a result of Baldwin's scathing presentation of generic, mass-produced, commercial sexuality.

In addition to shifting the subject of discussion in photo-text works, Baldwin also calls attention to the tone that others have used in such works. In this context, the passionate intimacy with which he always writes takes on new significance. Although this tone is rather conventional for Baldwin's work, his manner of argumentation—somehow merging the preacherly and the confessional—is highly unusual compared to other works of this genre. Working against the grain of scientific and historical authorities (both of whom he deeply mistrusted) that documentaries traditionally have utilized, Baldwin moves from anecdote to argument and back again as he surveys "the myth" of American rhetoric:

> It is, of course, in the very nature of a myth that those who are its victims and, at the same time, its perpetrators, should, by virtue of these two facts, be rendered unable to examine the myth, or even to suspect, much less recognize, that it is a myth which controls and blasts their lives. (383)

This pregnant passage contains Baldwin's central argument in the text of *Nothing Personal,* a point reflected in Avedon's photography: Illusions and unexamined myths are most effective when they are invisible, when they are taken for granted. The iconography that both the writer and photographer challenge is the set of myths presumed by U.S. national rhetoric around sexuality and race, "whatever, by this time, in this country, or, indeed, in the world, this word may mean" (386). Baldwin's own rhetoric is designed to surprise, to counter the presumptions about how African Americans and gay men often are depicted, not in the least by documentary art itself.

The anecdote that forms the basis of the second text section of *Nothing Personal* turns into a parable of the inevitability of violence as a result of American racial polarities. "Looking for a taxi" on Broadway, Baldwin and a visiting Swiss friend are arrested and quickly separated by plainclothes policemen. Baldwin says that he is not concerned for himself, "I am an old hand at this—policemen have always loved to pick me up and, sometimes, to beat me up," but for his friend whose limited English probably does not include "the somewhat special brand used by the police" (385). When it becomes clear that the officers have the wrong men, they explain that they are looking for suspects, "two guys who looked just like" Baldwin and his friend. "White and black, you mean?" Baldwin wants to ask, but the twisted logic of domestic racial binaries is even more bizarre. In fact, the policemen took the Swiss man for a Puerto Rican (because he was walking with an African American) and were "baffled" when the man "turn[ed] out to be exactly what he said he was." That the officer presumed the Swiss man was lying, Baldwin points out, "contains its own comment . . . concerning the attitudes Americans have toward one another." Misreading appearances, however, is only the symptom of a much larger cause, a much larger lie. Despair, Baldwin argues, makes it "absolutely indispensable to discover, or invent—the two words, here, are synonyms—the stranger, the barbarian, who is responsible for our confusion and our pain" (386). This invented, mythologized outsider provides reassurance that "the evil came from without and is in no way connected with the moral climate of America" (387).

The reassurance of familiar, discretely external enemies is, partly, what Walter Benjamin means when he writes that the rise of photography as historical evidence lends the images themselves "a hidden political significance" (226). This significance is that the photographs come with external instructions for interpretation. Harnessing photographs to do the work of persuasion changes the nature of photographs themselves, according to Benjamin.[20] They appear with captions in magazines and newspapers so that readers cannot miss the "meaning" of the image, the singular purpose of its existence: illustration or amplification of a point already articulated textually. Captions are "directives" to the reader that "prescribe" the meaning of pictures even more explicitly. Benjamin's point is that prescribing meaning constrains readers/viewers from creatively contemplating the meaning or value of art. By equating the existence of an image with an instructional purpose (conveying evidence) the viewer is less likely to interrogate the picture's creativity and artfulness, and more likely to treat it as simply another code, another language.

Baldwin and Avedon seek to unhouse the photo-text work from the confines of documentary evidence. The pedagogical prejudices of most photo-text combinations presume a single, undivided purpose for both the images and the text. Thus, in *How the Other Half Lives,* the pictures and the text tell the same story. The photographs merely shine more light on the problem that the author wants to examine, urban poverty. Similarly, *Let Us Now Praise Famous Men,* regardless of its authors' coyness, uses a similar metaphor of bringing invisible lives, the people ignored or forgotten by society, into the light of historical visibility. Baldwin explicitly avoids this metaphor of bringing light to the darkness, making visible that which has been invisible. Rather than this progressive narrative that presumes historians or storytellers can peer into the misty distance of time and arrange the "true" narrative of events, Baldwin and Avedon cherish the mystery. *Nothing Personal* constitutes an attempt to detach photographic images from the evidentiary purpose; the text steadfastly refuses to hew to a single, unitary purpose that the photographs can be seen to uphold. Instead, both artists seek the Benjaminian purpose: To evoke more than they express in the images and words set on the page, to allow (and even encourage) readers to construct their own meanings from the conjuncture they offer up.

It seems a rather melancholy observation to note that Benjamin's argument of the encompassing "age" of mechanically reproduced art is nonetheless upheld by the publication history of Baldwin and Avedon's book. If, as I have argued, the point of this photo-text collaboration is—in part—to regain for photography the premechanical state of nondidactical meaning, the age has bitten back. *Nothing Personal* has been out of print since its first edition in 1964. If art in the age of mechanical reproduction is endlessly reproducible, it seems fitting (however unfortunate) that a work acting against this impulse is deemed *un*worthy of reproduction.

"We have," Baldwin concludes, "a very curious sense of reality" or, to put it another way, "a striking addiction to irreality" (390). Waking up at four in the morning and staring into the haze of dawn, he "peeks through the blinds" at the new day outside and then looks through the "limbo of the bathroom steam and fog, one's face comes floating up ... unreadable as ever" (389–90). One's face, like the dawning day and the historical past, has no particular meaning until its bearer creates one for it. Until "one selects the uniform" for the day, one's body remains "unreadable" and "crypt[ic]." The uniform "is designed to telegraph to others what to see so that they will not be made uncomfortable and probably hostile by being forced to look on another human being" (390). But being forced to look on, at, and into other human beings is precisely what motivates this collaboration between disconcerting photographs and unsettling text. Clothing, in this sense, is much like Benjamin's idea of the caption; it is a guide to interpretation, a prescribed way of seeing someone.

When Baldwin invokes the traditional polarity of light and dark, he does so to make a rather untraditional point. "One discovers the light in darkness," he writes, "that is what darkness is for; but everything in our lives depends on how we bear the light" (392). Coming on the heels of Avedon's overwhelming series of photographs of patients in a mental institution, the concept of bearing light takes on a variety of meanings: hopeful, historical, resistant, and regenerative. Life remains, as it must, "dependent, entirely, on things unseen" (392). No matter how determined the impulse to weld singular, unitary meanings to images and words, to read history as only one version of one story, *Nothing Personal* remains an eloquent gesture toward the complication that arises from the knowledge that "nothing is fixed, forever and forever and forever, it is not fixed; the earth is always shifting, the light is always changing" (393).

NOTES

Acknowledgments: For their insight, suggestions, and support, I am deeply grateful to Ann Douglas, Robert G. O'Meally, D. Quentin Miller, Timothy P. McCarthy, Deborah M. Levy, Martin and Ylana Miller. I am especially indebted to Richard Avedon for sharing both his photographs and his observations with me. I also would like to acknowledge the generous support of Elizabeth Baer of Gustavus Adolphus College. The photographs that appear with this essay are reprinted with the following permissions: Richard Avedon; The Museum of the City of New York, Jacob Riis Collection; The Library of Congress.

1. Since *Nothing Personal* is unpaginated, I cite Baldwin's text from his collection of nonfiction, *The Price of the Ticket*. I refer to Avedon's photographs according to which of the five photo sequences they appear (i.e., wedding set, portraits I, portraits II, hospital, conclusion).

2. One of the classic studies of this history is Sander Gilman's essay, "Black Bodies, White Bodies: Toward an Iconography of Female Sexuality in

Late Nineteenth-Century Art, Medicine, and Literature." Although less explicit about the role of visual images, Hazel Carby's work also is exemplary, particularly her essay "'On the Threshold of Woman's Era': Lynching, Empire, and Sexuality in Black Feminist Theory" in the same volume, *'Race,' Writing, and Difference*. Please see also Elizabeth Alexander's essay on more recent examples of African American bodies, violence, film, and photography, "'Can you be BLACK and look at this?': Reading the Rodney King Video(s)."

3. Walter Benjamin's comments in *Illuminations* on the use of captions around this time also is significant in regard to photo-text works: "For the first time, captions have become obligatory. And it is clear that they have an altogether different character than the title of a painting. The directives which the captions give to those looking at pictures in illustrated magazines soon become even more explicit about more imperative in the film where the meaning of each single picture appears to be prescribed by the sequence of all preceding ones" (226).

4. For a wide variety of interdisciplinary considerations on the subject of evidence, please see *Questions of Evidence: Proof, Practice, and Persuasion across the Disciplines* edited by James Chandler, Arnold I. Davidson, and Harry Harootunian). For alternative meditations on photography as evidence, see Richard Avedon's *Evidence,* and Luc Santé's *Evidence.*

5. Carol Shloss highlights Riis's portrayal of space by pointing out that his photographs implicitly call for the destruction of urban tenements and the construction of public parks and other open areas. "Space," says Shloss, "itself signalled the defeat of the landlord class" (122). Her book is an invaluable survey of a century of U.S. writing on, about, and around photography.

6. Sara Blair contextualizes this moment of competition and collusion between photo and text in her work on Henry James, Lewis Hine, and Jacob Riis. Blair suggests that James wrote *The American Scene* by both "aligning" himself and "competing with the emerging documentary modes of mass visual culture," i.e., photography (160). Please see also Alan Trachtenberg's account of Hine, Alfred Stieglitz, and John Dewey, "Camera Work/Social Work" in his *Reading American Photographs.*

7. Paula Rabinowitz's account of reportage and documentary forms has greatly illuminated this text to me. Her chapter on Evans and Agee, "Voyeurism and Class Consciousness," provides a detailed analysis of the class and gender dynamics between the two uneasy documentarists and their subjects (35–55). For another astute perspective on the complex relationship between the documentary genre and its subjects, see Chandan Reddy, "Home, Houses, Non-identity: *Paris is Burning.*" More recent examples of this form of documentary are also important to note, particularly the photography of Jean Mohr, who has worked with John Berger *(Another Way of Telling)* and Edward Said *(After the Last Sky).*

8. An excellent source of criticism on contemporary documentaries is *Theorizing Documentary,* edited by Michael Renov. Although the essays in this 1993 collection consider more recent examples of the genre, the juxtapositions of documentary form with science, history, and philosophy are useful for thinking through both its presumptions and its legacy.

9. Houston Baker lays out some of the deeply problematic gendering that Wright's narrative, particularly in this final section "Men in the Making," reifies. As Baker notes, "*12 Million Black Voices*'s conclusion is not only utopian, but also aggressively masculine" (115).

10. In her analysis of documentary fiction, Barbara Foley makes a similar point regarding text-based narratives: "The Afro-American documentary novel continues to adopt the familiar representational strategies of realistic and modernist documentary fiction, but it introduces documentation in ways that subvert rather than reinforce certain aspects of bourgeois hegemony. In the Afro-American documentary novel, the two main types of documentary validation—veracious and verifying—are characteristically blended" (234).

11. Baker's analysis of *12 Million Black Voices* focuses on Wright's use of "PLACE" and African American displacements—geographical, textual, historical (105–24). As I indicate earlier, space/place representations are crucial to all photo-text works. A provocative way to bear this out would be to compare the pervasive sense of absence and exteriority that I discuss in Walker Evans's photographs in *Let Us Now Praise Famous Men* with the dialectic of absence and presence, intimacy and interiority, in the photographs that make up Wright's work. These salient differences suggest that the authors and artists have very different (political and aesthetic) ends in mind for their projects.

12. Evidence of this crucial nexus between visuality and race emerges from the article that follows the piece by Wright and Miller in *Ebony*. Titled "'Evil-Eye' Ingram," the article recounts the story of an African American "Tobacco farmer [who] gets [a] two-year sentence for 'looking' at [a] white girl" (33). In this 1950 legal proceeding, a forty-four-year-old North Carolina father of nine was sentenced to two years of hard labor "for 'attempted assault on a female,'" although according to the woman, Mack Ingram's crime was "merely looking at white Willa Jean Boswell from a distance of 75 feet" (33). That a look could be considered dangerous enough to be classified as an "attempted assault" speaks volumes about the need for the photography projects by Wright.

13. The genre has continued to produce complex articulations of race and culture. Albert Murray's 1976 book, *Stomping the Blues,* integrates its photographic and textual material so completely that the book seems to be in conversation with its subjects. Murray's unconventionally detailed captions also are worth noting. I am grateful to Robert G. O'Meally for leading me to this rich and insightful example of the photo-text genre.

14. I am, of course, taking some liberty with the title of Avedon's major collection, *Evidence, 1944–94.* Although I did not have Avedon's title in mind, it indicates Avedon's interest in playing with the boundaries of this crucial term in photographic history. His massive *An Autobiography* is wordless, aside from a brief introduction and captions at the end. Avedon consistently has subverted viewers' expectations for "evidence" in his photographs (of power, wealth, beauty, not to mention madness, poverty, and indigence), whether verbal or visual.

15. Richard Avedon, interview by author, 16 April 1998.

16. Ibid.

17. Baldwin felt strongly that the book should conclude on a note of redemption. "The end of the book was Jimmy's necessity," Ibid.

18. For a wider discussion of the Baldwinian witness in the context of African American literature and the Cold War, please see Joshua Miller, "The Discovery of What it Means to be a Witness: James Baldwin and the Dialectics of Distance."

19. W.J.T. Mitchell sets up a useful distinction in his consideration of photo-text works. Thinking primarily of William Blake, Mitchell writes that the relationship between the image and the text ranges "from the absolutely disjunctive ('illustrations' that have no textual reference) to the absolutely synthetic identification of verbal and visual codes (marks that collapse the distinction between writing and drawing" (91). Mitchell's summation of the general relation between image and text as "an unstable dialectic that constantly shifts its location in representational practices" seems particularly apt in regard to *Nothing Personal* (83).

20. Another particularly acute critic of the history of photography is Sigfried Kracauer. In *Critical Realism,* Dagmar Barnouw provides a useful philosophical framework in which to consider Kracauer's work on photography, documentary, and "objective truth." See especially her chapter on "Image, Imagination, and Historical Evidence" (200–64).

WORKS CITED

Agee, James and Walker Evans. *Let Us Now Praise Famous Men.* 1941. Reprint, Boston: Houghton and Mifflin, 1960.

Alexander, Elizabeth. "'Can you be BLACK and look at this?': Reading the Rodney King Video(s)." In *Black Male: Representations of Masculinity in Contemporary Art,* 91–110. New York: Whitney Museum of American Art, 1994.

"American Gothic." Review of *Nothing Personal,* by James Baldwin and Richard Avedon. *Time* 6 November 1964, 108–10.

Avedon, Richard. *An Autobiography.* New York: Random House, 1993.

———. *Evidence: 1944–94.* New York: Random House, 1994.

Baker, Houston. *Workings of the Spirit: The Poetics of Afro-American Women's Writing.* Chicago: University of Chicago Press, 1991.

Baldwin, James and Richard Avedon. *Nothing Personal.* New York: Atheneum, 1964.

Baldwin, James. *The Price of the Ticket: Collected Nonfiction 1948–1985.* New York: St. Martin's, 1985.

Barnouw, Dagmar. *Critical Realism: History, Photography, and the Work of Sigfried Kracauer.* Baltimore: Johns Hopkins University Press, 1994.

Barthes, Roland. *Camera Lucida: Reflections on Photography.* Trans. Richard Howard. New York: Hill and Wang, 1981.

Benjamin, Walter. *Illuminations.* Trans. Harry Zohn. New York: Schocken, 1968.

Berger, John and Jean Mohr. *Another Way of Telling.* New York: Pantheon Books, 1982.

Blair, Sara. *Henry James and the Writing of Race and Nation.* New York: Cambridge University Press, 1996.

Brustein, Robert. "Everybody Knows My Name." Review of *Nothing Personal,* by James Baldwin and Richard Avedon. *The New York Review of Books,* December 1964, 10–11.

Campbell, James. *Talking at the Gates: A Life of James Baldwin.* New York: Viking, 1991.

Carby, Hazel. "'On the Threshold of Woman's Era': Lynching, Empire, and Sexuality in Black Feminist Theory," In *'Race,' Writing, and Difference,* ed. Henry Louis Gates, Jr., 301–16. Chicago: University of Chicago Press, 1986.

Chandler, James, Arnold I. Davidson, and Harry Harootunian, eds. *Questions of Evidence: Proof, Practice, and Persuasion across the Disciplines.* Chicago: University of Chicago Press, 1994.

"Dark Exposure." Review of *Nothing Personal,* by James Baldwin and Richard Avedon. *Times Literary Supplement* 10 December 1964, 1122.

DeCarava, Roy, and Langston Hughes. *The Sweet Flypaper of Life.* 1955. Reprint, Washington, D.C.: Howard University Press, 1984.

Ellison, Ralph. "Letter to Richard Wright," 3 November 1941. *Richard Wright Papers: Personal Correspondence.* Beinecke Rare Book and Manuscript Library. JWJ MSS 3, Series II, Box 97, Folder 1314.

Fabre, Michel. "Paris as a Moment in African American Consciousness." In *The Black Colombiad: Defining Moments in African American Literature and Culture,* ed. Werner Sollors and Maria Diedrich, 123–38. Cambridge, Mass.: Harvard University Press, 1994.

———. *The Unfinished Quest of Richard Wright.* 2d ed. Trans. Isabel Barzun. Urbana: University of Illinois Press, 1993.

Foley, Barbara. *Telling the Truth: The Theory and Practice of Documentary Fiction.* Ithaca, N.Y.: Cornell University Press, 1986.

Gilman, Sander. "Black Bodies, White Bodies: Toward an Iconography of Female Sexuality in Late Nineteenth-Century Art, Medicine, and Literature." In *'Race,' Writing, and Difference,* ed. Henry Louis Gates, Jr., 223–61. Chicago: University of Chicago Press, 1986.

Gilroy, Paul. *The Black Atlantic: Modernity and Double Consciousness.* Cambridge, Mass.: Harvard University Press, 1993.

Kirstein, Lincoln. "Art Books of 1964." Review of *Nothing Personal,* by James Baldwin and Richard Avedon. *The Nation* 14 December 1964, 470–72.

Leeming, David A. *James Baldwin: A Biography.* New York: Knopf, 1994.

Lenz, Gunter H. "Symbolic Space, Communal Rituals, and the Surreality of the Urban Ghetto: Harlem in Black Literature from the 1920s to the 1960s." *Callaloo* 11, no. 2 (Spring 1988): 309–45.

Levine, Laurence W. "The Historian and the Icon: Photography and the History of the American People in the 1930s and 1940s." In *The Unpredictable*

Past: Explorations in American Cultural History. New York: Oxford University Press, 1993.

Miller, Joshua L. "The Discovery of What it Means to be a Witness: James Baldwin and the Dialectics of Distance." In *James Baldwin Now,* ed. Dwight A. McBride. New York: New York University Press, 1999.

Minh-ha, Trinh T. "The Totalizing Quest of Meaning." In *Theorizing Documentary,* ed. Michael Renov, 90–107. New York: Routledge, 1993.

Mitchell, W.J.T. *Picture Theory: Essays on Verbal and Visual Representation.* Chicago: University of Chicago Press, 1994.

Murray, Albert. *Stomping the Blues.* New York: McGraw-Hill, 1976.

Nelson, Emmanuel S. "James Baldwin's Vision of Otherness and Community." In *Critical Essays on James Baldwin,* ed. Fred L. Standley and Nancy V. Burt. Boston: G. K. Hall, 1988.

Parks, Gordon. "The Atmosphere of Crime." *Life,* 9 September 1957, 53–58.

Rabinowitz, Paula. *They Must Be Represented: The Politics of Documentary.* London: Verso, 1994.

Reddy, Chandan. "Home, Houses, Non-identity: *Paris is Burning.*" In *Burning Down the House: Recycling Domesticity,* ed. Rosemary Marangoly George. Boulder, Colo.: Westview, 1998.

Reilly, John M. "Richard Wright and the Art of Non-Fiction: Stepping Out on the Stage of the World." *Callaloo* 9, no. 3 (Summer 1986): 507–20.

———. "Richard Wright Preaches the Nation: *12 Million Black Voices.*" *Black American Literature Forum* 16, no. 3 (Fall 1982): 116–19.

Renov, Michael, ed. *Theorizing Documentary.* New York: Routledge, 1993.

Riis, Jacob A. *How the Other Half Lives: Studies Among the Tenements of New York.* 1890. Reprint, New York: Dover Publications, 1971.

Robbins, Bruce. "Feeling Global: John Berger and Experience." In *Postmodernism and Politics,* ed. Jonathan Arac, 145–61. Minneapolis: University of Minnesota Press, 1986.

Rowe, John Carlos. "Eye-Witness: Documentary Styles in the American Representations of Vietnam." In *The Vietnam War and American Culture,* ed. John Carlos Rowe and Rick Berg, 126–50. New York: Columbia University Press, 1991.

Said, Edward, and Jean Mohr. *After the Last Sky: Palestinian Lives.* New York: Pantheon, 1986.

Santé, Luc. *Evidence.* New York: Farrar, Straus Giroux, 1992.

Shloss, Carol. *In Visible Light, Photography and the American Writer: 1840–1940.* New York: Oxford University Press, 1987.

Standley, Fred L. and Louis H. Pratt, eds. *Conversations with James Baldwin.* Jackson: University Press of Mississippi, 1989.

Stovall, Tyler. *Paris Noir: African Americans in the City of Light.* Boston: Houghton Mifflin, 1996.

Thorsen, Karen. *James Baldwin: The Price of the Ticket.* Movie. American Masters and Maysleys Films, New York, 1989.

Trachtenberg, Alan. *Reading American Photographs: Images as History Mathew Brady to Walker Evans.* New York: Hill and Wang, 1989.

Troupe, Quincy, ed. *James Baldwin: The Legacy.* New York: Simon & Schuster, 1989.

Weatherby, W. J. *James Baldwin: Artist on Fire.* New York: Donald I. Fine, 1989.

Wright, Richard. "The Shame of Chicago." Photo by Wayne Miller. *Ebony,* December 1951, 24–31.

———. *12 Million Black Voices.* 1941. Reprint, New York: Thunder's Mouth Press, 1988.

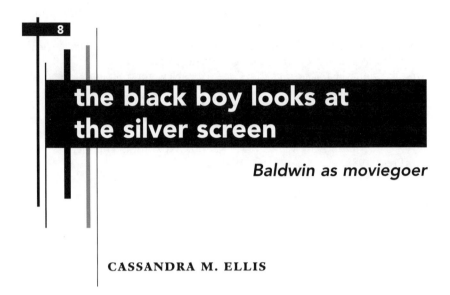

the black boy looks at the silver screen

Baldwin as moviegoer

CASSANDRA M. ELLIS

When asked how he characterized his role as one of the nation's most acclaimed African American writers, James Baldwin often replied that he wanted to be regarded not as an activist or a spokesperson for the black community, but as its witness. The term *witness* ensues from his fiercely pious upbringing in scriptural tradition, resonating in the apocalyptic language of *The Fire Next Time* (1963), a vocabulary in which he became well-versed as a teen-aged storefront preacher in Harlem. When he finally left the pulpit, it was because he already had converted to a different theatrical (and, some would say, religious) arena. One Sunday, instead of attending service, he sneaked off to a matinee on Forty-second Street. From that day on, Baldwin remained a devoted cinefile. "I don't know if I have any [interests]," he admitted as he introduced himself when his first collected essays appeared in 1955, "unless the morbid desire to own a sixteen millimeter camera and make experimental movies can be so classified" (*Notes of a Native Son,* 8–9).[1] Although he never seriously fulfilled this "morbid desire" to be a filmmaker, Baldwin spent his life witnessing cinema by reviewing films, admiring stars and directors, taking his fictional characters to the movies, and even struggling to get Hollywood to do justice to his vision of Malcolm X.

Baldwin's frustration with the movie industry's incapacity to fulfill what he saw as a transformative relation between literature and film led him to abandon production of his Malcolm X screenplay,[2] but his dismay inspired a long essay on American cinema. *The Devil Finds Work* eloquently chronicles how studios perpetuated racist ideologies for decades, yet it is perhaps most remarkable because Baldwin refuses to reduce cinema to a transparent narrative medium. Instead, he offers the personal testimony of an eyewitness, and we feel his presence in a dynamic, dark arena. Here, and throughout his writings, Baldwin foregrounds cinematic space in order to negotiate identity through negation and celluloid traces of human images. By so witnessing cinema, he testifies to racial, gendered, and sexual identifications that exceed existing paradigms of spectatorship, identification, and visual pleasure within both cinema studies and literary theory.

Witnessing entails a process of retrospection, recuperation, and finding one's voice. "The life of a witness," as Baldwin's friend and most authoritative biographer, David Leeming, reminds us, "usually has its self-doubting, self-searching side" (49). Etymologically, *witnessing* originated in the black church, then slipped across cultural spheres until it was appropriated into more secular black English discourses (Smitherman 93–94, 150, 231–32, 257).[3] Its movement thereby parallels Baldwin's conversion from storefront preacher witness to a witness of a Forty-second Street matinee. By interchanging the church and cinema in his writings, Baldwin calls attention to their close correlation as cultural sites that often find their way into the pages of African American literature. Through this exchange, he mediates the distinctions of sacred and profane, high and low, literature and popular culture.

To be a witness, one must both see and linguistically perform that act of seeing. A witness, that is, must testify. Witnessing integrates notions of the gaze (the visual and aural pleasures of cinema) with performative testimony (spoken or written words) that reifies film-viewing as a collective experience. The term *witnessing* therefore not only serves as a useful paradigm to frame the moviegoing of Baldwin, a self-described witness, but also fills theoretical and discursive gaps in the critical treatment of spectatorship. Witnessing cinema paradoxically entails both the embodiment and disembodiment of the viewer. A witness looks more actively than a passive spectator, but nevertheless must subvert the act of viewing to the greater purpose of testifying to events. When he writes about cinema, Baldwin documents a cultural history wherein seemingly unlikely identifications have been forged. He does not merely watch, he *witnesses,* and in so doing, he provides a singular model for marginalized spectators. His witnessing legitimizes the experience of watching, and he testifies, sometimes reluctantly, both to exhilarating pleasure (as in witnessing a miracle) and in order to indict. As the last and most sustained of Baldwin's testaments to the power of popular cinema, *The Devil Finds Work* stands as a prophetic text that offers fresh insights for re-imagining the critical dimensions of spectatorship and identification.

Semiotic and psychoanalytic readings of films proliferated during the seventies, as did many examinations of Hollywood's representations of blacks; yet neither approach seemed aware of the other.[4] Published in 1976 as the culmination of Baldwin's views on film, *The Devil Finds Work* synthesizes these disparate trends, although film theory has yet to contend rigorously with the essay. Instead of offering an abstracted theory of viewing or a catalogue of on-screen distorted images, Baldwin testifies about his own viewing experiences within a significant black cultural space. He bears witness to the ways filmic constructions of race and identity are constituted through the cinematic apparatus as it operates in a particular cultural context.

Reviewing Baldwin's essay when it first appeared, Donald Bogle noted that some of its observations seemed rather passé after his *Toms, Coons, Mulattoes, Mammies, and Bucks: An Interpretive History of Blacks in Films* (1973) and other studies like it had begun to cast film into the light of black consciousness. "Hip" readers, warned Bogle, already assured in their demystification, might dismiss Baldwin as "witty and damnably intelligent but somewhat old hat." Seeking to narrow the generational gap, Bogle pointed out, however, that viewers' "new cynicism is no more than a new form of romanticism tinged with some old-fashioned, self-righteous masochism" (107), equally nostalgic but less honest than Baldwin's testimony. Bogle presumably counts himself among the "hip" viewer he admonishes, but his own derivative studies cannot be considered acts of witnessing. Since Baldwin's account is more self-conscious about its pleasures, *The Devil Finds Work* is a more personally invested project than its contemporary film studies professed to be. Baldwin's witnessing approach also lent his essay a strong prophetic dimension, which also set it apart from the sociologically based work of its time.

The cynicism of those analyses to which Bogle's review alludes, moreover, remained unexamined until fairly recently when scholars took a renewed interest in spectatorship. As Judith Mayne attests in her ground-breaking *Cinema and Spectatorship* (1993), Baldwin's essay, far from being dated, was in many respects ahead of its time. Stressing that spectatorship is a necessarily paradoxical phenomenon, Mayne insists on entangling the abstracted, disembodied subject of apparatus theory with sociology's favorite statistic—the actual film viewer. She maintains that spectatorship only can be understood as a mediation of the two personae. *The Devil Finds Work*, she contends, breaks down the "facile opposition" that film theory upheld in the seventies between subject and viewer by incorporating both the subject ("as ideological entity . . . and psychic one") and real historical audiences (156).[5]

Pursuing Mayne's estimation of Baldwin's significance to theorizing spectatorship, this chapter will trace some of Baldwin's inscriptions of moviegoing, alongside his development as a writer, to their culmination in *The Devil Finds Work*. Baldwin's essay deserves reexamination because it raises crucial implications for a host of current cultural debates, particularly those surrounding *whiteness* and *identification*. At the outset of her pursuit of new conceptions for identification in *Performance Anxieties: Staging Psychoanalysis, Staging Race*, Ann Pellegrini recognizes the "double direction" into which her inquiry will lead her. Like Mayne in her refusal to study spectators in oppositional terms, Pellegrini prepares herself for "optimism at what identifications across difference may enable; painful awareness of who and what go missing in the scene, and the 'seen,' of difference" (11). *The Devil Finds Work* traverses both paths by highlighting a lifetime of writing about moviegoing: Baldwin's own and that of others.

Yet despite this essay's value and currency, even theorists of spectatorship who have looked to Baldwin as a moviegoer have missed his relevance to their projects by underestimating and even misreading him. Although Mayne mentions *The Devil Finds Work* in her comprehensive study of spectatorship, lauding its foresight, she references it as a kind of audience response survey form, completed by the most gifted, eloquent, and, therefore, eminently qualified member among African Americans. She values the essay's historical and sociological aspects, mentioning Baldwin's experiences at uptown and downtown screenings of *The Defiant Ones* (1958), for example, but overlooks the ways Baldwin's witnessings also might transform the more theoretical or psychic dimensions of spectatorship. In so neglecting to abstract much from Baldwin, Mayne fails to observe him at a personal level. Instead, she locates *The Devil Finds Work* within the tradition of seventies scholarship on black film, distinguishing Baldwin from those positive and negative image seekers with only an off-handed compliment to his acumen and reputation. Mayne concedes that Baldwin is a much better writer than most black Hollywood critics, yet he both is and is not making the same points by using different words. What intones Baldwin's different tune in *The Devil Finds Work* is his first-person testimony, which carries with it the greater context of his artistic and spiritual development.

Like other contemporary scholars who have mined *The Devil Finds Work* for new insights into the effects of the cinematic apparatus, Mayne also deflects the religious dimension of Baldwin's witnessing. In doing so, she overlooks a focal point that may alert us to a great deal more about how piously Americans of all traditions (not just those of the black church) see film through and against, not necessarily in direct opposition to, their faiths, theologies, and the degrees to which they practice them. Laurence Goldstein similarly underrates the essay's value to current inquires into the impact of film on American writers. In his lucid critical study of *The American Poet at the Movies*, Goldstein reads *The Devil Finds Work* as Baldwin's renunciation of his youthful attitudes toward movie pleasures (216–22).

It is well known that Baldwin embraced his vocation as literary artist to work through the contradictory yet integrated aspects of his identity, thereby demonstrating the inextricably linked identities of all Americans. My goal is to show how his love of moviegoing played an instrumental role in that development (216–22). Ever aware of moviegoing as a unique practice with its own set of pleasures, conventions, and cultural trappings, Baldwin treated the movies as a vernacular through which he sought to bridge the linguistic communities of black and white America. By watching and writing about film, Baldwin was able to absorb his background in the black church into the cinema. For Baldwin in 1976, the cinema was the appropriate arena for wrestling with the demons of American history because—unlike either the black church or the white liberal intellectual establishment—film demanded extensive exchanges between black and white images, whether on-screen or, with Baldwin as witness, between audience and screen.

Although I wish to underscore that Baldwin's legacy as American author depends on his being a movie buff, I also must stress that he never confuses the movie theater with the library, nor does he conflate literature and film; rather, he always is acutely aware of the differences of narrative media. Recounting his impressions of MGM's 1936 *A Tale of Two Cities*, he notes that, even as a child and would-be novelist, he was well-versed enough in moviegoing to disbelieve suspense and suspend disbelief simultaneously:

> For while believing it all, and really believing it, I still knew that Madam Defarge was really an actress named Blanche Yurka and that Lucie

Mannette was really an English girl, named Elizabeth Allan. Something implacable in the set of Yurka's mouth probably reminded me of my grandmother, and I knew that Elizabeth Allan-Lucie Mannette reminded me of my music teacher, a Miss Taub, with whom I was desperately in love. . . . This was the first time in my life that I had seen a screen rendition (so the ads and press put it) of a novel, which, considering my age, I could claim to know. And I felt very close to the actors. (564)

Shuffled between images of characters and white actors, yet all the while secure in his seat in the theater, Baldwin gets safely returned to the world of the familiar: to the face of his grandmother, a former slave, and to the realms of his own experiences. His memories of *A Tale of Two Cities,* however, clue us into the first problem with imaging Baldwin as a black film scholar. He discusses a film that seems to be not at all about race. It is a Hollywood version of a European masterpiece, which features no black characters. Indeed, all the actors to whom Baldwin "felt very close" were white.

Most critical inquiries concerning race in the cinema typically have been limited to what is on-screen, and they analyze images rather than viewers. They tend also to confine themselves to black images in films that treat race in terms of settings, geographical and historical, and depict black characters *or*—not necessarily *and*—black actors. Understandably, critics have chosen to focus on race as explicit subject matter, calling attention to the neglected histories of black actors, Hollywood's all-black features, and independent black filmmakers rather than accentuating what seems all too obvious: the fact that classical Hollywood cinema so often omits African Americans entirely.[6] Excluded from the screen, blackness is coded "absent" so that whiteness too gets rendered seemingly invisible, ensuring that these films cannot possibly be about race. That Baldwin's cinematic perspectives include all-white films, as well as films that represent black bodies, forces us to confront the historical fact that although blacks too often were absent from Hollywood's screens, they were not absent from the audiences that watched those screens.[7]

Baldwin adores white screen icons from an early age, not out of any overdetermined self-hatred or a desire to pass for white, but for the enigmatic instability of their star quality and the awe of alluring human presences these icons instilled in him. Their elusive quality, in fact, seemed gloriously resilient to the bounds of cultural divisions, racial or otherwise. The earliest film he recalls, for instance, is the 1931 gangster thriller *Dance, Fools, Dance,* starring Joan Crawford, which the seven-year-old Baldwin attended with either his mother or his aunt. The image of Crawford's "small, lonely back" must have lingered in his imagination some forty-five years before he transcribed it in the first sentence of *The Devil Finds Work.* Shortly after having seen the film, Baldwin encountered a "colored woman—who looked exactly like Crawford" shopping in a Harlem store. Baldwin became so utterly entranced, for "she seemed to be wearing the sunlight, rearranging it around her head from time to time, with a movement of one hand, with a movement of her head, and with her smile" (558), that he followed her into the street. Captivated, he had managed to project Crawford's radiant gestures onto a woman from his own neighborhood. Hollywood backlighting may have cast a glow on Crawford, but in Baldwin's eyes this "colored woman" could manipulate the very rays of the sun.

In a 1961 radio interview with Studs Terkel, he generalized from these impressions to address the "psychological hazards of being an American Negro":

> You go to the movies and, like everyone else, you fall in love with Joan Crawford, and you root for the Good Guys who are killing off the Indians. It comes as a great psychological collision when you realize all of these things are really metaphors for your oppression, and will lead into a kind of psychological warfare in which you may perish. (5)

Accordingly, the radiance of the Crawford look-alike you saw in Harlem may or may not be altogether extinguished by the realization that falling in love with Joan Crawford signifies a "metaphor for your oppression." That woman's image, in fact, may cast doubt on that realization, but either way, forging such an identification with a white female star does, without question, engage you in some form of "psychological warfare."

Determined not to perish in the psychic battles he fought, Baldwin's "great psychological collision" nonetheless came not as a single moment but as an ongoing struggle. That struggle, moreover, he waged not only by interacting with the whiteness on screen, but also with the white faces that surrounded him in the cinema. In his 1968 novel, *Tell Me How Long the Train's Been Gone,* when the narrator Leo remembers going to a film in Times Square as a teen-ager in the forties, his retrospective voice is identical to Baldwin's in *The Devil Finds Work.* In the interval between the newsreel and the Warner Brothers feature, Leo considers the white faces belonging to

Strange people, sitting, mainly, all alone. There were one or two cou-
ples, very, very young: the boy's hair still bright from the water, the girl's
hair still bright from the heat; they sat very close together, and as to the
popcorn, chewing gum, and candy, the boys were attentive indeed,
climbing the titled steps from time to time to call on the usherettes. I
was between fourteen and fifteen then, and the boys and girls could not
have been much older. But they impressed me as being children, children forever, children not as a biological fact, but as a perpetual condition. I am sure that I was a very disagreeable boy in those days, for I
really despised them for their blank, pimpled faces and their bright,
haunted eyes. it had not occurred to me—partly, no doubt, indeed,
because it had not occurred to *them*—that they had to shit, like I did,
and they jerked off sometimes, like I did, and were just as frightened as
I. It had not yet occurred to me that the mask of my bravado was very
much like theirs, concealed though it was, and most effectively, by the
mask of my color, and by the reflexes which this mask occasioned in
them and in me. No: I simply despised them because I thought it might
have been better for me if I had been like them. (176–77)

Like Baldwin, Leo's "mask of . . . color" necessitates hatred, occasioned
by an as yet unselfconscious identification that separates blacks and
whites within the very theaters in which they physically come together
to watch movies. Although the movie theaters in New York City where
Baldwin grew up were not legally segregated as in the South, as late as
the 1930s ushers in theaters owned and managed by whites such as
Loew's in Harlem would routinely seat black and white patrons in separate sections (Gomery 159). More pervasively, however, New York's
cinemas were segregated by neighborhood and by "residential patterns
of use," a trend that became more marked with the suburbanization and
white flight of the postwar decades (Gomery 165). By the sixties, when
movie theaters finally were integrated in the South, theaters in the
major northern cities not only were becoming more exclusively black,
but those theaters also were considerably busier than their suburban
counterparts. In 1961, *Ebony* estimated that urban blacks attended
movies more often than any other group in the population (Gomery
165). According to *Variety,* although blacks constituted between 10–15
percent of the U.S. population in the sixties, they bought half of all
movie tickets, especially in the major cities (Gomery 169). That trend
has persisted. In 1991, for example, African Americans accounted for
12 percent of the population and for 25 percent of commercial film
audiences (Mayne 154). Baldwin comments upon this long-standing

situation by assuming his ironic child-spectator pose: "I did not yet know that virtually every black community in America contains a movie house, or, sometimes, in those days, an actual theater, called the Lincoln, or the Booker T. Washington, nor did I know why: any more than I knew why The Cotton Club was called The Cotton Club" (*Devil Finds Work* 561). As he tried to become conscious about the historical and ideological significance of his community's predilection for moviegoing, Baldwin's own viewing habits first had to lead him both into and away from the theaters in his own neighborhood. His own "residential-use pattern" of various New York neighborhood theaters broadened as he matured and pursued his artistic vocation. On his way to becoming a writer, he saw movies in Harlem, on Forty-second Street, and in Greenwich Village.

Baldwin's religious acumen was instilled at home, but it continually conflicted with the cultural contacts to which his schooling exposed him. At school he met white friends with whom he would go to the movies, both in and beyond Harlem. In *The Devil Finds Work*, Baldwin paid tribute to one of his teachers at P.S. 24, Orilla "Bill" Miller, the person who first influenced his attitudes toward white people and the movies.

Although he thought his striking young teacher beautiful, Baldwin acknowledged that she was somehow neither white nor beautiful in the same ways as Joan Crawford. Nor, I would infer, was she alluring in the same way as the black woman he saw "wearing the sunlight" in the Harlem store, resembling Crawford. He does not describe Bill performing or gesturing in an "unwhite" way, the way that he perceived, for example, some white actors like Sylvia Sidney or Henry Fonda.[8] Baldwin claimed that Sidney and Fonda were the only American actors who reminded him of blacks and so "reminded me of reality;" all the others "moved me at a distance" (*Devil Finds Work* 569–70). He mentions that Fonda's walk at the close of *The Grapes of Wrath* did not look like the walk of a white man, and maintains that a combination of Fonda's and Sidney's looks, gestures, roles, and contexts into which they were cast—in films such as *Dead End* and *You Only Live Once*—contributed to this impression. Knowing that Bill Miller lacked the wealth and glamour that produced an icon, however, Baldwin called her whiteness into question on the basis of his having observed police and landlords treat her "just like a nigger."

Bill and Baldwin both loved Dickens, and when she took him to see *A Tale of Two Cities* at the Harlem's Lincoln Theater, teacher and student were not escorted to segregated sections. During the storming of the Bastille scene, when Bill whispered to Jimmy that every body plummeting from the drawbridge signified the end of a human life (*Devil Finds Work* 564), she was more concerned with teaching him how to discern who the "good guys" really were than in confirming or dissuading his attractions to *femmes fatales*, yet she was pointing him toward the contradictions and inherent difficulties underlying Hollywood metaphors for oppression as well as liberation. Although Baldwin had a great deal yet to ponder about the stakes of revolution, when he saw Sydney Carton prepare for the guillotine, performing the ultimate self-sacrifice in another man's place, the climactic scene conjured not an image but a text for him: *Greater love hath no man than this.* Ronald Colman thus became Christ in his young viewer's eyes, even before MGM confirmed the analogy by flashing before audiences suffering the zenith of the Great Depression what Baldwin termed its "sprawling enormity" of a postscript: *I am the resurrection and the life, saith the Lord: he that believeth in me, though he were dead, yet he shall live; and he that believeth in me shall never die.* Although he had not yet become a preacher, Baldwin indeed had "lived with this text all [his] life, which made encountering it on the screen of the Lincoln Theater absolutely astounding" (*Devil Finds Work* 562). He was mesmerized by the epigraph flashed on the screen of this most sinful place, which his father reviled yet was powerless to oppose in the face of his son's white schoolteacher. What he once had thought antithetical realms and allegiances—home and school, black and white, church and theater—were synthesized by watching a film, revealing themselves, for now, as interpenetrable.

Initially, the influence of his fathers—both earthly and heavenly—prevailed, and young Jimmy, the preacher, lost Bill Miller's respect by telling her he no longer could see her. A few years later, however, just before graduating from DeWitt Clinton High School in the Bronx, Baldwin was convinced by another of his white friends, Emile Capouya, that his preaching had become nothing more than a disappointing exercise in hypocrisy, that he could not go on preaching what he no longer believed himself. In 1941, after Baldwin preached what would be his last sermon, he sneaked out before the end of service to meet Capouya for a matinee at Times Square. This anticonversion proved a pivotal event in his life, and Baldwin reworked it several times to maximize its dramatic effect. In the sixties, he recalled meeting Capouya for a Gilbert and Sullivan operetta, but in *The Devil Finds Work,* he changed the matinee in question to the stage version of *Native Son,* starring Canada Lee. Capouya, trying to recall the specifics after Baldwin's death, doubted whether the two could have afforded theater tickets. "It wouldn't have been a Broadway play," he qualified, "just a cheap moviehouse, perhaps another Russian film. The war had started and the Russians were our allies and the Russian films downtown were very cheap" (Weatherby 36).

While Baldwin was growing up in New York City, movies always had presented him with the complicated task of image-sorting, displaying a range of images and identities, offering up pleasures that always were somehow integrated—whether as a social outing or as a force that threatened at once to destroy the values and culture of home (including his religious identity), and oddly, to mirror, replicate, even reconstitute them. Baldwin's viewing experiences throughout New York thus are quite different from those of another young preacher—Bliss in Ralph Ellison's posthumous novel *Juneteenth*—who sneaks off to the movies in Atlanta one afternoon and discovers, by virtue of his admission to the segregated theater, that he can pass for white (*Juneteenth* 257–66). In an earlier scene, Bliss fears having his preacher father, Daddy Hickman, take him to his first picture show (233–45). Bliss hopes to preserve the images of sin in his imagination, and Hickman's hypocrisy is revealed gently in his role of persuasive escort who must instruct the boy, just this once, in the knowledge of temptation.[9] Cinema confronted Baldwin, in contrast, with an affirmation of his black identity both in contestatory and complementary relation to film images and to mixed audiences. Moreover, Baldwin's persistent wrestling with Hollywood's contradictory metaphors undoubtedly influenced his development as an author.

In Baldwin's first and most autobiographical novel, *Go Tell It On the Mountain,* the protagonist, John Grimes, celebrates his fourteenth birthday by going to a matinee on Forty-second Street. Unlike Ellison's Bliss, John goes unaccompanied, for it is impossible to imagine that either Gabriel Grimes or Reverend David Baldwin would resort to Daddy Hickman's tactics of confronting sin on screen. Once inside, however, John experiences the same sort of ambivalence as Bliss. He becomes transfixed by the transgressive allure of the film's villainess, not because she is like him but because she represents what he cannot be. She is not only white and female, but blasphemously powerful, and he envies her pride and her relentless rhetorical sadism. She is also a much whiter devil than any with whom John could hope to wrestle on the threshing floor of the black church.

Although its title is never mentioned in *Go Tell It on the Mountain,* the film Baldwin describes John watching is RKO's 1934 rendition of W. Somerset Maugham's novel *Of Human Bondage.* The film stars Leslie Howard as Philip Carey and Bette Davis, in the role that catapulted her rise to stardom, as Mildred Rogers. *Life* magazine lauded Davis's portrayal as "the best screen performance ever recorded" by an American actress, so John certainly was not alone in his ambivalent captivation. Davis reportedly had to beg Jack Warner to lend her out for the role, which he and others close to her were certain would ruin her career, causing the public to forever identify Davis with her evil character. But Davis persisted, and the studio arranged to trade her for Irene Dunne. Given what she called her rather sheltered upbringing, Davis claims that she herself was shocked at her ability to bring Mildred to life, to understand what motivated her "vileness" and "machinations" to the point that a viewer like John Grimes could empathize with her. *Go Tell It on the Mountain*'s narrator does not conjecture about what motivates Mildred's actions, but given that she is an uneducated, impoverished waitress with a Cockney accent manipulating a comparably affluent artist-turned-medical student, it is not difficult to conceive of John's connection to her disadvantaged state. To a certain extent, she was like Bill Miller who, making her way in the big city, knew how to give the cops a piece of her mind. Although it was known as "the white plague," one of John's relatives had died of consumption, so he knew it to be a disease common among the wretchedly poor and admired how "particularly grotesque" Mildred appeared on her deathbed. Hollywood lore has it that Davis did her own makeup for the scene, insisting that "Mildred was not going to die of a dread disease looking as if a deb had missed her noon nap." She quipped that "the last stages of consumption, poverty, and neglect are not pretty, and I intend to be convincing looking" (Spada 138).[10] Baldwin forever would admire those who sought to use cinema as a medium for revealing truths, and Davis's "intend[ing] to look convincing" marked the first time a female star actually sought to make herself look ugly.

Bette Davis reappears as one of Baldwin's favorite stars in *The Devil Finds Work*. Baldwin delights in the resemblance he found between his own "frog eyes," which his stepfather, Reverend David Baldwin, had deemed the marks of his ugliness and illegitimacy, and Davis's legendary eyes:

> So, here, now was Bette Davis, on that Saturday afternoon, in close-up, over a champagne glass, pop-eyes popping. I was astounded. I had caught my father, not in a lie, but in an infirmity. For, here, before me, after all, was a *movie star: white:* and if she was white and a movie star, she was *rich:* and she was *ugly.* (560)

Baldwin's ability to forge an identification with an icon of white femininity—whether on her deathbed or, more curiously perhaps, over champagne—on the basis of equating her most prized, fetishized, and star-like attribute with his ugly mark of self-hatred represents a remarkable feat of spectatorial projection. Not only does it unsettle the notion of a monolithic male gaze,[11] but Baldwin's look at Davis also defies viewing along racial axes.

According to the ways film theorists such as Mulvey chart gender and race with respect to spectatorship, Baldwin's gaze thus is both female and somewhere between self-denyingly white and racially unmarked. From the perspectives of both feminist and black Hollywood film scholarship, that is, Baldwin represents a doubly "marginalized" spectator. Feminist discourse values such a position for the way it allows a subject to view cinema against the ideological grain, whereas in accounts of racialized spectatorship, alignment with any ideology of whiteness is typically represented as a psychologically devastating, politically reprehensible, and complicit way of seeing. Marginalized subjects abound in feminist film theory, but nonwhite viewers who take pleasure in white images virtually go unmentioned. It is tempting, therefore, to want to explain away Baldwin's identification with Davis the way film theory has been accustomed, as an effect of his homosexuality—the same way, for example, that Judy Garland's cult status in the gay community has been documented (see, for example, chapters devoted to Garland in both Dyer and Staiger). In this context, whether he is black or white becomes inconsequential and deferent to questions surrounding his sexuality.[12] In other words, we might be inclined to want to explain the way Baldwin sees Davis as an attribute of a gay male gaze, one that has nothing to do with of his blackness. We recall, for instance, how Baldwin recollected his anticonversion matinee, revising it from the cheap Russian film he probably saw with Emile Capouya, to *HMS Pinafore,* and subsequently to *Native Son.* Baldwin's reconstruction of his moviegoing indicates an increasing awareness of its being perceived as a sign of something other than his racial identity. His anxieties about these shifting perceptions, however, like the inclination to oversimplify his looking at Davis, not only belies how homophobia and racism implicate one another, particularly in the case of how Baldwin often gets read, by assuming that his sexuality eclipses his blackness; it also is symptomatic and indicative of a pervasive critical desire within film theory to deny racial differences among spectators and to privilege categories of gender and sexuality instead.[13] Baldwin's cinematic witnessing indeed proves that, as Ann Pellegrini puts it, "there is nothing straightforward about identification" (4).

In any case, because race, gender, and sexuality cannot be so readily extricated in determining visual pleasure, the cause of Baldwin's identification with Bette Davis, must be because he is, among other things, both gay *and* black. Those other things are significant if, following Kobena Mercer, we seek to transcend the race, gender, sexuality "mantras" and account for what he terms "between contingent spaces" of viewers' identities (215). We also must be willing to look beyond the mantra triad altogether, having noticed, for example, how John Grimes sees Bette Davis/Mildred Rogers through a religious lens and not, as we might expect, in terms of social class allegiance. The cinema scene, however, also often has been read to signal John's emergent homosexual identity (and an allusion to Baldwin's) in the same way that his wrestling with his Sunday school teacher, Elisha, gets coded (see, for example, Macebah, 52–67).

Like Bette Davis and his own writings, Baldwin the film viewer resists simple classification. As he continues to describe his reaction to one image of Davis, it is clear that what fascinates him is the *combination* of her race and gender, constituted in her transcendent intelligence-made-visible. As her identity as a white woman renders itself tenuous and unstable before his eyes, both viewer and image are sustained and "held" by their mutual intelligence:

> Out of bewilderment, out of loyalty to my mother, probably, and also because I sensed something menacing and unhealthy (for me, certainly) in the face on screen, I gave Davis's skin the dead-white greenish cast of something crawling from under a rock, but I was held, just the same, by the tense intelligence of the forehead, the disaster of the lips: and when she moved, she moved just like a nigger. (560)

Here we see Baldwin trying to cope with his daring and presumptuous attempt to identify with the white female star, as if he suddenly has become aware of the need to avert such a transgressive look and its consequences. Davis's face has become "menacing and unhealthy" because it appears both excessively sexualized and racially marked. Turned on by the inescapable knowledge that she is sexy because she "move[s] just like a nigger" without becoming one, Baldwin's only recourse is to accentuate her grotesque whiteness to the point of monstrosity so that her ugliness marks her as a threatening other. The only problem is that his projected disgust ultimately cannot contain either Davis's image or his desire to see himself in it.

If indeed this effect of seeing Davis—entrapment in a seemingly inevitable, sadomasochistic double bind—proves the only possibility for black identification with a white image, then we only can assume the pleasure of such a look to be the pleasure of passing or of (at least physically) assimilating. Discussing the ways spectatorial desire is structured in *King Kong* (1933), James Snead concludes:

> It is not true that we identify only with those in a film whose race or sex we share. Rather, the filmic space is subversive in allowing an almost polymorphically perverse oscillation between possible roles, creating a radically broadened freedom of identification. *But this freedom only increases the guilt that comes from looking at that which should remain hidden.* (23, italics added)

The admission that transforms Davis's skin into the "dead-white greenish cast of something crawling from under a rock . . . out of loyalty to [his] mother" affirms that Baldwin's identification indeed has increased his guilt. The pleasure of his freedom cannot, however, as Snead would have us believe, be reduced to guilt, nor does it *"only"* serve to "increase" guilt.

Baldwin demonstrates yet another transformation of his gaze when he speculates about the lasting impression Davis (who cries in Spencer Tracy's arms at the end of *20,000 Years in Sing Sing*) must have made on him:

> I had not yet heard Bessie Smith's "why they call this place Sing Sing?/Come stand here by this rock pile, and listen to these hammers ring," and it would be seven years before I would begin working on the railroad. It was to take a longer time than that before I would cry; a longer time than that before I would cry in anyone's arms; and a long long long long time before I would begin to realize what I myself was doing with my enormous eyes—or vice versa. This had nothing to do with Davis, the actress, or with all those hang-ups I didn't yet know I had: I had discovered that my infirmity might not be my doom; my infirmity, or infirmities, might be forged into weapons. (*Devil Finds Work* 560)

Baldwin's vow to "forge his infirmities into weapons," having seen his Bette Davis eyes, almost inspires a liberatory battle cry. It ensures that marginalized spectators can create their own images in triumph. There are, of course, plenty of moments in Baldwin's writings about film in which he manages to read mainstream film images in ways that we might not have expected. A rather striking illustration of such a moment comes in *Tell Me How Long the Train's Been Gone,* when two young brothers end up at a screening of the 1941 melodrama *King's Row* and find themselves snickering at its incestuous subtext:

> When it developed, coyly enough indeed, and with tremendous laments from the mighty music, that her father had been interfering with her, had lain between her thighs, had, in short, been screwing her, thus causing her to become mentally unbalanced—which we both felt then, was a somewhat curious result—and we watched Robert Cummings' plum-pudding reactions, Caleb had his face in his hands, which was thoughtful of him, for otherwise we would have been thrown out of the theater. (176–77)

Because they keep no secrets from one another, the boys are able to identify the "curious" secret of *King's Row* as incest, which, while never explicitly revealed as the key to the film's central enigma, nonetheless remains among its likely possibilities. The narrator, Leo, emphasizes the difficulty of drawing the inference of incest, while his brother Caleb uncovers the source of its cinematic repression: "When we finally picked up the story line—so to speak, it was by no means an easy matter—Caleb whispered, 'Shit. They acting just like niggers. Only they ain't got as much sense about it as *we* got'" (177).

Caleb's remark, especially given its sexual context, typifies an instance of *signifying.* Caleb reacts to *King's Row* by signifying, thereby contextualizing his reading of the film in terms of the brothers' "sense" of their own relationship. By this point in the novel Caleb and Leo have been sexually intimate, yet their intimacy is a source of empowerment, not madness or guilt. When they finally discover that the film's plot is about incest, a cultural experience with which they are familiar because it is understood, if not spoken, and nonetheless is not a veiled taboo, they can amuse themselves with the spectacle of white hysteria, secure in the knowledge that it is not something they will ever experience.

Seeing the whiteness of *King's Row* becomes an affirming experience for the brothers, just as Baldwin's gaze at Bette Davis inspired him to forge his infirmities into weapons. Yet those instances should no more lead us toward taking a totalizing view of the liberatory possibilities of black spectatorship than claims that posit any gaze at whiteness as a sign of utterly complicit masochism. I wholeheartedly agree with Mayne's contention that film viewing ought not to be conceived in dualistic terms—wherein "dominant" viewers always are properly sutured, while the "marginalized" only can produce resistant readings.[14] Although I insist on underscoring that Baldwin's looks at the silver screen often confess visual pleasures that are effectively guilt-free, I nevertheless am not suggesting that his viewings are ever either purely recuperative or utterly contestatory.[15] To do so would only be to diminish their brilliance and to limit their scope.

To begin to appreciate the range of that scope, I now turn to Baldwin's witnessing of black performers in Hollywood films. As Baldwin repeatedly insisted, he had to travel to Paris to gain a vantage from which he could properly envision himself as artist and to "discover what it means to be an American." It was from Paris, therefore, that he reviewed two all-black musicals of the fifties, designed to appeal simultaneously to the increasingly numbers of black urban audiences and to cross over to entertain, without offending, white audiences. Reviewing these films, Baldwin transposes the ritual of witnessing, a cultural practice he learned in the church, to the cinema. Hollywood so distorts its representations of black experience that the presence of black actors often, as Baldwin bears witness, exposes those distortions. Launching his scathingly brilliant attack on *Carmen Jones,* which transposed Bizet to a sanitized Chicago where apparently, to quote the review's title, "the dark is light enough," Baldwin glimpses in Pearl Bailey's pained caricature "such a murderously amused disdain" that he "cannot quite avoid suspicion that ... she is commenting on the film" ("Carmen Jones" 108). Similarly, he witnesses buried truth as it emerges "in Ruth Attaway's miming of 'My Man's Gone Now'" in the 1956 screen version of *Porgy and Bess,* noting that through her "miming" of the song, "some genuine depth is touched which has nothing to do with the vulgar production in which she is, for the rest of the time, quite thanklessly trapped" ("On Catfish Row" 180–81).

Generalizing about black actors working under white directors, Baldwin claims that "they know ... they are going to be ill-used and they resign themselves to it with as much sardonic good nature as they can muster" ("On Catfish Row" 179). In certain cases, they are ill-used because they are miscast. Baldwin thought, for example, that Sidney Poitier's star qualities—his strength, virility, and intelligence—made him an unconvincing Porgy, but he prefaces this assessment by qualifying that "no one can admire Sidney Poitier more than I do" ("On Catfish Row" 181). Perhaps the Poitier performance Baldwin most admired was the one delivered opposite Tony Curtis in *The Defiant Ones.* After Baldwin had returned in 1957 to live in the United States, to visit the South for the first time, and to join in the civil rights movement, he went to see this Hollywood message movie, purportedly inspired by the struggle for racial equality. After seeing *The Defiant Ones* twice in two of his old New York neighborhoods, he was convinced that Poitier's presence defiantly challenged the film's "buddy formula" premise:

> The irreducible difficulty of this genuinely well-meaning film is that no one, clearly, was able to see what Sidney Poitier would do with his role— nor was anyone, thereafter, able to undo it—and his performance, which lends the film its only real distinction, also, paradoxically, smashes it to pieces. There is no way to believe both [Poitier's character] and the story. (*Devil Finds Work* 595)

Baldwin goes on to describe how different audiences witnessed the contradictions Poitier embodies when, at the end of the film, he relinquishes his last chance for freedom in order to remain at his wounded white friend's side. Amongst a predominantly white, downtown audience, Poitier's loyal gesture was applauded wildly; amidst the Harlem audience, however, the same moment occasioned shouts of "Get back on that train, you fool!" (*Devil Finds Work* 596). Downtown they believed the story, but uptown Poitier had managed to make them believe his character in spite of it. As collective witness, the black audience senses an affinity with Poitier in excess of its liberal heroics. It recognizes enormous sacrifice, the insurmountable "price of the ticket" that the black performer must sacrifice at the expense of creating that white hero for whom downtown audiences cheer.

Baldwin continues witnessing Hollywood's distorted representations of real African Americans and their lives later in *The Devil Finds Work*. Beginning his discussion of the film version of Billie Holiday's autobiography, Baldwin—while acknowledging the credit due its stars, Diana Ross, Billy Dee Williams, and Richard Pryor, given the limitations of a script otherwise "empty as a banana peel"—claims that "*Lady Sings the Blues* is related to the black American experience in about the same way, and to the same extent that Princess Grace Kelly is related to the Irish potato famine" (*Devil Finds Work* 620). He supports his assertion by contrasting the ways Hollywood portrays white versus black heroines. All the Joan Crawford vehicles he watched as a child taught him that despite the "brutally crass and commercial terms," which always dictate white heroines' survival, those social forces always are subsumed and subverted by love, their primary desire. Consequently, Grace Kelly's displaying her fatal marksmanship skills at the end of *High Noon*, as Baldwin reminds us, does not render her a murderess for the simple reason that "the situation of the white heroine must never violate the white self-image. Her situation must always transcend the inexorability of the social setting, so that her innocence may be preserved" (*Devil Finds Work* 629).

For a black heroine like Billie Holiday, unfortunately, crass social settings are primary no matter how unrealistic they are. Baldwin notes that although Holiday wrote a beautifully honest account of her life, the film industry remains unable to risk representing black experience as private, personal, or in any way truthful. Instead, Hollywood reduces Holiday's autobiographical account to an effective protest novel starring a heroine who must be judged didactically: "A gifted, but weak, self-indulgent woman brought about the murder of her devoted Piano Man because she was not equal, either to her gifts, or to society which had made her a star and, as the closing sequence proves, adored her" (*Devil Finds Work* 630). On-screen her innocence must be destroyed at all costs.

In analyzing the failure of a film like *Lady Sings the Blues* to even approach representing black experience, Baldwin opposes the all-black film to the "a star is born" genre of classic Hollywood cinema and thereby calls attention to its dependence on upholding the sanctity of whiteness. Hollywood's heroines depend on their white self-imaging and can never violate the whiteness they project; neither, it seems to Baldwin in 1976, can Hollywood's black heroines. Baldwin realizes that to ignore whiteness's constructedness, even when contextualizing a black-cast film like *Lady Sings the Blues,* is to risk complicity with its ideological invisibility. Even when he looks more directly at whiteness on screen, he manages to avoid two interrelated effects of ignoring black spectators: first, the essentializing of black subjectivity, and secondly, the assumption that spectatorial pleasure is, in this context, only possible through assimilation to white identity.

In his discussion of the last film in *The Devil Finds Work,* Baldwin tests and dispels any lingering doubts concerning his deliverance from both essentialism and assimilation at the movies. He tells us that when he went to see *The Exorcist* (1975), he attempted to see the film, in effect, through the eyes of John Grimes, hoping to "relive [his] adolescent holy-roller terrors" (635). What he saw, however, actually contradicted the way he and his church understood the test of a Satanic visitation. Baldwin therefore could not identify with the film's lack of faith, "the terror of its unbelief" (632), which he found utterly alienating. Seeing *The Exorcist* as an allegory about race and American identity, Baldwin concludes that "the mindless and hysterical banality of the evil ... is the most terrifying thing about the film. The Americans should certainly know more about evil than that; if they pretend otherwise, they are lying" (635). Baldwin notes a preponderance of filial guilt in *The Exorcist*, in both the mother and the priest. The same kind of guilt, we recall, caused the young Baldwin to transform the face of Bette Davis into a that of a demon "out of loyalty to [his] mother": "This uneasy and terrified guilt is the subtext of *The Exorcist*, which cannot, however, exorcise it since it never confronts it. But this confrontation would have been to confront the devil" (*Devil Finds Work* 635).

Recalling Snead's comment about the only possibility for identifying with an "other" images as increased guilt, Baldwin's witnessing of *The Exorcist* qualifies the process. Although never explicitly referring to *The Exorcist*'s guilt as white liberal guilt, Baldwin nevertheless asserts that his identifications no longer are guilty (as they may have been for John Grimes), but are instead designed to confront guilt, to delight in the pleasures of battling Satan. What *The Exorcist* fails to do, he argues, film viewers must do: They must confront the guilt they experience when confronted with images of difference.

Ultimately, the impossibility of assigning a positive or negative message to Baldwin's essay makes it an ideal text for any theory of spectatorship trying to free itself from the same dialectical shackles. Moreover, by gleaning contradictory impulses within the same Baldwinian identifications, we eradicate our self-delusions that moviegoing ever can pretend to shed issues of race, gender, sexuality, family history, nation, religion, or any aspects of our identities we bring with us into the cinema.

Baldwin's witnessing in *The Devil Finds Work* remains therefore not so much polemical as homiletic, despite prevailing critical tendencies now, as in the seventies, to dismiss it as rather trite didacticism. We can accept Goldstein's regard for the essay as "among other things ... a denial of credibility and authenticity of the medium" (220), only so long as we do not ignore the many "other things" among which it also professes. Goldstein remains eager to uncover a moral in Baldwin's essay: "Baldwin does not advise any reader to withdraw from the movies; but his book is a cautionary one, warning black readers that the medium is part of the problem, not part of the solution" (220). To the extent that it does resound a "cautionary" message, that message is hardly reserved exclusively for black readers. More importantly, we must recognize that the book bears witness to a lifetime at the movies. Baldwin revisits all his scenes of viewing—white images, his forging infirmities into weapons, his own affinities with black performers— before retracing his genesis in the black church to see through America's paranoia in *The Exorcist*. His essay is not simply a journey from the bliss of mythic universality in the movies toward an angry, moralistic denouncement of, in Ishmael Reed's phrase, their "poison light" (Goldstein 216). Although its gaze remains devilishly critical, it makes no attempt to renounce, justify, or apologize for its author's ongoing love affair with the movies. *The Devil Finds Work* witnesses and preaches the same lesson bell hooks currently teaches in her educational film: "The issue is not freeing ourselves from representations," as hooks stresses before the camera. "It's really about being enlightened witnesses when we watch representations." When it comes to interrogating American cinema, anytime we really want to get ourselves a more enlightened witness, we need look no further than to James Baldwin.

NOTES

1. Although Baldwin seemed to deflect the implied question about his hobbies, he was much less hesitant about voicing his ambitions at the outset of his first nonfiction book: "I want to be," he announced laconically, "an honest man and a good writer" (*Notes* 9).

2. The screenplay was published as *One Day, When I was Lost*. For a detailed account of Baldwin's 1968 stint in Hollywood, see David Leeming's *James Baldwin: A Biography*, 285–302.

3. As part of his entry on "black identity" for the *Encyclopedia of African American History and Culture*, Cornel West stipulates, "To bear witness is to make and remake, invent and reinvent oneself as a person and people by keeping faith with the best of such earlier efforts, yet also to acknowledge that the very new selves and peoples to emerge will never fully find a space, place, or face in American civilization—or in Africa. This perennial process of self-making and self-inventing is propelled by a self-loving made possible by the overcoming of a decolonized mind, body, and soul." Reading the conversion scene at the end of *Go Tell it on the Mountain* compels West to define witnessing this way, and he thus inscribes Baldwin as representative, consummate witness to black identity. Furthermore, as a sensory perception, witnessing also retains its mystical, devotional allure and approaches conjuring, as Theophus Smith defines that process (4, 134).

4. James Snead in *White Screen/Black Images: Hollywood from the Dark Side* characterizes those "black Hollywood" studies as having taken "a binary approach, sociological in its position" (1). Snead lists these titles chronologically as follows: Edward Mapp's *Blacks in American Films* (1972), Donald Bogle's *Toms, Coons, Mulattoes, Mammies, and Bucks: An Interpretive History of Blacks in American Films* (1973), James P. Murray's *To Find an Image* (1973), Gary Null's *Black Hollywood: The Negro in Motion Pictures* (1975), Daniel Leab's *From Sambo to Superspade: The Black Experience in Motion Pictures* (1975), and Thomas Cripps's *Slow Fade to Black* (1977).

5. See Judith Mayne's *Cinema and Spectatorship* for her argument tracing the "paradoxes of spectatorship." For her discussion of *The Devil Finds Work,* see 155–56.

6. Here I am referring mainly to the "black Hollywood" tradition of the seventies and projects like those of Cripps, Bogle, and others. See especially the titles mentioned in note 4 above.

7. Nor, of course, were African Americans absent from film production, whether they worked for Hollywood studios or, like Oscar Micheaux, produced independently. See Cripps, Bruce Tyler's *The Struggle for Racial and Cultural Democracy, 1920–1943,* and Manthia Diawara's edited work *Black American Cinema.*

8. Mayne quotes a remark from a lesbian viewer describing Greta Garbo, recalling gazing at the screen and finding the truth about their shared sexuality revealed. Mayne points out that such a projection has nothing to do with discovering any fact about Garbo's sexuality, and everything to do with the viewer's self-projections (163). The same can be said for Baldwin's comment, since it is so obviously not staking any claims about the "real" racial heritages of Sidney or Fonda.

9. Ellison published each of Bliss's moviegoing episodes in only slightly different form than they now appear in *Juneteenth:* the Atlanta passing episode as "Night Talk," *Quarterly Review of Literature* 16 (1969): 317–29, and the prelude to Bliss and Daddy Hickman's nickelodeon excursion as "The Roof, the Steeple, and the People," *Quarterly Review of Literature* 10 (1960): 115–28. In Callahan's readers' edition of *Juneteenth,* these two movie scenes are bridged by Daddy Hickman's taking Bliss to the circus. There the six-year-old preacher gets infuriated by the self-debasement of a midget clown in blackface, with whom he identifies, and lashes out violently (see chapter 12, 246–54). This rebellious outburst prefigures Bliss's straying off into the Atlanta matinee. Hickman recalls that on that particular afternoon, "I thought you might have been kidnapped. In fact, we were already headed along a downtown street when, lo and behold, we look up and see you coming out of a picture house where it was against the law for us to go!" (*Juneteenth* 255–66). Hickman hoped his popular culture adventures would distract Bliss from the traumatic implications of his attempted kidnapping by a white woman who claims to be his mother, but the movies have the opposite effect, offering Bliss the image of his lost mother through their heroines and an extended metaphor for his identity crisis; he loses himself "between the frames in blackness" (*Juneteenth* 265). Bliss's psychic struggles with the screen stand out as among Ellison's most powerfully written fragments in *Juneteenth,* but their connection to a larger theme of Bliss as "Mister Movieman" and to the design of the unfinished novel Ellison imagined is, like *Juneteenth* itself, inchoate. *Juneteenth* supplements Bliss's childhood spectatorship by offering a brief glimpse of him as a young man who works behind the camera; we meet him shooting on-location silent Westerns as a young man, apparently years before he reinvents himself as the notorious U.S. senator Adam Sunraider (see chapter 5, 64–94).

10. For further details on Davis's career and the production of *Of Human Bondage,* see James Spada's *More Than a Woman: An Intimate Biography of Bette Davis,* 133–41, and Whitney Stine's *Mother Goddam,* 57–62.

11. I am alluding of course to Laura Mulvey's watershed 1975 article "Visual Pleasure and Narrative Cinema" and to the overwhelming critical responses it generated through the eighties (set off by Mulvey's "Afterthoughts" written in 1981) from feminist film theorists including Teresa DeLauretis, Tania Modleski, Mary Ann Doane and the writers in the collection she co-edited with Patricia Mellancamp and Linda Williams, *Re-vision: Essays in Feminist Film Criticism* (1984), and Contance Penley and the selections in her collection *Feminism and Film Theory* (1988). Following Mulvey, the "male gaze" is supposed to revel in the pleasure of fetishizing "to-be-looked-at-ness," thereby confirming both its distance and difference from her. The source of Baldwin's pleasure, however, proves his discovery of a narcissistic affinity to Davis's image, which, in Mulvey's scheme, could be classified only as masochistic.

12. I am deliberately invoking Michael Jackson's "Black or White" song lyrics here, since a parallel tendency to obscure race with sexuality inflects readings of Jackson's star persona. For a compelling, if flawed (in part because its publication predates Jackson's sex scandal and his finite marriage to Lisa Marie Presley) reading of the tensions comprising Jackson's sexual and racial imaging, see Michael Awkward's *Negotiating Difference: Race, Gender, and the Politics of Positionality,* 175–92.

13. For an enlightened contextualization of Baldwin's "victimization" through homophobic discourses of the Black Arts Movement of the sixties, see Henry Louis Gates, Jr., "Looking for Modernism," in Diawara (200–207). Perhaps not so ironically, the same categories of classification problems that apply to Baldwin also inform the dimensions of Bette Davis's star personae. Davis's enigmatic sexuality signified alternately as tough leading lady opposite leading man as well as through rivalries with strong female co-stars like Miriam Hopkins and Mary Astor. Just as these rivalries simultaneously both confirmed and undermined Davis's monopoly on heterosexual prowess, so her racial identity also was rendered disputable through her performances of it both on and off the screen. Layers of sexual and racial power thus doubly veil Davis's stardom, obscuring any single attributable cause—be it any one form of her whiteness or sexuality—for her enigmatic allure. For a broader sketch of Davis-as-icon, see Mayne's illustrative arguments in her chapter entitled "Star Gazing," 123–41.

14. As Mayne variously enumerates the distinction in: "Critical spectatorship is not the same as a politicized audience, even though it may be a necessary condition for it" (165). . . . "Spectatorship and advocacy are not the same; however much they may inflect each other—as they should—they are never reducible one to the other" (167). . . . "There is no simple, pure site of resistance, and the complicated forms that spectatorship takes makes this clear" (171).

15. When reprinting his article "Black Spectatorship: Problems of Identification and Resistance" (1986, 1988) for a collection on black film he edited in 1993, Manthia Diawara noted how "totalizing" its claims for resistance seemed in retrospect (219–20). It is precisely this trap to "totalize" spectatorship that, following Diawara, Mayne, and informed by Baldwin himself, I am seeking to avoid through conceptualizing Baldwin's viewing practices.

Works Cited

Awkward, Michael. *Negotiating Difference: Race, Gender, and the Politics of Position-ality.* Chicago: University of Chicago Press, 1995.

Baldwin, James. "Carmen Jones: The Dark Is Light Enough." In *The Price of the Ticket: Collected Nonfiction, 1948–1985.* New York: St. Martin's, 107–12. Originally published as "Life Straight in De Eye," *Commentary,* January 1955.

———. *The Devil Finds Work.* 1976. Reprint in *The Price of the Ticket: Collected Non-fiction 1948–1985,* 557–636. New York: St. Martin's, 1985.

———. *Go Tell it on the Mountain.* New York: Knopf, 1953.

———. *Notes of a Native Son.* Boston: Beacon, 1955.

———. "On Catfish Row: Porgy and Bess in the Movies." In *The Price of the Ticket: Collected Nonfiction 1948–1985.* New York: St. Martin's, 1985. Orig-inally published in *Commentary,* September 1959.

———. *One Day, When I Was Lost: A Scenario Based on "The Autobiography of Mal-colm X."* New York: Dial, 1972.

———. *Tell Me How Long the Train's Been Gone.* New York: Laurel, 1968.

Bogle, Donald. "A Look at the Movies By Baldwin." *Freedomways* 16, no. 2 (1976): 103–8.

———. *Toms, Coons Mulattoes, Mammies, and Bucks: An Interpretive History of Blacks in American Films.* 1973. Reprint, with updates. New York: Continuum, 1989.

Cripps, Thomas. *Slow Fade to Black: The Negro in American Film 1900–1942.* New York: Oxford University Press, 1977.

Diawara, Manthia, ed. *Black American Cinema.* New York: Routledge, 1993.

Doane, Mary Ann. *The Desire to Desire: The Woman's Film of the 1940's.* Bloom-ington: Indiana University Press, 1987.

———. "Film and the Masquerade—Theorising the Female Spectator." *Screen* 23, nos. 3–4 (1982): 74–88.

Doane, Mary Ann, Patricia Mellencamp, and Linda Williams, eds. *Re-Vision: Essays in Feminist Film Criticism.* Frederick, Md.: University Publications of America and the American Film Institute, 1984.

Dyer, Richard. *Heavenly Bodies: Film Stars and Society.* New York: St. Martin's, 1986.

Ellison, Ralph. *Juneteenth.* Ed. John F. Callahan. New York: Random House, 1999.

———. "Night Talk." *Quarterly Review of Literature* 16 (1969): 317–29.

———. "The Roof, the Steeple, and the People." *Quarterly Review of Literature* 10 (1960): 115–28.

Goldstein, Lawrence. *The American Poet at the Movies.* Ann Arbor: University of Michigan Press, 1994.

Gomery, Douglas. *Shared Pleasures: A History of Moviegoing in the United States.* Madison: University of Wisconsin Press, 1992.

hooks, bell. *Cultural Criticism and Transformation.* Video. Northampton, Mass.: Media Education Foundation, 1996.

Leab, Daniel J. *From Sambo to Superspade: The Black Experience in Motion Pictures.* Boston: Houghton Mifflin, 1975.

Leeming, David A. *James Baldwin: A Biography.* New York: Knopf, 1994.

Macebuh, James. *James Baldwin: A Critical Study.* New York: Okapaku, 1973.

Mapp, Edward. *Blacks in American Films: Today and Yesterday.* Metuchen, NJ: Scarecrow, 1972.

Mayne, Judith. *Cinema and Spectatorship.* New York: Routledge, 1993.

Mercer, Kobena. "Skin Head Sex Thing: Racial Difference and the Homoerotic Imaginary." In *How Do I Look? Queer Film and Video,* ed. Bad Object-Choices. Seattle: Bay Press, 1991.

Modleski, Tania. *Loving with a Vengeance: Mass-Produced Fantasies for Women.* Hamden, Conn.: Archon, 1982.

Mulvey, Laura. "Afterthoughts on 'Visual Pleasure and Narrative Cinema' Inspired by *Duel in the Sun.*" *Framework* nos. 15, 16, 17 (1981): 12–15.

———. "Visual Pleasure and Narrative Cinema." *Screen* 16, no. 3 (1975): 6–18.

Murray, James P. *To Find an image: Blacks in Films from Uncle Tom to Superfly.* Indianapolis: Bobbs Merrow, 1973.

Null, Gary. *Black Hollywood: The Negro in Motion Pictures.* Secaucus, NJ: Citadel Press, 1975.

Pellegrini, Ann. *Performance Anxieties: Staging Psychoanalysis, Staging Race.* New York: Routledge, 1997.

Penley, Constance, ed. *Feminism and Film Theory.* New York: Routledge, 1988.

Smith, Theophus. *Conjuring Culture: Biblical Formations of Black America.* New York: Oxford University Press, 1994.

Smitherman, Geneva. *Talkin and Testifyin: The Language of Black America.* Detroit, Mich.: Wayne State University Press, 1977.

Snead, James. *White Screen/Black Images: Hollywood from the Dark Side.* Ed. Colin McCabe and Cornel West. New York: Routledge, 1994.

Spada, James. *More Than a Woman: An Intimate Biography of Bette Davis.* New York: Bantam, 1993.

Staiger, Janet. *Interpreting Films: Studies in the Historical Reception of American Cinema.* Princeton, N.J.: Princeton University Press, 1992.

Standley, Fred and Louis H. Pratt, eds. *Conversations with James Baldwin.* Jackson: University Press of Mississippi, 1989.

Stine, Whitney with Bette Davis. *Mother Goddam.* New York: Berkeley, 1974.

Tyler, Bruce. *The Struggle for Racial and Cultural Democracy, 1920–1943.* New York: Garland, 1992.

Weatherby, James. *James Baldwin: Artist on Fire.* New York: Donald I. Fine, 1989.

West, Cornel. "Black Identity." In *Encyclopedia of African American History and Culture,* ed. Jack Salzman, David Lionel Smith, Cornel West, et al., 356. Vol 1. New York: Macmillan, 1996.

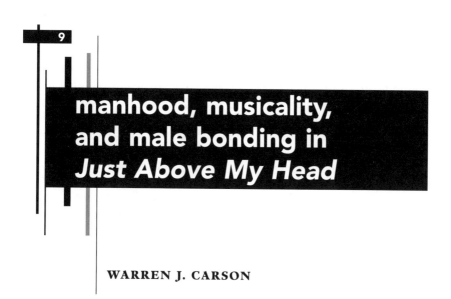

manhood, musicality, and male bonding in *Just Above My Head*

WARREN J. CARSON

Long before it became fashionable to bemoan the plight of the black male or to mourn the demise of the black family, the always prophetic James Baldwin already had examined both concerns in work after work, beginning with his earliest novel, *Go Tell It On the Mountain* (1953) where he introduces these themes, and continuing through *Tell Me How Long the Train's Been Gone* (1968), which, at the time of its publication, was his "most directly political novel . . . regarding the question of the relation of men to society and to each other" (Gibson 14). However, nowhere does Baldwin address these twin issues more fully or as excruciatingly than in his last novel, the sprawling 1979 work *Just Above My Head* that chronicles the interconnected lives of two families, the Montanas and the Millers, over more than thirty years. The lives of these families connect on a number of levels, as do the lives of an extended family, the members of the Trumpets of Zion, a male gospel quartet. In the final analysis, the Montana family is presented as the paragon of stability, while the Miller family emerges as totally dysfunctional. Baldwin examines innumerable theses in *Just Above My Head*, but among the most prominent is the argument that black males largely are responsible for preserving the African American family. Unless black men can rely on one another for strength and support, then individual black males will be incapable of supplying the strength and stability needed to ensure the family's survival.

For Baldwin, the bonding of males—and for African American males in particular—is a natural process toward a shared sense of unity and fraternity, but one whose development has been inhibited, if not altogether thwarted, by society's sexism, racism, and unrealistic expectations for men. Thus Baldwin advocates, strongly in many places, dangerously in others, that men must be allowed to bond in ways that men themselves deem necessary and beneficial without fear of criticism and without being made to feel guilty or less masculine for needing or wanting male companionship, male support, and male acceptance. This idea is stated most succinctly in *Tell Me How Long the Train's Been Gone* when the protagonist, Leo Proudhammer, observes that "men . . . need each other as comrades, need each other for correction, need each other for tears and ribaldry, need each other as models, need each other indeed, in sum, in order to be able to love women" (68). Leo's assertion echoes Baldwin's idea of the male prison, an idea he had advanced in 1954 when he wrote that "when men can no longer love women they also cease to love or respect or to trust each other, which makes their isolation complete" ("The Male Prison" 105). In his works, Baldwin explores such relationships as father-to-son, brother-to-brother, friend-to-friend, or lover-to-lover, and in *Just Above My Head* he attempts to bring together all of the strands of black male experience into a definitive statement of black masculinity. Baldwin's ever-present operative problem, as he so eloquently states in "The Male Prison," "is how to be—in the best sense of that kaleidoscopic word—a man" (103). In an attempt to define that problem, Baldwin posits that if men are to have truly meaningful relationships as men among men, they must be "honest, open, and self-accepting" (Gibson 12). This sounds simple enough, but the simplicity is both deceptive and elusive, so much so that most critics have missed the nuances of male-to-male experiences in Baldwin's works and thus fail to appreciate fully or articulate precisely Baldwin's testimonies to the presence of a "powerful masculinity" ("The Male Prison" 105). This is true of the several white male biographers who have written on Baldwin and his works since his death in 1987; it is true of the early black male old-guard establishment critics who seemed intent upon distancing themselves from what seemed to them an unhealthy obsession on Baldwin's part; and it is true of the several female critics who, for all their admiration of Baldwin or their insight into his shortcomings of female characterization, do not, perhaps cannot, speak convincingly of his definition of masculinity.

Clearly, Baldwin extends these thoughts in *Just Above My Head* as he attempts to lay an intricate foundation of true bonding and brotherhood in his portrait of the Trumpets of Zion. Furthermore, Baldwin notes a certain musicality to true bonding among men, for when the Trumpets of Zion bond through music and manhood, the product is an unmatchable amen-corner symphony. With more than one hundred references and allusions to song titles and song texts, Baldwin composes a multilineal, multivocal, multitextual narrative that Hall Montana, the retrospective, introspective, and speculative narrator, calls "a love song to my brother" (443). Moreover, Baldwin employs song texts, music style, technique, and performance with a deep and abiding permeation as he seeks to articulate the essential truth of black manhood.

The Trumpets of Zion is a gospel singing group of four Harlem teen-agers ranging in age from fifteen to nineteen. Arthur Montana, the youngest member, later embarks on a solo gospel career as "The Soul Emperor," but branches out into rhythm and blues in his later years. The epigrammatic introductions to the five books of *Just Above My Head* add to a greater understanding of the novel's thematic development. Headings such as "Have Mercy," "Twelve Gates to the City," "The Gospel Singer," "Stepchild," and "The Gates of Hell," chart the development of Arthur's life from adolescent soloist to teen-age quartet singer with the Trumpets of Zion to civil rights activist and commercial success as a solo gospel singer to critical and popular dismissal, debauchery, heartbreak, and death at age thirty-nine after having "branched out" from gospel music to the blues. Simultaneously, we are led through a progression of Arthur's homosexuality, from his childhood molestation by an older man, to his torrid love affair with Crunch (the guitarist for the Trumpets of Zion), to deepening unfulfillment with man after man, to comfort and despair in a fourteen-year relationship with his pianist and childhood acquaintance, Jimmy Miller.

The chapter epigrams, each taken from "traditional" gospel lyrics, not only segmentize an otherwise digressionary narrative, but characterize and codify the various experiences of the characters as well. For example, the epigram for book one, "Work: for the night is coming," is cautionary. It suggests that despite how dark one's past and present experiences may be, darker times are sequential and the darkest of those times is perhaps yet to come. Each of the characters experiences a descent into darkness in search of the light, but only Hall Montana, Julia Miller, and Jimmy Miller survive, though not without "trying on their robes at the gates of Hell," as the gospel epigram of the last book confirms.

Arthur's life and death form the focus of *Just Above My Head*, and the novel begins with an examination of his life against the backdrop of the lives of his singing companions. During the period covered by their singing together, the other Trumpets—Jason Hogan, called Crunch; Alexander Theophilus Brown, called Peanut; and Red, whose given name is not known—along with Arthur, learn that not only does a good song require the best individual effort for complete success, but that a successful life, a meaningful life, particularly for African American males, requires the love, support, understanding, and acceptance from other African American males. The Trumpets of Zion are able to supply that talent, energy, and discipline to make themselves a superb quartet; indeed, their harmony frequently is impeccable. Furthermore, at least for the time they are together, the young men create a tremendously strong bond—they love, support, criticize, work through problems, and defend one another, both from within and without. The quartet, in fact, is a support mechanism, one that establishes a familial environment for three of its members who come from far less than ideal family circumstances, and it sustains them through some of their most crucial developmental years. Unfortunately, when the quartet is broken up and its members dispersed by the Korean War draft, they face the tragedies that all too often have become the fates of contemporary African American males: Crunch goes insane; Red becomes a heroin addict; Peanut is abducted and killed by white supremacists; and Arthur is left to attempt expiation of guilt and loneliness in alcohol and in one affair after another, sometimes with women, but most often with other men.

A closer examination of the dynamics of the relationships among the members of the Trumpets of Zion yields a deeper understanding of Baldwin's ideas about the natural presence and necessary development of bonds between and among males. It also unveils the ubiquitous threat of an all-engulfing darkness and destruction that looms over the young men. Indeed, their early small problems seem inconsequential compared to the payments that life ultimately exacts from each of them.

Crunch and Red, for example, are distant cousins who grew up together as best friends. They share, therefore, not only a familial bond, but one that transcends the fraternal bond. Each one, for instance, describes the other as his "heart." A more acceptably masculine reference is "bosom buddies," yet Baldwin specifically chooses to let his men say "heart" because it elicits a more visceral and deeply emotional response from its witnesses. Crunch is from an unstable background in which he is the oldest of five siblings, each of whom apparently has a different father. He tearfully describes his mother as "a whore" (163). However, Crunch understands that he and his brothers and sisters love her because "she's our *mama*. . . . the men came and went, but she stayed, she raised us" (164). Despite the love and devotion Crunch demonstrates for his mother, he is unable to reach her. This fact, along with the absence of a male figure in the household to depend upon, only deepens his emotional bond to Red and leads directly to Crunch's falling in love with Arthur, who is nearly five years his junior.

Their love affair is presented as anything but uncommon and unnatural, although the two young men are sophisticated enough to understand the taboo that the larger society places upon such unions. Clearly, Baldwin goes to great lengths to portray the members of the Trumpets of Zion as clean-cut, average guys—the boys next door. This is especially true of Arthur, who is not characterized as a stereotypical effeminate male homosexual, although he is cast in the feminine role. In fact, Baldwin often "treat[s] homosexuality as a normal or super-normal behavior [and] he sharply differentiates [in *Just Above My Head*] between phallic confrontation and overt effeminacy" (Lash 49). Darryl Pinckney notes that "it is clear that [Arthur] is very different from the subversive heroes of Baldwin's earlier novels. He is homosexual, but seen sentimentally, continually as a member of a family, the doting younger brother, the loving son. He is meant to be a kind of artist hero, hardworking, dedicated, tragically undone by the rages of their lives" (163). Crunch, in contrast, is described as looking like a combination of thunder and innocence, if either could be seen: "He was skinny, but powerful, played basketball, and was the boy who made out best with 'the ladies,'" one who "appear[ed] to be born for the purpose of ignit-ing desire" (74). Crunch is an example of Donald Gibson's assertion that "there is some suggestion that the bisexual male is for Baldwin the apogee of human development" (12). However, a tragic disillusionment results from Crunch's failure to "know his [own] incredible beauty" (Traylor 221) and from people who misunderstand Crunch's intentions, that perhaps his function on earth "is to fulfill desire" (74). Ultimately, Crunch's misgivings as the son of a whore pale as he lives out the tragedy "of being treated like something hanging on the edge of a prick" (75) and being "treated with an unbelievable brutality, a brutality made all the more hideous by presenting itself as love" (74). After trying unsuccessfully to satisfy the desires of men, women, and the U.S. Army, Crunch's growing bewilderment at being used and misused finally over-whelms him, and he goes mad and is institutionalized. Before this tragic turn of events, though, Crunch finds in Arthur someone to love uncon-ditionally and someone who returns that love unconditionally and completely. Sex becomes just another way to express their love and does not, for Baldwin, compromise the masculinity of either partner;

rather, sex is presented as a new route to empowerment, an act that makes them stronger and more sensitive to the fuller dimensions of manhood. Furthermore, as George Kent observes, "sex, for Baldwin, is obviously a metaphor for the act of breaking one's isolation and, properly experienced, responsibly entering into the complexity of another being" (22), in other words, a way of escaping the male prison. The love affair between Crunch and Arthur—"the fusion of the male with the male" (Lash 51)—confirms this argument as they employ "sex and love as instruments in the achievement of full being" (Kent 24).

The clearest example of the harmony created by their love affair is present in the call-and-response pattern that informs a song sung by the two as members of the Trumpets of Zion that precipitates their first sexual encounter and that is described in identical terms. What Baldwin insists on, however, is that the song, whatever its genre—blues, gospel, or jazz—is inspired by an emotion, one emotion that eventually must reach the surface and free itself regardless of the consequences. Only by freeing the emotion and emptying that emotion through song is there any salvation for the soul. Such is Baldwin's argument in *Just Above My Head*.

The aforementioned example is taken from a familiar gospel song performed by the Trumpets of Zion in a Birmingham church while the quartet is in Alabama on a southern tour. "Take me to the water to be baptized" is the title and refrain of the song, which initially is sung in a call-and-response pattern with Arthur "[answering] Crunch's echo" (172). As the two labor with the song, sweat gathers as Crunch and Arthur begin to "[move] together . . . in song, to some new place . . . laughing and crying at the same time [finally] ending together, as though on a single drum" (172–73). After being "dragged, kicking, through a miracle," the boys "[dare] look at each other" and then burst into another singing celebration, "Somebody touched me and . . . it must have been the hand of the Lord!" (173). Baldwin renders the performance in obviously sexual imagery, and these overtones are confirmed and emphasized by the fact that this performance leads directly to the sexual consummation of Crunch and Arthur's feelings for each other. While in Atlanta, the next stop on the tour, Hall describes this consummation:

> Arthur was afraid in one way, and Crunch in another. It was also as though they had expended so much energy to arrive at this moment that . . . this moment was almost enough. But . . . the train was boarded, the engine ready to roll . . . pulsing . . . slamming . . . moving. (178)

As they reach their climax, Baldwin writes, "it was as though each were coming through the other's sex" (179), an obvious allusion to ending together as in song. In comparison to the relief they felt after singing about religious baptism, Baldwin writes that, after being baptized in love and sex, Crunch and Arthur experience "a peculiar joy" that was best described as "peace like a river" (182), yet another allusion to a gospel lyric, "It is well with my soul." Moreover, this "peculiar joy" confirms what John Lash sees as Baldwin's argument

> that the search of man for self-realization comes ultimately to a point of genital cognition, that a morality and an ethic gonadic in inception are instinct in the bodily intercourse of man with man, that in the naked moment of sexual confrontation between man and man are to be found truth stripped of hypocrisy and deceit, self-fulfillment beyond the necessity for proof and measurement, peace and security reuniting the male and masculine flesh and spirit. (48)

Similarly, although it does not develop beyond adolescent sexual curiosity, an early reciprocal masturbation between Red and Peanut is described by Peanut as "something new I could do for him, that we could do for each other" (365) to show how much they loved each other. Thus, like many of Baldwin's male characters, Peanut and Red turn to "the phallic experience for spiritual gratification" (Lash 50). Unlike the love affair between Crunch and Arthur, the bond between Red and Peanut is mostly fraternal. Like Crunch and Red, Peanut and Red are "distant cousins" (360). They are extremely close and are best friends who shared everything they discovered. Peanut's mother had died in childbirth, and his father deserted him. As a result, he was raised by his maternal grandmother, a woman he describes as "too *old* to be raising a young kid" (360) and who really does not know how to deal with him. It is a relief, a godsend, then, when Peanut meets his slightly older cousin, Red. Red becomes the older brother, the "heart," the bosom buddy, the almost father figure so long missing from Peanut's life. This immediate bonding sustains both until they are separated by war, a split that not only spells disaster for their relationship, but also for them as individuals. Red becomes a junkie who steals from his mother, from Peanut, from Peanut's grandmother, and who alienates his wife and sons because of his inability to kick his drug habit. Their collective love, support, and patience cannot rescue Red. Peanut observes, "The worst this is that you slowly begin to hate, to despise this person, this person that you loved. You hate him because he hates himself. And that's horrible, I swear, to feel your love drip out of you drop by drop, until you empty of it and there's just a big hurting hole where that love used to be" (366). Here, two lives that were mutually loving and supporting are both destroyed by hopelessness and despair. Red ultimately destroys his family and finally dances a slow dance with death on a methadone treatment program. Only then, Baldwin tells us, does he begin to understand "the [gospel] songs he was singing—way back there—but he can't sing no more, and he don't want to anyway" (30). Similarly, Peanut, the pianist, loved and victimized by colorstruck relatives—being too light for some, not light enough for others—pays a far greater price for his color when he is abducted from a Georgia outhouse by white racists and presumably is murdered for asserting his rights as a black man. Although their lines of experience are sometimes parallel, more often than not their experiences tangle and twine among themselves and with other characters. Indeed, this tragic symphony is composed of an intertextual movement/countermovement, call-and-response narratology, "voices [that form] a kind of rumbling, witness wailing wall" (77). Before their individual tragedies, however, Baldwin emphasizes that the young men are strong because they have each other. The bonds they share as men are "as deep as that inarticulate connection between [Arthur] and Peanut and Crunch and Red when they sang" (155). Unfortunately, this bonded strength does not last, for "what they might have longed to endure together each would . . . [be] forced to endure alone" (188). In a sense, a stronger reality moves in and shapes their greater experience.

The rift between Red and Peanut echoes another example of hearts once bonded but subsequently torn asunder by changes in circumstance. In Baldwin's portrayal of the Proudhammer brothers, Caleb and Leo, in *Tell Me How Long the Train's Been Gone,* Caleb is cast as keeper and caretaker for Leo, who is seven years younger. Leo adores, respects, loves, and admires his older brother. When Caleb is seventeen, he is sent to prison for stealing, but not before a tragic scene in which the brothers, who always have been affectionate, "clung together as [they] never had before" (*Tell Me* 92). Caleb returns from prison when he is twenty-one, spiritually broken because of "what they did to [him]" in prison (161). In an effort to give Caleb back a measure of his manhood, Leo assumes the role of the "big brother" (161). Leo remembers, "I knew, I knew, what my brother wanted, what my brother needed, and I was not at all afraid. . . . I held my brother very close, I kissed him and caressed him and I felt a pain and wonder I had never felt before. My brother's heart was broken; I knew that from his touch. In all the great, vast, dirty world, he trusted the love of one person only, his brother, his brother, who was in his arms" (162). But in this supreme sacrifice of love between men, between brothers, Leo and Caleb only temporarily can abate the disillusionment that threatens to destroy them both. While Caleb joins the army and afterward devotes himself to a Pentecostal religious denomination, Leo pursues his artistry in a lifelong dream to become an actor, and gives himself over to affairs with Barbara King and Christopher Hall as well as numerous anonymous sexual encounters. While Caleb and Leo attempt to communicate, to understand each other, they grow further apart, even though they "hope for daylight, hope for reconciliation" (298). Although they have internalized society's attitudes toward religion and sex and such a reconciliation, according to Baldwin, can never take place because of the inherent dishonesty in society's position. Thus the Proudhammer brothers fail to achieve the wholeness promised by the bonding of men as men. In other words, Baldwin's idea that "sexual honesty contained healing possibilities for the disturbed psyche" (Pinckney 164) fails to ring true for Leo and Caleb, just as it fails to sustain the various male pairs in *Just Above My Head.*

That Arthur outlasts the other Trumpets is the greatest tragedy of all, for his longevity, such as it was, means only that Arthur's funeral march is made to a longer and slower dirge as he witnesses the destruction of the loved ones around him. In the process, Arthur becomes more emotionally mutilated as pieces of himself are torn away and he is powerless to do anything about it. Initially, Arthur could not sing because had not hurt enough—"an adolescent malady" (75) that soon passed. Ultimately, Arthur could not sing because he had hurt too much—music could not sustain him because it no longer could convey his grief and pain. The opening epigram thus fulfills its awful prophecy for the Trumpets of Zion—"Work: for the night is coming when no man can work."

Nor does Arthur's unquestioning faith seem rewarded in the end. The lyrics of his debut song are instructive here:

> *Beams of heaven, as I go*
> *Through this wilderness below*
> *Guide my feet in peaceful ways*
> *Turn my midnights into days.*
> *When in darkness I would grope*
> *Faith always sees a star of hope:*
> *And soon from all life's grief and danger*

> *I shall be free someday*
> *But I do not know*
> *How long it will be*
> *Or what the future may hold for me:*
> *But this I know*
> *If Jesus leads me*
> *I shall get home someday.*

In an apparent subversion of this gospel song text, Arthur's life—as well as the lives of the Trumpets of Zion—is not sustained by this faith: His feet do not find peaceful ways, his days are so many midnights, there is little hope attendant, darkness abounds, grief and danger are omnipresent, and his freedom from pain and despair comes only as a result of a hemorrhaging death. Arthur pours a lament into the last song he sings before dying, "Boy, you sure took me for one big ride." While the song was, on the surface, sung for Jimmy Miller, his lover who was conspicuously absent from Arthur's final concert, it is just as possible that it was addressed to God, who had been conspicuously absent from Arthur's life—or so he felt. Baldwin acknowledges this apparent blasphemy and presumption early in the novel when he writes, "Maybe all gospel songs begin out of blasphemy and presumption . . . out of entering God's suffering, and making it your own, out of entering your suffering and challenging God to have or withhold mercy" (8). Unfortunately, such understanding comes too late for Arthur to save himself, and he sings—like Pete in *Tell Me How Long the Train's Been Gone*—of "the faithless loves, the lost loves, the hope of love; the many deaths, and the fear of death; in all of this, some style evolving, some music endlessly played, ringing inexorable changes on the meaning of the blues" (241). And like the unnamed young saxophonist in *Another Country*, Arthur is "full of a need that he can express only indirectly" through a song, but it is clear that "he has been irreparably damaged by the bitter necessity to survive alone in an uncaring world" (Collier 40). Eleanor Traylor points out that "we see . . . the slow dissolution of Arthur . . . whose attempt to harmonize his sacred song with the cacophony of his secular life finally breaks his willing but unequal heart" (221). Finally, David Leeming argues that "Arthur's music, his anguish and his death . . . are all notes in the larger blues song" (350).

While Baldwin presents the Trumpets of Zion as the model of male bonding in a group situation, there are a number of one-on-one male relationships described as exemplary. These relationships focus on how Hall, the novel's narrator, bonds with his younger brother, Arthur; his best friend, Sidney; his father, Paul; and his son, Tony. During the course of the narrative, Hall not only reconciles his feelings about his brother's life and death, but also learns to appreciate himself for who he is in the process. Baldwin says much about brotherhood and the special bonds of brothers in his customary intrusive and digressionary manner. In one instance, Hall pronounces that "a brother . . . you love him, in the shit or out of the shit, and you clean him up if you have to, and you know he's got to go the way his blood beats because that's *your* blood beating in those veins, too" (215). Furthermore, Hall shows he is acutely aware of an older brother's special responsibility when he argues, "It is taken for granted that the younger brother needs the older brother: this need defines the lover brother's role, and older brothers remain older brothers all their lives" (331). Baldwin had explored the role of the older brother in an earlier short story, "Sonny's Blues." In that work, the mother admonishes the older brother/narrator/witness "to hold on to your brother . . . and don't let him fall, no matter what it looks like is happening to him and no matter how evil you gets with him" (1305). The quality of brotherhood that Baldwin advocates in *Just Above My Head,* then, is scriptural—Hall, indeed, is his brother's keeper, for in so doing, he keeps himself. He is protector, defender, and nurturer, for in so doing, he protects, defends, and nurtures himself. And in the sense that he describes his narrative as "a love song to my brother," he is lover—not in a merely physical or emotional way as Trudier Harris argues (166), but in a purer, more unconditional, fraternal manner, for in so doing, Hall comes to love himself and "come[s] to terms with his own identity as a black man in America" (Shin and Judson 255).

The way the Montana brothers communicate reveals the mutual regard they have for one another. Arthur, an overt homosexual, is open with Hall, and he does not hide even the sordid aspects of his life that he suspects will revolt his brother. That is not to say that he flaunts his openly gay lifestyle, because he respects Hall too much to risk embarrassing him. On one occasion when the two are "pub crawling," Arthur says, "I've always looked up to you, and I love you, and I wouldn't be able to live, man, if I thought you were ashamed of me" (48). Hall realizes, years later, that Arthur had spent most of life trying to make himself worthy of his family's love.

Likewise, Hall has tremendous respect for Arthur, for his right to choose his own lifestyle, and for his right to privacy. And while he agrees, at Arthur's insistence, to manage his brother's singing career, he makes conscious efforts not to manage his life. In this respect, "the boys take their cue from their father Paul" (Shin and Judson 256) by refusing to be authoritarian with each other. Furthermore, while Hall is open and candid with Arthur, his relationship with his younger brother is based on love, respect, and responsibility; therefore, Hall always is circumspect because he does not "want to be a bad example to Arthur" (73). Thus, Baldwin's concept of ideal brotherhood is based on wholesome factors; the bonds between the Montana brothers are special, even sacred, and are devoid of the treachery and selfishness that marred relationships between Cain and Abel or Jacob and Esau in the Bible, or the guilt, mistrust, or resentment that destroyed the fraternal bonds between John and Roy in *Go Tell It On the Mountain* and Leo and Caleb in *Tell Me How Long the Train's Been Gone*. Hall commits himself to being his brother's keeper, and Arthur, happily and with relief, commits himself to being kept. As Arthur tells a reluctant barmaid while ordering drink after drink, "It's all right. I'm with my brother" (51).

Thematically, the title perhaps provides the best insight into one of the novel's central problems. "Just Above My Head" is taken from the lyrics of an old gospel song that joyously proclaims "Just above my head I hear music in the air/ There must be a God somewhere!" Baldwin, however, reverses this emphatic hopefulness in his application of the lines to the experiences of the Montana brothers. For both of them, the "something" just above their heads is not something to long for or celebrate; rather, it is something irrepressible, something suffocating, something ominous. For Arthur, it is mainly his inability to reconcile his homosexuality with his "calling" as a gospel singer. For Hall, because he is neither homosexual nor a musician, it is his inability to understand or articulate his brother's pain. In both cases, knowledge and truth, while often elusive, just as often conspire to suck the marrow of happiness from their lives until they kill Arthur and very nearly kill Hall. Although Hall achieves a considerable degree of affirmation at the end of his narrative, it comes at a tremendous price.

The relationship between Hall and Sidney is another example of male bonding, and, for Baldwin, constitutes a further extension of the ways that men can love and support one another. Sidney is a bartender at Jordan's Cat, a Harlem bar that Hall visits one Christmas. The fact that they meet on Christmas Day suggests that Sidney is, in a sense, a savior for Hall by rescuing him from a situation in which he has no male friends to provide comfort and camaraderie. Although Sidney is considerably older, the bond between the two men is immediate. After a couple of drinks and a little small talk, Hall experiences the joy of having found a friend: "For that moment, leaning on the bar, caught in the

New York sunlight . . . [Sidney's] face changing like a fountain of water spinning in the air, his eyes bottomless and bright and flashing, the white teeth in the dark chocolate face . . . he was incredibly beautiful and I felt myself flow toward him" (107). Likewise, Hall saves Sidney from the loneliness of having no family: His mother had given him away when he was a child; his grandmother, who had raised him, had recently died; and his brother is in prison. Hall treats Sidney like a brother, and over time he is "adopted" by the Montana family. Further, Sidney gives Hall something to hang on to when it is time for him to leave home for his tour of duty. In response to Hall's request that "I'd like to have a friend, [Sidney] took [Hall's] hand in his and gripped it hard. 'You got it baby,' he said. . . . 'That's just the way it's going to be'" (107). After Hall enters the army, Sidney looks out for Arthur but also becomes engaged to Martha, Hall's girlfriend. Hall knew that he himself would never marry Martha although he loved her; however, he is happy that she has found happiness with his best friend. Baldwin wants us to know that only a friendship between real men could accommodate such a change in circumstance without being threatened, compromised, or destroyed. Hall and Sidney are examples of Baldwin's heroes—"real and practicing men, who have no desire or intention to employ the trappings of conventional maleness as a facade" (Lash 50), who are comfortable with themselves and with each other.

The bonding between Hall and Sidney is reminiscent of the bonding between John Grimes and Brother Elisha in *Go Tell It On the Mountain*. With an absent brother and hostile stepfather, John reaches out to Elisha who prays him through his threshing-floor experience as his witness. In the aftermath of John's salvation experience, as John and Elisha struggle to define their relationship, Elisha "kiss[es] John on the forehead, a holy kiss" (221), a saving kiss, for "the sun had come full awake. It fell over Elisha like a golden robe, and struck John's forehead, where Elisha had kissed him, like a seal ineffaceable forever" (221). While sexual overtones may be read into this relationship, and perhaps into the relationship between Hall and Sidney, Baldwin emphasizes that bonding can take place between men on spiritual levels as well as those that are purely social in nature so long as those who bond are honest with themselves and with those with whom they seek companionship.

The necessary bonding between fathers and sons is another issue that receives considerable attention in *Just Above My Head*. Where these relationships are stable, the families tend to remain intact; where fathers and sons do not bond, the family unit suffers irreparably. Paul Montana, for example, is in many ways a model father for Hall and Arthur.

A blues and jazz pianist, he is comfortable and secure with himself, loves his wife, and cherishes his sons. He is warm and gentle, yet firm and supportive. A powerful presence loved and respected by his family, Paul sets the appropriate example for his sons and expects them to adhere to the same high standards. Furthermore, he trains his sons to be men through example, such as when he buys Hall a drink in an act of initiation to legal manhood, thus expanding the father-son relationship to a new level of mutual acknowledgement and respect. Similarly, Paul encourages Arthur's artistry, although he "refuses to play the role of mentor, deeming it too authoritarian, allowing Arthur instead to cultivate his own voice in gospel music and the blues" (Shin and Judson 256). Paul, in fact, is so secure in his relationship with his sons that he also can serve as surrogate father for the rest of the Trumpets of Zion without feeling that he is neglecting his sons and without his sons feeling abandoned.

In a true testament to Paul's influence, Hall becomes a successful father to his own son, Tony. It is, in fact, fifteen-year-old Tony's questions about Arthur's gay lifestyle that precipitates the reminiscence by Hall that comprises *Just Above My Head*. Because Hall can look his son in the face and answer his questions without making excuses, but more importantly, because Tony can *ask* the tough questions of his father and expect the truth without fear of rejection, the bond between them grows stronger. As the episode closes, both father and son are standing tall and firm in their love, admiration, and respect for themselves and for each other.

Bonds between fathers and sons have occupied Baldwin's other novels as well. In *Go Tell It On the Mountain,* for example, Gabriel Grimes cannot bond with either of his biological sons and refuses to bond with his stepson. In the case of Royal, whom Gabriel never acknowledges and who later is killed in a gambling game, they are "two black men alone in the dark ... [who are] swallowed up in silence" (141). Gabriel's other natural son, Roy, holds his father in contempt because of his brutal behavior toward Elizabeth, and what relationship they might have had dissolves in anger and violence. The "son" that Gabriel could have bonded with most easily—his stepson, John—is emotionally tormented by Gabriel's distance and hostility. Even when John received the gift of salvation, Gabriel "did not move to touch him, did not kiss him, did not smile. They stood before each other in silence, while the saints rejoiced" (207). Because of these dysfunctional relationships, Royal dies an early violent death, Roy is headed for destruction as well, and John, "a boy filled with guilt, hatred, fear, [and] love, amidst the stern, religious frustrations of his elders and the pagan rebelliousness of his brother Roy" (Kent 21), must reach out to other men for the love, comfort, and encouragement that he cannot receive at home.

In *Tell Me How Long the Train's Been Gone,* the situation between the Proudhammer brothers and their father is not as bleak, but it is just as ineffectual. Mr. Proudhammer is a Garveyite, "a ruined Barbados peasant, exiled in a Harlem which he loathed . . . [who] brought with him from Barbados only black rum and a blacker pride, and magic incantations which neither healed nor saved" (11). Because he cannot adapt to the city and the hardships of supporting his wife and sons, Mr. Proudhammer cannot be a strong father. Leo and Caleb refuse to follow his "impossible lead," and Leo admits that "it was because of our father . . . that Caleb and I clung to each other" (13). Ultimately, though, Caleb cannot perform the multiple roles of brother, father, and lover for the younger Leo, and must choose to save himself instead. Moreover, Leo eventually "comes to resent" Caleb's authority as older brother; indeed, "the day comes when [Leo] is willing to destroy his older brother simply because he has depended upon him for so long" (14). Their early bond is not strong enough to withstand such a fracture. Even after Leo's heart attack, Caleb admits, "I returned to my brother, I longed for him. I needed him: but the fire raged between us" (258). Clearly, the absence of a positive example set by the father for the sons spells disaster for the Proudhammer brothers. It is this situation that Baldwin tries to reverse through the example of the bonding of the Montana men in *Just Above My Head.*

Nevertheless, for all the emphasis on male bonds that work in *Just Above My Head,* Baldwin does not fail to acknowledge those male relationships where bonding does not occur. Baldwin is exceedingly critical of these, as he rails against the selfish, insincere motives of men who will use other men or allow themselves to be used for destructive and disingenuous purposes. For Baldwin, such actions are not expressions of manhood; rather, they are expressions of malefaction and malignity for which he has neither appreciation nor patience. One such example is Webster, the music teacher who serves as impresario for the Trumpets of Zion on their southern tour. A closet homosexual, Webster responds to the genuine affection among the boys with suspicion, lechery, and greed, on one occasion even asking Crunch and Arthur, "What's going on between you two?" He continues, "I'm a very understanding guy. . . . I might want to do it, too" (185). In response to Webster's disingenuity, Crunch threatens to beat his brains out. Here Baldwin implies that those interested only in sex for sex's sake—actually he says that fucking must "become something more than fucking" (73)—and who will use others merely to obtain sex perhaps deserve such violence. This pronouncement is repeated in the episode that recounts Hall's sexual escapades with other men while in the army because Hall "used somebody merely as a receptacle and had allowed [himself] to be used merely as a thing" (272). The indictment is repeated yet again in Faulkner Grey's pursuit of Hall, in which the sexual overtures are cloaked as business maneuvers. Baldwin vehemently dismisses Grey's interest in Hall as another example of white interest in the stereotypical well-hung black male stud, which is, for Baldwin, white inhumanity, deception, and racism at its worst.

Baldwin continues his assault on the weak and ungenuine males in *Just Above My Head* through the example of Joel Miller's relationship—actually, his lack of a relationship—with his son, Jimmy. For reasons that are not altogether clear, Joel despises Jimmy. It could be that Joel sees in Jimmy a certain softness and sensitivity that undermines his own masculine perceptions as a "zoot-suited stud of studs" (70). According to Trudier Harris, "Joel's sexuality represents the stereotyped image of the superstud who wins feminine favors as a result of flashy clothing and superficial charm" (182). Therefore, Joel's resentment of Jimmy may just as well be grounded in his resentment of being dominated by the women in his house, especially his holy, terrible preacher daughter, Julia Miller, who maintains her preferred central position in the family at the expense of Jimmy's emotional and physical well-being, her mother's health (and eventually her life), and her own dysfunctional family's relationship with the far more stable Montanas. Although Julia pays for her juvenile treachery and insincerity through a violent incestuous rape by her father, it is Joel who bears the brunt of Baldwin's criticism. It is Joel's hardness and general lack of acceptance toward Jimmy that makes his childhood miserable and that drives him, in part, into the arms of other men to seek the solace he could never experience at home. According to Trudier Harris, "Hall stresses the sexuality, laziness, ineffectualness, and spinelessness of Brother Miller . . . and makes clear the distinction between . . . Joel and other black men, especially himself" (182–83). According to Hall, "Joel appalled the man in me, he made me sick with shame; but I placed with speed, so vast a distance between his manhood and my own that he could not threaten me" (*Just Above* 317). Joel finally is dismissed by Paul, Hall, Florence, Amy, Julia, Jimmy, Crunch, and Arthur as a weak man who has no self-respect, no love for himself or for others, who is incapable of saving his family, and who, finally, deserves no pity.

Just Above My Head is a brooding, sometimes angry novel. Baldwin's narrator/witness struggles through a labyrinthine narrative that calls attention to the many factors that affect black males in contemporary society, and by bringing together disparate threads from previous narratives in a culmination of themes and characters, Baldwin "generates an alternative vernacular of black American masculinity" (Shin and Judson 256). Also, in an effort to explore the depths of black male joy and suffering, Baldwin asserts that both begin internally from love, desire, panic, or pain; the resultant music that conveys those feelings may be gospel or blues, spiritual or jazz—it does not matter which one, or whether it is a combination of two or more forms—and the expression is valid and valuable because of its powers of salvation. Thus, Baldwin's conclusion about song in *Just Above My Head* is one that challenges each of us to save ourselves:

> I will testify that, to all the gods of the desert, and, when they have choked my throat with sand, the song . . . will bring water back to the desert, that's what the song is supposed to do, and that's what *my soul is a witness* is about. . . . Think about where you would have had to go, to put those five words [my soul is a witness] together, and make of the connection, a song. (494)

Despite myriad digressions, Baldwin arrives, mercifully, at one of the essential truths in the development of the black male psyche—that men must be men, but more importantly, that men must define, for themselves, in consort, collaboration, and bonding with other men, what manhood really is.

WORKS CITED

Baldwin, James. *Go Tell It On the Mountain.* 1953. Reprint, New York: Dell, 1973.

———. *Just Above My Head.* New York: Dial, 1979.

———. "The Male Prison." In *The Price of the Ticket: Collected Nonfiction, 1948–1985.* New York: St. Martin's, 1985. 101–5.

———. "Sonny's Blues." In *Call and Response: The Riverside Anthology of the African American Literary Tradition,* ed. Patricia Liggins Hill et al. Boston: Houghton Mifflin, 1998. 1298–1316. Originally published in *Partisan Review* 24 (Summer 1957): 327–58.

———. *Tell Me How Long the Train's Been Gone.* 1968. Reprint, New York: Dell, 1969.

Collier, Eugenia W. "The Phrase Unbearably Repeated." In *James Baldwin: A Critical Evaluation,* ed. Therman B. O'Daniel, 38–46. Washington, D.C.: Howard University Press, 1977.

Gibson, Donald B. "James Baldwin: The Political Anatomy of Space." In *James Baldwin: A Critical Evaluation,* ed. Therman B. O'Daniel, 3–18. Washington, D.C.: Howard University Press, 1977.

Harris, Trudier. *Black Women in the Fiction of James Baldwin.* Knoxville: University of Tennessee Press, 1985.

Kent, George E. "Baldwin and the Problem of Being." In *James Baldwin: A Critical Evaluation,* ed. Therman B. O'Daniel, 19–29. Washington, D.C.: Howard University Press, 1977.

Lash, John S. "Baldwin Beside Himself: A Study in Modern Phallicism." In *James Baldwin: A Critical Evaluation,* ed. Therman B. O'Daniel, 47–55. Washington, D.C.: Howard University Press, 1977.

Leeming, David A. *James Baldwin: A Biography.* New York: Knopf, 1994.

Pinckney, Darryl. "Blues for Mr. Baldwin." In *Critical Essays on James Baldwin,* ed. Fred L. Standley and Nancy V. Burt, 161–66. Boston: G. K. Hall, 1988.

Shin, Andrew, and Barbara Judson. "Beneath the Black Aesthetic: James Baldwin's Primer of Black American Masculinity." *African American Review* 32, no. 2 (Summer 1998): 247–61.

Traylor, Eleanor. "I Hear Music in the Air: James Baldwin's *Just Above My Head.*" In *Critical Essays on James Baldwin,* ed. Fred L. Standley and Nancy V. Burt, 217–23. Boston: G. K. Hall, 1988.

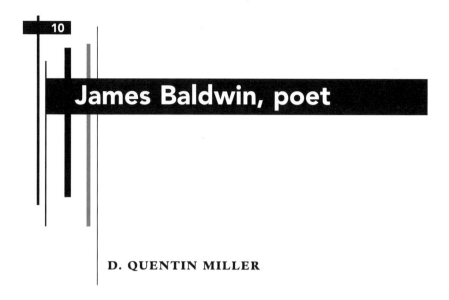

10

James Baldwin, poet

D. QUENTIN MILLER

The tug-of-war over James Baldwin's legacy continues more than two decades after his death, and as critics dig in their heels and resign themselves to ropeburn, a sense of the complete author is lost. Many camps try to claim him for their own, yet few are willing to consider his entire career: Queer theorists hold up *Giovanni's Room;* civil rights scholars arm themselves with *The Fire Next Time;* humanists champion *Another Country;* modern essayists cite *Notes of a Native Son;* aesthetes praise *Go Tell It on the Mountain,* and so forth. Everyone has an ax to grind, of course, and everyone can find in Baldwin a useful sharpening stone. This situation underscores how versatile a writer Baldwin was and how relevant he continues to be. But as I argue in the introduction, the tendency to pigeonhole Baldwin also jeopardizes his place in literary history. If he wrote for all of those causes and many more, who was he, really?

Even if we concentrate on the debate over Baldwin's primary strength as a literary craftsman, we begin to see how literary criticism has fragmented the scope of his vision. During his lifetime, critics and reviewers tried to argue that he was either a novelist or an essayist.[1] No one seemed to be satisfied with the idea that Baldwin could be both; in a 1970 interview with Baldwin in *The Transatlantic Review,* John Hall expresses this division as a "dilemma" (Standley and Pratt 98). Aware of this so-called dilemma, critics and reviewers wanted Baldwin to become one type of writer or the other, and they criticized him for being a writer divided: His novels were accused of being too polemical, and his essays of relying too much on narrative.

In the debate over Baldwin's strengths as a novelist or essayist, no one has labeled him a playwright, a short story writer, a screenwriter, or (until this moment) a poet. The reasons for avoiding these labels have something to do with sheer numbers: Baldwin published six novels and seven books of nonfiction prose, as opposed to two plays, one collection of stories, one screenplay, and one book of poetry.[2] But more is involved in this process than just numbers. The tendency to label Baldwin *anything* runs counter to his fundamental beliefs. In a 1965 interview he states, "If one's going to live at all, one's certainly got to get rid of the labels" (Standley and Pratt 55). My labeling him "poet" in the title of this chapter is really an ironic counterlabeling: I am calling him something that no one ever has called him before as a way of demonstrating how misleading such labels can be. At the same time, I also hope to bring attention to his critically neglected collection of poetry, *Jimmy's Blues* (1985), to inquire about the reasons for its neglect, and finally to analyze it not as some anomalous afterthought to the rest of his career but as an important work that contains the essence of his vision, and which could (and perhaps should) be an introduction to Baldwin rather than the book one reads when one has read everything else. Unified by the motif of blindness converted into action, *Jimmy's Blues* is a powerful rendering of Baldwin's most persistent message: that love involves suffering, and that singing the blues makes that suffering bearable. These spare, pointed verses—markedly different from his prose works in style and tone—are his blues, as the title of the collection makes clear. Critics have overlooked Baldwin's poetry completely, and in doing so they have failed to complete his portrait.

Baldwin's poetry never has been collected in a major literature anthology. Baldwin's poetry is not even *mentioned* in a major literature anthology. One of Baldwin's most prominent scholars, Trudier Harris, overlooks his poetry in her introduction to Baldwin in the third edition of the *Heath Introduction to American Literature,* arguing, as many critics do, that Baldwin's greatest strengths were perhaps his essays rather than his novels, and that he also wrote a couple of plays (2221). More troublesome is the fact that the list of Baldwin's primary works on the next page also omits his poetry. The ninth edition of McGraw Hill's *American Tradition in Literature* also fails to mention *Jimmy's Blues* in both the narrative introduction to his works and the list of his other published works (1533–34). *The Norton Anthology of African American Lit-*

erature, despite the fact that its introduction to Baldwin is considerably longer than these others, also neglects to mention Baldwin's poetry. The problem goes well beyond literature anthologies; even Baldwin's friend and colleague Maya Angelou, one of the twentieth century's most renowned African American poets, does not consider his poetry as she contemplates how others will remember him: "Someone will speak of the essayist James Baldwin in his role as the biblical prophet Isaiah admonishing his country to repent from wickedness and create within itself a clean spirit and a clean heart. Others will examine Baldwin the playwright and novelist who burned with a righteous indignation over the paucity of kindness, the absence of love, and the rippling hypocrisy he saw in the streets of the United States and sensed in the hearts of his fellow citizens" (Troupe 41). Another poet, Eugene B. Redmond, states, "Poetry flourishes across the Baldwin canon. Poetry of blues. Poetry of sermon. Sermonical essays. Sermonical assayer that he was. Poetry of tumult. Poetry of narrative. Poetry of rebellion. Great poetry gets uttered as motherwit and wisdom. . . . Poetry, technical mastery (of many forms and feelings), insight, love, tolerance, genuine concern, fundamental passion, longstanding care, succor, embrace" (Troupe 92). Bold though this pronouncement is, Redmond's examples are not from Baldwin's actual *poetry,* but from his essays, plays, and novels. Even while he proclaims that Baldwin is a poet, Redmond does not call our attention to the fact that Baldwin is a Poet.

The critical neglect of Baldwin's poetry can be seen as an outgrowth of the neglect of all of his later works. As Henry Louis Gates, Jr. and Nellie McKay summarize this trend, "Many critics allege that, by the end of his career, Baldwin was spouting rhetoric that compromised the moral persuasion and authority that had made his earlier works so powerful and compelling. Others charged that the line between his artistic preoccupations and his own personal and psychic life had become embarrassingly blurred. Still others observed that, in resorting to abstract sociological categories, Baldwin was flattening what had once been a richly complicated view of race and racialism in America and thus committing the same ideological excesses he had once condemned in Richard Wright" (1653). But *Jimmy's Blues* stands out as *particularly* neglected among his later works, and it easily can be explained by the fact that no one was prepared, by the twilight of Baldwin's career, to accept the fact that he was a Poet, since they still were trying to resolve the question of whether he was really a novelist or an essayist. In a retrospective article in *The New York Review of Books,* Darryl Pinckney writes of Baldwin, "his later essays and his last, very pro-family novels failed to convince a large part of his audience that his work still held the revelatory subtleties so long associated with his name" (64). No one expected that these revelatory subtleties could have come in the form of poetry. One review of *Jimmy's Blues* sarcastically begins, "As a poet, James Baldwin makes a pretty good novelist" (Booklist 1655). Another review also chides Baldwin's poetry for not being his prose: "One would expect a prose stylist as intense and sophisticated as James Baldwin to turn out a dense, fiercely ironic, unfailingly elegant lyric poetry. Instead, his verses are discursive, loosely cumulative in structure, and haunted by the rhetorical ghosts of Black Power." This review ends as it begins, by dismissing the collection: "One wonders what got into the author of *Go Tell It on the Mountain* and *Notes of a Native Son,* that he permits himself such stuff, but one doesn't wonder very long" (Virginia 99–100). In both cases, the reviewers' sneers are made possible entirely by their comparison of Baldwin's poetry to his best-known prose works.

The general dismissal of Baldwin's poetry may stem from his own dismissal of himself as a poet early in his career. In the autobiographical notes at the beginning of *Notes of a Native Son,* he admits that verse is not his forté. He recalls writing poetry at a young age, but treats it as a joke by simply stating "the less said, the better" (3). Baldwin recalls how he was "intimidated by his high school French teacher, Countee Cullen. 'I showed him one of my poems once . . . and he said it was too much like Langston Hughes. . . . [laughing] I never showed him anything again'"[3] (Troupe 58). It's easy enough for famous writers to dismiss their early literary efforts, particularly when these efforts took the form of poetry. We should recall, though, the scene from *Go Tell It on the Mountain* in which fourteen-year-old John Grimes dreams about an existence in the world beyond his father's church: he fancies himself "a Great Leader of His People . . . a *poet,* or a college president, or a movie star" (19, italics added). It would seem that Baldwin's earliest aspirations to become a writer were rooted specifically in poetry, not prose. But by his own admission, one of the driving forces behind his becoming a writer was "to become rich and famous simply so no one could evict [his] family again" (Standley and Pratt 89), and Baldwin knew that the only *poet* from Harlem who ever became that rich *was* Langston Hughes. Not even Harlem's second most famous poet, Countee Cullen, ever approached the financial success of Hughes. For Baldwin, for practical reasons, poetry would have to wait until he was famous for his other writings, except insofar as his novels, stories, essays, and plays can be considered "poetic," as Redmond has pointed out.

While these practical reasons count for something, it is clear that Baldwin was less a writer motivated by the demands of the marketplace and more an artist striving for honesty and clarity. In one sense of the word, "poet" has different connotations than "writer," the latter being a literal profession, the former being a figurative calling. People have described Baldwin repeatedly as a witness, a prophet, and an artist. These are, at least, the connotations of the word "poet" that John Grimes had in mind when he fantasized about becoming a poet rather than a writer, and also what Baldwin had in mind when he described the role of the poet in 1962:

> The problem of the American identity has everything to do with all the things that happened in this country but never have been admitted or dealt with. We are facing problems so grave that we may not survive them; if we don't deal with the facts, the truth, then obviously we are doomed. The importance of an image is that this country has never really been described, never discovered. It is not up to politicians to do this, it is up to the people who really care about it, who in one way or another are always the poets. (Standley and Pratt 27)

In another interview eleven years later Baldwin refined his definition:

> A change, a real change is brought about when the people make a change. The poet or the revolutionary is there to articulate the necessity, but until the people themselves apprehend it, nothing can happen. . . . When I say poet, it's an arbitrary word. It's a word I use because I don't like the word artist. Nina Simone is a poet. Max Roach is a poet. There is a whole list of people. I'm not talking about literature at all. I'm talking about the recreation of experience, you know, the way that it comes back. (Standley and Pratt 155)

The role of the poet as Baldwin has described it here in fact resolves the "dilemma" that I spoke of earlier between the essayist and social activist who must act publicly in the service of the nation's conscience and the fiction writer and dramatist who must, in the words of the interviewer, "remain faithful to the complexities of life in order to create a true image" (Standley and Pratt 98). Baldwin responds to the question about the essayist/novelist dilemma, "if one is forced, for whatever reason, to ally oneself with a public cause, it is still necessary to maintain a private point of view about it" (98). In the search for the perfect rendition of this formula between private and public points of view in the Baldwin œuvre, critics never have managed to train their gaze on Baldwin's poetry, which does indeed strike this balance succinctly and eloquently.

Far from a primary consideration of Baldwin criticism, *Jimmy's Blues* is barely mentioned in any of the book-length studies, collections of essays, or biographies. In *Talking at the Gates*, James Campbell does not even mention *Jimmy's Blues*. David Leeming affords some room for discussing the collection in his biography *James Baldwin*, especially focusing on the first poem in *Jimmy's Blues*, "Staggerlee wonders," and he acknowledges that although Baldwin's early attempts at poetry were not as successful as his prose, "he genuinely liked some of his more recent attempts" (360). Yet Leeming devotes far less attention to *Jimmy's Blues* than to Baldwin's other writings, and the same certainly can be said of W. J. Weatherby, who pauses over the poetry collection only briefly before dismissing it outright in his biographical portrait of Baldwin:

> For years [Baldwin] had wanted to publish a collection of his poetry; Dial [Press] was not interested. Eventually Michael Joseph in Britain published a very slim collection entitled *Jimmy's Blues*, which included "The Giver," dedicated to his mother—"For Berdis." It was free verse, almost conversational and sometimes so cryptic as to be like shorthand notes to the author. Few of Baldwin's great qualities as a writer were present in his poetry. Dial obviously classed the Atlanta book *[The Evidence of Things Not Seen]* with the poetry as being unpublishable. (359)

In spite of Baldwin's jocular dismissal of his own poetic abilities 30 years before the publication of *Jimmy's Blues*, these poems certainly deserve more critical attention than a mere mention of the fact that one poem is dedicated to his mother. Yet Baldwin's poetry continues to fall into a critical blind spot that would have disappointed the author to no end because the poems are largely about invisibility, and the speaker sings the blues because he has been ignored.

Baldwin considered his penultimate book an important and worthy project, and he persisted in getting it published despite Dial's refusal to do so. To counter Weatherby's assessment, the poems in *Jimmy's Blues* are far from cryptic, they are not all free verse, and as to their "almost conversational" tone, that just may be the point. Baldwin's poetry delivers its message as clearly and sensibly as if it were presented as a conversation, or a song. Its spare rendering on the page underscores its theme of invisibility: If the reader cannot see Baldwin's message, it is because of willed blindness. The reason that the poems have been overlooked is not because they are not "poetic": they rely heavily on repetition and allusion, though not symbol or metaphor, except for the central metaphor of blindness. Baldwin was not a writer who relied heavily on metaphor, though, especially toward the end of his career, and even more especially when he was singing the blues. His prophetic voice is the most prominent feature of his poetry, and he uses it effectively to take on the related themes of race relations in America and the tribulations of personal love.

Nearly all of Baldwin's works—from *Go Tell It on the Mountain* and *Giovanni's Room* through *The Evidence of Things Not Seen*—concern themselves with either the consequences of refusing to love or with the racial strife that plagues his country. In general, love is a more prominent theme in his fiction, and race relations are more frequently the province of his essays. In *Jimmy's Blues*, Baldwin brings these themes together through the metaphor of blindness. Love for Baldwin is not always a pretty business; as Giovanni tells David in *Giovanni's Room*, we must accept the "stink of love" if we are to love properly. Because love in Baldwin's world is often conflicted, and because of the conflicted state of race relations in the United States, it is not surprising that he invents the persona of America's rejected lover who tells his country,

> *I*
> *do not ask you why*
> *you have spurned,*
> *despised my love*
> *as something beneath you [. . .]*
>
> *you do not know*
> *how desperately I hoped*
> *that you would grow*
> *not so much to love me*
> *as to know*
> *that what you do to me*
> *you do to you.* ("A Lover's Question" 23–28, 47–53)

The complexities of Baldwin's definition of love and the unity of his messages regarding both love of country and romantic love are stated clearly and concisely in this poem. By understanding the clear-eyed message of this poem and of others in *Jimmy's Blues*, we are closer to understanding two related themes that evolve in Baldwin's work throughout his career: learning to love and America's failed attempts at national unity through the fulfillment of the promise of equality. His frequent use of blindness as a metaphor for these failures reifies the connection between Baldwin's work and the majority of African American literature following World War II. Although Baldwin's contributions were unique, this metaphor of blindness in *Jimmy's Blues* demonstrates his alliance with the theme of invisibility that dominates African American literature from Ellison on.

One can pick up virtually any of Baldwin's works and find an exploration of one of two themes I have mentioned: the failure of America, with its racial blind spot, to fulfill the promise of its nationhood, or the difficulties of learning to love. In his most ambitious and accomplished works, such as *Another Country*, these themes come together and inform one another. Both themes are evident throughout *Jimmy's Blues*, and, read as a collection, the two themes intertwine; yet in individual poems, one theme generally takes precedence over the other.

The striking opening poem, "Staggerlee wonders," is an extended meditation on race relations in America. The speaker, the irreverent and candid trickster Staggerlee, pretends to be wondering, or simply musing about America. In reality, he is delivering a prophetic sermon. In *Understanding the New Black Poetry*, Stephen Henderson writes, "A step toward objectification and distancing of personal involvement occurs when the poet depicts either real or imaginary Black figures" including in this category "larger-than-life figures such as Stack O'Lee" (23). Mississippi John Hurt's "Stack O'Lee Blues" (and many variants of it) describes Stack O'Lee as "cruel," a "bad man" who everyone was glad to see die. Other versions of the story have Stack O'Lee knocking "the devil down with a big black stick" and taking charge of Hell (Gates and McKay 50). Antisocial, unfeeling, and self-serving, he is a figure of ironic rebirth and relentless power. But Baldwin, in his attempt to objectify his opinion of America through Staggerlee, gives this mythical figure a prophetic voice, more preacher than murderer. Like any good preacher, Staggerlee draws examples from history, tracing a line of the modern horrors of Manifest Destiny, from Charles Manson ("Mad Charlie man's son" [1.46]) through John Wayne to Ronald Reagan. This vision culminates in an ironic mantra of empty patriotism:

> *Salt peanuts, salt peanuts,*
> *for dear hearts and gentle people,*
> *and cheerful, shining, simple Uncle Sam!* (1.67–69)

Echoing Ellison's Invisible Man in his dream of his grandfather, Staggerlee breaks off from this portrait of the hollowness of his fellow citizens and shouts to his black audience,

> *Nigger, read this and run!*
> *Now, if you can't read,*
> *run anyhow!* (1.70–72)

The speaker exposes the dangers and the hypocrisy that continue to plague his country, and he also explains to a degree Baldwin's choice of poetry as a medium for delivering his message: The addressee may not be able to read, but he can certainly listen.

For his white audience, Staggerlee chooses a different metaphor to describe poetry. "Kinsmen," he tells them, "Quite a lot has been going on / behind your back, and, / if your phone has not yet been disconnected, / it will soon begin to ring" (4.79, 85–88). Staggerlee's poem is either a shouted diatribe or a wake-up call. In either case, his message is clear: We cannot be a nation until we have begun to rise above that which separates us, or to remove the impediments to our vision. Referring to white America, Staggerlee states his theme concisely:

> *My days are not their days.*
> *My ways are not their ways.*
> *I would not think of them,*
> *one way or the other,*
> *did not they so grotesquely*
> *block the view*
> *between me and my brother.* (2.13–19)

This theme is a *leitmotif* for the collection: blindness, brought on either by one's own will or the actions of others, is the reason America remains a divided nation. Staggerlee suggests that the problem is not a racial division so much as one between those who can see clearly and those who refuse to do so. He continues:

> *And, so, I always wonder:*
> *can blindness be desired?*
> *Then, what must the blinded eyes have seen*
> *to wish to see no more!*
>
> *For, I have seen,*
> *in the eyes regarding me,*
> *or regarding my brother,*
> *have seen, deep in the farthest valley*
> *of the eye, have seen*

> *a flame leap up, then flicker and go out,*
> *have seen a veil come down,*
> *leaving myself, and the other,*
> *alone in that cave*
> *which every soul remembers, and*
> *out of which, desperately afraid,*
> *I turn, turn, stagger, stumble out,*
> *into the healing air,*
> *fall flat on the healing ground,*
> *singing praises, counselling*
> *my heart, my soul, to praise.* (2.20–39)

These lines are reminiscent, in diction, theme, and even language ("For I have seen ... flicker and go out ... desperately afraid") of T. S. Eliot's Prufrock, another speaker who sees what others do not. But unlike the painfully static Prufrock, Staggerlee is not eternally paralyzed by his situation. He is a seer, but he also is capable of action, as when he stumbles out of the "cave / which every soul remembers," a cave which, in this context, must represent at least partially the dark past of American history. Vision for Staggerlee is the first step toward healing, and we are all *capable* of it, but, he asserts, many do not *desire* it. The conversion from sight to action results in the blues; as Baldwin writes in "The Uses of the Blues,"

> I know, I watched, I was there. . . . I have seen it all, I have seen that much. What the blues are describing comes out of all this. . . . The person to whom these things happened watched with eyes wide open, saw it happen. So that when Billie or Bessie or Leadbelly stood up and sang about it, they were commenting on it. . . . You have to do something about it. (152)

Staggerlee wants us to do more than to nod our heads in agreement or shake them while muttering, "America, what a shame." As in many works in which Baldwin calls on his audience to see and hear what lies below the surface of America's mythic exterior,[4] the tone of "Staggerlee wonders" becomes apocalyptic at the end of the poem:

> *During this long travail*
> *our ancestors spoke to us, and we listened,*
> *and we tried to make you hear life in our song*
> *but it matters not at all to me*

whether you know what I am talking about—or not;
I know why we are not blinded
by your brightness, are able to see you,
who cannot see us. I know
why we are still here.

Godspeed.
The niggers are calculating,
from day to day, life everlasting,
and wish you well;
but decline to imitate the Son of the Morning,
and rule in hell. (4.146–160)

Staggerlee's laconic wondering has turned into prediction, and he has become a prophet: one who knows because he can see. Although his role has been augmented from ponderer to prophet since the beginning of the poem, his voice has remained steady, aloof, even conversational, allowing the message to be delivered in simple verse instead of the language of the pulpit. If we consistently have refused to hear the spiritual and the sermon, or if we have overlooked reality, we are forced by the poem's simplicity to hear the message and see the truth.

"Song (for Skip)," the poem immediately following "Staggerlee Wonders" in the collection, presents itself in the form of a song more in the tradition of William Blake or an English Renaissance poetic song than of a blues song or spiritual, though the latter two are suggested by the content. "Song (for Skip)" is rendered simply, going so far as to address a child of ten in the second stanza. The voice is even more straightforward than Staggerlee's, yet the message is similar to that of "Staggerlee wonders," and the poet returns to the same metaphor:

We, who have been blinded,
are not blind
and sense when not to
trust the mind. (1.53–56)

Again, the poet intimates that blindness is a self-imposed condition that prohibits us from getting past superficiality, and that confuses us as to the true nature of reality:

At least, we know
a man, when we see one,
a shackle, when we wear one,

> *or a chain, when we bear one,*
> *a noose from a halter,*
> *or a pit from an altar.* (1.47–52)

Those who categorically "trust the mind" as opposed to those who attend to the sense or emotions cannot always accurately discern reality. This condition points toward the poem's final vision of self-destruction, described as "the great temptation / beckoning this disastrous nation" (3.23–24).

The poet distances himself from those who are blind and uses his power of sight to change the reader's perception, hoping that blindness is not irrevocable, that past refusal to see does not necessarily denote permanent blindness. He attacks our misconception on the level of the cliché, repeating the phrase "Time is not money. Time is time" three times in "Song (for Skip)." In doing so, he rejects metaphor in favor of emphasizing obvious, literal reality in order to make reality less obscure. With the repetition of the "time" phrase, he also causes us to call into question our sense of history, addressing past time in section 1, present in section 2, and future in section 3, (this structure is, as in "Staggerlee wonders," apocalyptic) while never letting us forget that time is time, not money. We thus are forced to make historical or biblical connections rather than economic ones, which are shown to be empty clichés. He also states and repeats an obvious reality about the next generation:

> *Our children are.*
> *Our children are.*
> *Our children are:*
> *which means that we must be*
> *the pillar of cloud by day*
> *and of fire by night:*
> *the guiding star.* (1.61–67)

The future is depicted here as the motivation for our present actions and the reason it is imperative to see the reality of the past.

Once this theme of blindness to reality is firmly established in the first two poems, the poet feels free to vary the theme. Baldwin experiments with form throughout *Jimmy's Blues*. A poem entitled "3:00 a.m. (for David)" is not a sequence like the poems discussed above, but almost an epigram with a rhythm that could be compared to William Carlos Williams, or even to a nursery rhyme. It reads,

> *Two black boots,*
> > *on the floor,*
> *figuring out what the walking's for.*
> *Two black boots,*
> > *now, together,*
> *learning the price of the stormy weather.*
>
> *To say nothing of the wear and tear*
> *on*
> > *the mother-fucking*
> > > *leather.*

Despite the obvious stylistic departure from the sequence poems dis-cussed earlier, its theme is similar. Our attention is drawn away from the two black boots—which are superficial, or at least visible to every-one—and toward the "mother-fucking leather" in the second stanza. The reader may strive to attach significance to the black boots, the walking, the price, or the stormy weather, but what the poet forces us to see is that we ignore something vital when we look only at the sur-face of things, which is akin to willed blindness. In the second stanza, the speaker forces us to open our eyes by showing us evidence of things not seen. The reader's process is similar to that of the boots in the first stanza: "Learning . . . figuring out," and eventually seeing and reaching a realization. The poet's task, like the prophet's, is to instruct, to point the reader toward the hidden leather relentlessly and with clarity.

Like the authoritative "I" of his essays, Baldwin's poetic speaker is frequently one who sees, witnesses, and testifies: an "I" who is also an "eye." In "Confession," this speaker repeatedly questions whether any-one knows more about the downtrodden than he does. He also ques-tions God, man's role in God's scheme, and his own role in man's scheme:

> *Oh, Lord,*
> > *can these bones live?*
> *I think, Yes,*
> *then I think, No:*
> *being witness to a blow*
> *delivered outside of time,*
> *witness to a crime*
> *which time*
> *is, in no way whatever,*
> *compelled to see,*

> *not being burdened with sight:*
> *like me.* (23–34)

As in the other poems I have discussed, the speaker has special insight and thus can exist outside time. He is a witness to time's errors, and his privilege of sight becomes a burden since he has to act on it, just as Staggerlee does. His action is, again, to make us see what he has seen, to act as an intermediary between reality and the reader just as his persona in the poem is an intermediary between God and humanity. As in the other poems, he deemphasizes metaphor and removes cliché from language in order to deliver his message clearly:

> *nothing is not better than nothing:*
> *nothing is nothing,*
> *   just like*
> *everything is everything*
> *(and you better believe it).* (54–58)

The speaker quite definitely dispenses with our clouded notions of reality—things are the way they are—and parenthetically warns about the consequences of an unclear notion of reality. At the poem's conclusion, he reasserts his role as prophet and seer, and repeats his message for our benefit:

> *My Lord.*
> *I understand it,*
> *now:*
> *the why is not the how.*
>
> *My Lord*
> *Author of the whirlwind,*
> *and the rainbow,*
> *Co-author of death,*
> *giver and taker of breath*
> *(Yes, every knee must bow),*
> *I understand it*
> *now:*
> *the why is not the how.* (152–164)

We are encouraged to understand this mystery now just as the poet has, and the formula for understanding should be obvious: the why is the why, the how is the how. The reason something occurs is not the same thing as the circumstances surrounding its occurrence: Things are as they are, and we must learn to accept that simple reality before attempting to change it.

The burden of sight in "Confession" is examined more closely in "Christmas carol." In this poem, the speaker questions the biblical Saul, asking him how it feels to be Paul.[5] He goes on,

> *I mean, tell me about that night*
> *you saw the light,*
> *When the light knocked you down.*
> *What's the cost*
> *of being lost*
> *and found? (4–9)*

The speaker feels sympathy for Saul; he recognizes Saul's condition and its potential for penalty—"the cost"—yet he allies himself with the biblical figure:

> *No wonder you went blind.*
> *Like man, I can dig it.*
> *Been there myself: you know: (22–24)*

Once again, the speaker is a prophet, measuring his own conversion from blindness to sight against Saul's. His language is more colloquial than the converted Paul's,[6] though, and he presents himself more humbly than Paul does, perhaps to show that the experience of regaining sight is not reserved for the elite.

The speaker of "Christmas carol" sees his conversion as a struggle for which prayer will be his aid:

> *If I can get up off this slime,*
> *if I ain't trampled,*
> *I will put off my former ways*
> *I will deny my days*
> *I will be pardoned*
> *and I will rise*
> *out of the camel piss*
> *which stings my eyes*
> *into a revelation*
> *concerning this doomed nation. (61–70)*

Since this speaker is like Saul in that "the hand of the Lord has been laid on [him]" (94), he can foresee his own gift for prophecy. Sight has been denied him not through his own will but through the will of others. He has been forced into the camel piss, but in converting his stinging eyes into a revelation instead of blindness, he can begin to act on that which he has seen, like Staggerlee does, to "rise / out of the camel piss." He addresses his own concern about becoming a privileged seer:

> Sometimes I wonder about that night.
> One does not always walk in light.
> My light is darkness
> and in my darkness moves, forever,
> the dream or the hope or the fear of sight. (103–107)

The uncertainty ("wonder") that the speaker encounters here is what humanizes him and thus enables him to communicate with us, just as Staggerlee's wondering is how he speaks to us. Yet the speaker reaffirms his message and reasserts not only that one must struggle to gain sight, but also that conversion into sight needs to be experienced by each individual, not just by prophets like himself and Paul:

> No tongue can stammer
> nor hammer ring
> nor leaf bear witness
> to how bright is the light
> of the unchained night
> which delivered
> Saul
> to Paul. (122–129)

Each of us must be a witness to the reality of this doomed nation in order to begin to change it, for, as the poet states in "Mirrors (for David)," "I cannot act on what you see" (3).

The witness in Baldwin's poetry converts what he sees into action, and this action is parallel to the writing of the poem itself. The role of the witness is to testify to what he has seen, after all. Yet Baldwin's witnesses-turned-speakers do not train their gaze solely on America. Baldwin's other primary theme of the difficulties of learning to love also is prominent in *Jimmy's Blues*. Lovers, like Americans, are divided and blinded in Baldwin's poetry; no matter how close they are, they remain strangers, as the speaker of "Munich, Winter 1973" suggests in his opening lines:

In a strange house,
a strange bed
in a strange town,
a very strange me
is waiting for you. (1–5)

By the time love occurs in the last two lines of the poem, it is "in the middle of the terrifying air," hardly a comforting image. Love of another human being is just as challenging as love of country for Baldwin. He claims in 1955, "I love America more than any other country in the world, and, exactly for this reason, I insist on the right to criticize her perpetually" (*Notes* 9). He reaffirms this idea in general terms fifteen years later in *No Name in the Street:* "Whoever is part of whatever civilization helplessly loves some aspects of it, and some of the people in it. A person does not lightly elect to oppose his society" (194). Love is no less difficult and risky, in other words, than the critical patriotism of a witness who has been blinded. In "The giver," the poem dedicated to his mother, he reasons, "If the hope of giving / is to love the living, / the giver risks madness / in the act of giving" (1–4).

Baldwin believed that, despite the risk of love, it absolutely must be undertaken. There are at least as many impediments to our ability to love as there are impediments to our nationhood, though, and they are brought about by our imperfect vision. In "Guilt, Desire and Love," for instance, Baldwin personifies love and places it in a war between Guilt and Desire. The metaphor is again one of blindness; "Love [comes] slouching along, / an exploded silence / standing a little apart / but visible anyway" (9–12). Desire continually looks toward love, "hoping to find a witness" (18), but Guilt, who "flag[s] down a truckload / of other people" (25–26), overcomes Desire and entreats the truckload of other people to "look away, and [swear] that they / didn't see nothing / and couldn't testify nohow, / and Love move[s] out of sight" (29–32). According to Baldwin, we must face love, a sometimes ugly and disquieting thing, with wide-open eyes, but we rarely do because conflicting emotions like guilt prevent us from doing so. Baldwin's response to Staggerlee's rhetorical question, "can blindness be desired?" is implicit in this miniature play-in-verse: It is most often a willed affliction.

Baldwin exploits this connotation of blindness as a refusal, a fundamental human failing, in order to bring together the themes of the failure of the American dream and the failure to love in "A Lover's Question" toward the end of the collection. In this poem, Baldwin puts into practice the role of the artist as he had stated it in his 1962 essay

"The Creative Process," in which he writes, "Societies never know it, but the war of an artist with his society is a lover's war, and he does, at his best, what lovers do, which is to reveal the beloved to himself, and, with that revelation, to make freedom real" (*Ticket* 318). Baldwin enacts this artist's (or poet's) war in "A Lover's Question" so that his society, which increasingly disappointed him after he penned those lines in the early 1960s, can finally realize the position of this poet who regards his nation as a frustrated lover might.

The speaker of "A Lover's Question" begins by addressing his lover directly: "My country, / t'is of thee / I sing" (1–3). It is clear from the outset that this poem is no mere lover's question, and that the addressee is no mere lover. While there are a few questions, the overall tone is a more familiar one to readers of Baldwin's novels and essays: The poem is a sermon about love, but a sermon directed to all Americans rather than to an individual lover. The speaker, representing black America, describes more a lover's spat than a lover's question. He claims, "You do not love me. / I see that. / You do not see me: / I am your black cat" (62–65). Baldwin's speaker delivers his message in a simple, declarative style so that no reader (or lover) could ignore or misconstrue it. The failure to love—like the failure of the American ideal of equality when it comes to race—is a question of perception. The speaker is a witness ("I see that"), yet he knows that he is invisible to his country ("you do not see me").

The speaker's voice in "A Lover's Question" is similar to that of Staggerlee. For one thing, he is coyly prophetic, labeling his lover, who is also his country, the

> enemy of all tribes
> known, unknown, past,
> present, or,
> perhaps, above all,
> to come. (4–8)

This speaker also shares Staggerlee's ironic, mocking tone juxtaposed with shocking candor; he further addresses America as

> my dear,
>   my darling,
> jewel
> (Columbia, the gem of
> the ocean!)

> *or, as I, a street nigger*
> *would put it —: [. . .]*
> *You are my heart.* (10–16, 19)

This admission is more tender than anything that Staggerlee says about America. The heart—the seat of the tenderest emotions and the source of life—connects the speaker to his country in a way that unites them permanently. Unlike the scrappy and street-wise Staggerlee, this speaker is a lover, and he acknowledges his inextricable bond with America. Yet the speaker shares Staggerlee's penchant for reminding his country that he is governed in part by the roles that his lover assigns him: a street nigger, your black cat, your black dancer. This is how you perceive me, he seems to say, so this is how I am; Baldwin was fond of saying to white Americans, "I'm only black as long as you think you're white."

The lover's problem has to do with the way he is seen, then, and this problem of perception relates directly to America's failure to see both itself and its lover (that is, white America and black America) in relation to one another. The speaker asserts,

> *No man can have a harlot*
> *for a lover*
> *nor stay in bed forever*
> *with a lie.*
> *He must rise up*
> *and face the morning sky*
> *and himself, in the mirror*
> *of his lover's eye.* (53–60)

The self-examination he expects of America is complex because the mirror is within the lover's eye. You must see yourself through my perceptions of you, in other words. Blindness feeds on itself; America cannot see itself *and,* or perhaps *because,* it cannot see how it is perceived by one whom it cannot see in the first place. The poem, then, acts as a corrective to this misperception: If you refuse to see me, the speaker reasons, then you must at least hear my question.

The poem's final question reiterates in no uncertain terms the stanza I have just discussed: "How can you fail to look / into your lover's eye?" The first question in the poem is perhaps more direct, if less easily remedied: "Why / have you allowed yourself / to become so *grinly* wicked?" This question is not the same as a more conventional version of it in a lover's quarrel, "Why have you become so wicked?" In the first place, America has *allowed* itself to become wicked, recalling Staggerlee's question, "Can blindness be desired?" Refusal to see clearly is not so much an act of evil—becoming wicked—as it is a desire to maintain the status quo, allowing wickedness. In the second place, there is this neologism "grinly" to interpret, made even odder by the fact that it is in italics. "Grinly" calls attention to some of America's basic character flaws: its smugness and its bland complacency, its preference to see "cheerful, shining simple Uncle Sam" rather than to look at its "black cat." It is an adverb that connotes contempt on the part of the speaker rather than hatred. They are lovers, after all, and the speaker is hoping "to make freedom real," in Baldwin's words, by revealing the beloved to himself.

Yet the poem is not ultimately optimistic. The speaker also shares Staggerlee's apocalyptic pessimism for race relations in America. Similar to Staggerlee's final prediction from the underworld, "A Lover's Question" ends with a message from below for white America for whom

> enough [rope] hangs from
> your hanging tree
> to carry you
> where you sent me.
>
> And then, false lover,
> you will know
> what love has managed
> here below. (93–100)

Like any spurned lover, this speaker vows revenge. America has become a "false lover" and thus may be incapable of seeing itself. Baldwin refuses to tie up his vision of America with a pretty bow and to say, "Everything will be okay; we'll make it through this." Rather, he foretells the consequences of the refusal to love, as he has throughout his career. The artist, as Baldwin has said, is like a lover to his society, but a lover who is *at war* with his society. This lover's question may seem fatalistic, yet Baldwin's prophecies have begun to come true in the past dozen years. (The Rodney King riots in Los Angeles are just the most familiar example). Trouble will continue as long as we refuse to see. Love is not possible until we learn to confront its unpleasantries. The promise of equality in America is not possible until we learn to examine our shortcomings. And neither can happen, according to Baldwin the poet, as long as we fail to look in the mirror of our lover's eye.

This idea also can be gleaned from Baldwin's novels and essays, but it has a different value in these poems. It is not just that he has repackaged his message for us in verse, but that he has stripped it down to its essence: the purest form of the blues. Baldwin depicted and discussed blues singers throughout his career, from Sonny in "Sonny's Blues" to Arthur in *Just Above My Head* in his fiction, and from Bessie Smith to Billie Holiday in his nonfiction. In his poetry, though, he actually *sings* the blues. To miss the performance is to miss Baldwin's final act. We must not take him at face value when he dismisses his poetic abilities in his introduction to *Notes of a Native Son* with the phrase, "the less said, the better." He was a young writer at the time, distancing himself from an even younger version of himself. *Jimmy's Blues* is the work of a mature writer and a true poet. The more said about it, the better.

NOTES

1. The new *Library of America* editions of Baldwin underscore this division: one volume on his essays, the other on his stories and early (of course) novels.

2. Another collection of Baldwin's verse was published posthumously in 1989, two years after his death, copyrighted by his brother David. A limited edition entitled *Gypsy and Other Poems,* it contains seven poems, plus a portrait of Baldwin and other signed artwork by Leonard Baskin. The poems vary in style, tone, and theme, and are dated as far apart as 1970 and 1986; yet the themes I address in this essay are still evident: "It leads to hell, and more / than your blinded eyes can see" ("For A").

3. To be compared to Langston Hughes generally is not an insult. Baldwin may have recoiled from this assessment in retrospect because of the exchange that stemmed from his scathing 1959 review of a collection of Hughes's poems, to which Hughes responded with a satiric poem at Baldwin's expense.

4. See, for example, *The Fire Next Time, No Name in the Street,* or *The Evidence of Things Not Seen.*

5. See Acts 9, 22, 26.

6. I would like to emphasize that the speaker does not necessarily identify with either Paul or Saul; it is the *conversion* that interest him. Baldwin found Saint Paul (or at least his legacy) somewhat odious. In *The Fire Next Time,* he says that Paul, "with a most unusual and stunning exactness, described himself as a 'wretched man'" (32) and that "the real architect of the Christian church was not the disreputable, sun-baked Hebrew who gave it his name but the mercilessly fanatical and self-righteous St. Paul" (58). In *The Devil Finds Work,* Baldwin describes Paul as "helplessly paranoiac" (13).

WORKS CITED

Baldwin, James. *The Devil Finds Work*. New York: Bantam Doubleday Dell, 1976.

———. *The Evidence of Things Not Seen*. New York: Holt, Rinehart and Winston, 1985.

———. *The Fire Next Time*. New York: Delta, 1963.

———. *Giovanni's Room*. New York: Dial, 1956.

———. *Go Tell It on the Mountain*. New York: Dial, 1953.

———. *Gypsy and Other Poems*. Hadley, Mass.: Wild Carrot Letterpress, 1989.

———. *Jimmy's Blues*. New York: St. Martin's, 1985.

———. *No Name in the Street*. New York: Dell, 1972.

———. *Notes of a Native Son*. Boston: Beacon Press, 1955.

———. *The Price of the Ticket: Collected Nonfiction 1948–1985*. New York: St. Martin's, 1985.

———. "The Uses of the Blues." In *The Twelfth Anniversary Playboy Reader,* ed. Hugh M. Hefner, 150–59. Chicago: Playboy Press, 1965.

Gates, Jr., Henry Louis and Nellie Y. McKay, eds. *The Norton Anthology of African American Literature*. New York: Norton, 1997.

Henderson, Stephen. *Understanding the New Black Poetry*. New York: Morrow, 1973.

Review of *Jimmy's Blues,* by James Baldwin. *The Booklist* (August 1986): 1655.

Review of *Jimmy's Blues,* by James Baldwin. *Virginia Quarterly Review* 62 (Summer 1986): 99–100.

Lauter, Paul, ed. *The Heath Anthology of American Literature*. 3rd ed. Boston: Houghton-Mifflin, 1997.

Leeming, David A. *James Baldwin: A Biography*. New York: Knopf, 1994.

Perkins, George and Barbara Perkins, eds. *The American Tradition in Literature*. 9th ed. Boston: McGraw Hill, 1999.

Pinckney, Darryl. "The Magic of James Baldwin." *The New York Review of Books* 45, no. 18 (19 November 1998): 64–74.

Standley, Fred L. and Louis H. Pratt. *Conversations With James Baldwin*. Jackson: University Press of Mississippi, 1989.

Troupe, Quincy. *James Baldwin: The Legacy*. New York: Simon & Schuster, 1989.

Weatherby, W. J. *James Baldwin: Artist on Fire*. New York: Donald I. Fine, 1989.

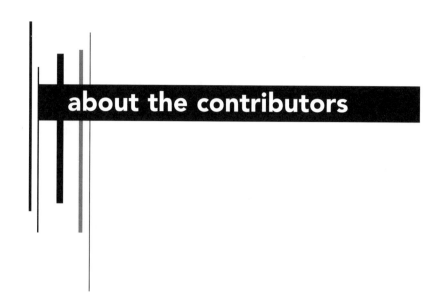

about the contributors

Richard Avedon is a photographer specializing in portrait photography whose work has been exhibited at major museums, including New York's Metropolitan Museum of Art and the Smithsonian Institution. In addition to *Nothing Personal* with James Baldwin, his books include *Observations* (1959) with Truman Capote and *In the American West* (1985). In 1992, he became the first staff photographer for *The New Yorker* magazine.

Warren J. Carson is associate professor of English at the University of South Carolina at Spartanburg. He has written about such twentieth century African American writers as Zora Neale Hurston and Albert Murray, and presented papers on Baldwin, Ralph Ellison, and Langston Hughes.

Yasmin Y. DeGout is assistant professor of English at Howard University. Her dissertation focused on the fiction of James Baldwin.

Kathleen N. Drowne is the managing editor of *a/b: Auto/Biography Studies*. As a Ph.D candidate at the University of North Carolina at Chapel Hill, she is writing a dissertation on legislating morality.

Cassandra M. Ellis is visiting assistant professor of American literature at the University of Alabama at Birmingham. She is currently writing a book on moviegoing in American fiction.

Susan Feldman is the managing editor of the journal *Umbr(a)*. She is a Ph.D. candidate at the State University of New York at Buffalo. Her dissertation focuses on racial and sexual difference in twentieth-century American literature.

David Adams Leeming is emeritus professor of English and comparative literature at the University of Connecticut at Storrs. His books include *James Baldwin: A Biography;* a biography of Baldwin's mentor, the painter Beauford Delaney, *Amazing Grace;* and *Stephen Spender: A Life in Modernism.*

Michael F. Lynch is associate professor of English at Kent State University and has written extensively on Baldwin.

D. Quentin Miller is assistant professor of English at Gustavus Adolphus College in Saint Peter, Minnesota. He has published reference entries and presented papers on Baldwin.

Joshua L. Miller is a Ph.D. candidate in English and Comparative Literature at Columbia University.

Saadi A. Simawe is assistant professor of English and African American Studies at Grinnell College in Iowa. He has presented several papers on Baldwin and is currently editing a volume of essays on music in African American fiction.

Charles P. Toombs is chair and associate professor of the Department of Africana Studies at San Diego State University. He presented a paper on Baldwin and is completing a book on the black gay male aesthetic in African American fiction.